SAMPLING
ESSENTIALS

To
Viola McLemore Daniel

SAMPLING
ESSENTIALS

Practical Guidelines for Making Sampling Choices

Johnnie Daniel
Howard University

Los Angeles | London | New Delhi
Singapore | Washington DC

Los Angeles | London | New Delhi
Singapore | Washington DC

FOR INFORMATION:

SAGE Publications, Inc.
2455 Teller Road
Thousand Oaks, California 91320
E-mail: order@sagepub.com

SAGE Publications Ltd.
1 Oliver's Yard
55 City Road
London EC1Y 1SP
United Kingdom

SAGE Publications India Pvt. Ltd.
B 1/I 1 Mohan Cooperative Industrial Area
Mathura Road, New Delhi 110 044
India

SAGE Publications Asia-Pacific Pte. Ltd.
33 Pekin Street #02-01
Far East Square
Singapore 048763

Acquisitions Editor: Vicki Knight
Association Editor: Lauren Habib
Editorial Assistant: Kalie Koscielak
Production Editor: Karen Wiley
Copy Editor: Jovey Stewart
Permissions Editor: Adele Hutchison
Typesetter: C&M Digitals (P) Ltd.
Proofreader: Jenifer Kooiman
Indexer: Sheila Bodell
Cover Designer: Bryan Fishman
Marketing Manager: Helen Salmon

Copyright © 2012 by SAGE Publications, Inc.

Printed in the United States of America

Library of Congress Cataloging-in-Publication Data

Daniel, Johnnie.
Sampling essentials: practical guidelines for making
sampling choices / Johnnie Daniel.

p. cm.
Includes bibliographical references and index.

ISBN 978-1-4129-5221-7 (pbk.)

1. Social sciences—Research. 2. Social sciences—
Methodology. I. Title.

H62.D229 2011
001.43—dc22
2011000546

This book is printed on acid-free paper.

11 12 13 14 15 10 9 8 7 6 5 4 3 2 1

CONTENTS

DETAILED CONTENTS

LIST OF TABLES, FIGURES, AND RESEARCH NOTES

TABLES

FIGURES

RESEARCH NOTES

ABOUT THE AUTHOR

 **Johnnie Daniel** earned a PhD degree from the University of Michigan, and a JD degree from the Georgetown University Law Center. He teaches courses in research methods and statistics at Howard University. He has also taught at Loyola University (Chicago), the University of Wisconsin-Milwaukee, Tuskegee University, and the University of Michigan. He presents workshops on evaluation research, survey research, and proposal writing for researchers and others in government and private industry. He has worked for the Division of Research and Statistics of the Social Security Administration, the Institute for Social Research at the University of Michigan, the legal newspaper *Los Angeles Daily Journal*, the District of Columbia Public Schools, and the Illinois Department of Public Aid. He has served as a scholar in residence for the Health Care Financing Administration, and as editor of the *Journal of Social and Behavioral Sciences*. Throughout his career he has conducted qualitative research, quantitative research, and mixed-methods research across a wide range of topics for such private and public organizations as the National Science Foundation, U.S. Department of Transportation, U.S. Department of the Treasury, U.S. Bureau of the Census, U.S. Department of the Army, U.S. Department of the Navy, U.S. District Court for the District of Columbia, District of Columbia Public Schools, DuPont Chemicals, Health Resources and Services Administration, World Bank, New York State Nursing Association, ACTION, D.C. Coalition for the Homeless, American Council on Education, March of Dimes, District of Columbia Office on Aging, D.C. Private Industry Council, Martin Marietta Corporation, the Institute for College Research Development and Support, Metropolitan Washington Council of Governments, and the Washington Urban League.

PREFACE

The choices made in selecting participants for a research study are critical to the validity and reliability of the findings of the study. Irrespective of the nature of the research, such choices must be made. The research may concern business, medical, educational, environmental, transportation, political, or other issues. This text provides guidelines for making such choices.

PURPOSE

Most research textbooks do not present a detailed and comprehensive coverage of sampling. Readers are left with incomplete and fragmentary information. On the other hand, textbooks on sampling are not written for those who have no desire to become sampling statisticians. As a result, students of research methods are not exposed to concepts and techniques that could assist them in doing quality work and making good sampling choices. This book attempts to reduce barriers between the non-statistical research practitioner and the sampling statistician by providing clear descriptions of sampling principles and guidelines as to how to use them.

This book attempts to improve the dialogue between the nontechnical researcher and the statistician (or technical researcher) in planning and executing effective sample designs, not by providing the nontechnical researcher a mathematical primer on sampling theory, but by providing a detailed, nontechnical description and guidelines with limited presentation of formulas as to how one might answer the following basic research questions:

- Should I take a census or sample?
- If I sample, should I select a nonprobability sample, a probability sample, or a mixed-methods sample?
- If I select a nonprobability sample, what type should I use?
- If I select a probability sample, what type should I use?
- If I select a mixed-methods sample, what type should I use?
- Should I use population-based sampling, telephone-based sampling, web-based sampling, address-based sampling, time-based sampling, or space-based sampling?
- What sample size should I target?

AUDIENCE

The intended audience for this text includes undergraduate students, graduate students, research practitioners, and all those who aspire to acquire a good understanding of sampling principles. Students and researchers in the social and behavioral sciences, marketing research, public health research, social work research, educational research, and related research areas are also targeted. Although many of the principles and guidelines presented can be applied to the natural and environmental sciences, the focus of the text is on social and behavioral research.

This book is designed for the nontechnical researcher or generalist who does not intend to have a career as a sampling statistician but has a need to have a good foundation in basic principles for conducting sound research and communicating with sampling statisticians. It is not intended for mathematical statisticians, sampling experts, or students taking advanced courses in sampling theory and design. Given its purpose and audience, this book does not cover variance calculations and the calculation of complex weighting schemes. Statistical procedures for estimating population parameters, analyzing complex sample data, and related topics are beyond the scope of this text.

ORGANIZATION

This book is organized around the sequence of choices a researcher must make in selecting study participants. The chapters of the book are the following:

Chapter 1. *Preparing to make sampling choices.* This chapter begins with a brief history of sampling and a description of the major steps in sampling, and then it leads into one of the main premises of the text: Sampling choices should be made only after careful and meticulous preparation. Such preparation should include careful review of the purpose of one's study, the nature of the population, available resources, research design considerations, and ethical and legal issues considerations. Guidelines for making these preparations are presented in this chapter.

Chapter 2. *Choosing between taking a census and sampling.* The first major sampling choice one has to make is whether to take a census or to sample. In making this choice and the other choices that must be made, it is important that one has a good understanding of the differences between random sampling error and systematic error. This chapter includes detailed descriptions of these error components and how they may be minimized. Guidelines are presented for choosing between taking a census and sampling.

Chapter 3. *Choosing between nonprobability sampling and probability sampling.* If one chooses to sample, the next choice to be made is whether to select a nonprobability sample, a probability sample, or a combination of these sampling procedures (mixed-methods sampling). This chapter describes the strengths and weaknesses of nonprobability sampling and probability sampling. Guidelines are presented for choosing between them.

Chapter 4. *Choosing the type of nonprobability sampling.* If one chooses nonprobability sampling, one next has to choose the type of nonprobability sampling to use. This chapter includes descriptions of the major types of nonprobability sampling, steps involved in their administration, their subtypes, and their weaknesses and strengths. Considering the strengths and weaknesses of the various methods, guidelines are presented for choosing among them.

Chapter 5. *Choosing the type of probability sampling.* If one chooses probability sampling, one next has to choose the type of probability sampling to use. This chapter includes descriptions of the major types of probability sampling, steps involved in their administration, their subtypes, and their weaknesses and strengths. Considering the strengths and weaknesses of the various methods, guidelines are presented for choosing among them.

Chapter 6. *Sampling characterized by the nature of the sampling unit and mixed-methods sample designs.* Sampling procedures may not only be classified according to their operational procedures, they may be classified according to the nature of the unit that is sampled. Although the unit of analysis of a study may be population-based, units of the population may not be available or practical to be used as sampling units. Alternative sampling units must be used. A number of sampling procedures characterized by the nature of the sampling unit have been developed. They include telephone-based sampling, web-based sampling, address-based sampling, time-based sampling, and space-based sampling. These sampling procedures are described in this chapter.

In addition to presenting description of sample designs distinguished by the nature of the sample unit that is used, description of mixed-methods sample designs are presented in this chapter. Instead of implementing a single-method sample design, a researcher may combine and mix different types of sample designs creating mixed-methods sample designs. Mixed-methods research designs are typically characterized by the mixing of qualitative and quantitative research designs. In this text, the term *mixed-methods sample design* is used to refer to a sample design that combines multiple nonprobability sample designs, combines multiple probability sample designs, or combines nonprobability sample designs and probability sample designs. Within-methods designs and cross-methods designs may be identified. Mixed-methods sample designs are described in Chapter 6.

Chapter 7. *Choosing the size of the sample.* There are a number of factors that should be considered in determining sample size. These factors are systematically reviewed in this chapter, and guidelines are presented for their application.

FEATURES

There are important features of this text that make it different from other texts.

- It is easy to read, and it is designed for the nontechnical reader in that the presentation of statistical formulas is minimized.
- It focuses on both nonprobability sampling and probability sampling.
- It systematically lists specific steps as to how to carry out the sampling procedures discussed.
- It describes the strengths and weaknesses of the sampling procedures and compares them to each other.
- It includes examples from research literature throughout the text.
- It provides detailed guidelines for making sampling choices.
- It presents a summary and review questions at the end of each chapter.

ACKNOWLEDGMENTS

I wish to acknowledge and thank teachers I have had who have made my study of sampling and related topics interesting, exciting, and challenging: Angus Campbell, Otis Dudley Duncan, Leslie Kish, Frank Andrews, and Graham Kalton. I give special thanks to my wife, V. Nadine Daniel, who edited the multiple drafts of this text, and whose emotional support made this text possible.

CHAPTER 1

PREPARING TO MAKE SAMPLING CHOICES

What you will learn in this chapter:

- Milestones in the history of sampling
- Major steps in selecting a sample
- Preparations important for making sampling choices
- Guidelines for preparing to make sampling choices

INTRODUCTION

The key to good research is preparation, preparation, and preparation. Hence, the key to making good sampling choices is preparation, preparation, and preparation. **Sampling** may be defined as the selection of a subset of a population for inclusion in a study. If done properly, it can save money, time, and effort, while providing valid, reliable, and useful results. On the other hand, if done poorly, the findings of a study may have little scientific and practical value. In order to increase the likelihood that the findings of a study will have value, preparations should be carried out *before* making sampling choices.

This chapter begins with a brief history of sampling, followed by a description of the major steps in selecting a sample. Preparation is the first of these steps. The preparation should include a careful review of the study's purpose, the nature of the population, the available resources, various research design considerations, and ethical and legal considerations. Guidelines for making these preparations are described in this chapter.

MILESTONES IN THE HISTORY OF SAMPLING

Although sampling probably has always been part of human history, many of the sampling procedures used today have a relatively short history. Governments have long collected population data for taxation, military purposes, and other objectives. Typically, total enumeration was sought. On the other hand, private pollsters tended to use availability sampling such as straw polling. However, by the end of the 19th century, "scientific" procedures for selecting a sample began to surface. U.S. governmental agencies, in particular, began experimenting with these procedures that later became known as probability sampling. Private pollsters, on the other hand, continued to rely on availability sampling until 1936.

Critical changes in sampling procedures used by private pollsters came about in 1936 and again in 1948. In 1936, the failure of the *Literary Digest* to predict the winner of the presidential election led to a movement away from availability sampling to quota sampling. Using availability sampling of millions of respondents, the *Literary Digest* was successful in predicting the winner in each U.S. presidential election that was held between 1916 and 1932. However, it failed to do so in 1936. On the other hand, using a new sampling procedure that later came to be known as quota sampling, pollsters George Gallup, Elmo Roper, Paul Cherington, and Richardson Wood were successful in predicting Franklin D. Roosevelt as the winner in that election. This caused pollsters to pay more attention to quota sampling and less attention to availability sampling (Bryson, 1976; Cahalan, 1989; Katz & Cantril, 1937; Squire, 1988). These sampling procedures are described in detail in Chapter 4.

The failure of the *Literary Digest's* prediction of the winner of the 1936 presidential election was primarily due to two factors: coverage bias and nonresponse bias.

- **Coverage bias** is the lack of a one-to-one correspondence between the elements in the target population and the elements encompassed by the respondent selection procedures used in a study. **Sampling frame bias** is the extent to which there are differences between the elements that are listed in the frame and the elements that make up the target population. The sampling frame of the *Literary Digest* consisted of its subscribers, listings in telephone books, and listings of automobile registrants. These lists were not representative of the 1936 voting population.
- **Nonresponse bias** is the extent to which there are significant differences between the respondents and nonrespondents in terms of the variables of

interest in a study. The proportion of Republicans among the respondents to the *Literary Digest's* straw poll was higher than the proportion of Republicans among the registered voters at that time. The magazine's straw poll was thereby not representative of voters throughout the country.

After the 1936 election, private pollsters increasingly used quota sampling instead of straw polling in predicting the results of elections. On the other hand, U.S. governmental statisticians and academic statisticians increasingly focused their attention on probability sampling. Probability sampling became a fixture of the U.S. decennial censuses in 1940. However, it took the failure of polls utilizing quota sampling to predict the winner of the 1948 U.S. presidential election to cause private pollsters to adopt this evolving sampling procedure. Using quota sampling, the major polling companies (Gallup, Crossley, and Roper) predicted that Thomas Dewey would beat Harry S. Truman in the presidential election of that year. On the other hand, academic researchers utilizing probability sampling predicted Truman would win. Truman won the election by more than 2 million votes and 114 electoral votes.

The failure of the pollsters using quota sampling in predicting the winner of the 1948 presidential election was due to several factors: basing projections on outdated data, stopping data collection too soon, the impact of interviewer bias, and changes in party identifications that were not factored into the projections.

- *The election projections were based on outdated data.* The quota sampling procedures used by the pollsters were based on the 1940 census, data collected 8 years earlier. As a result of major population changes during those 8 years, 1940 census data did not reflect the 1948 voting population.
- *The pollsters stopped collecting data too soon.* Gallup and Crossley stopped collecting data mid-October. Roper stopped in August. At the time they stopped polling, there were yet many voters undecided. A large proportion of these voters decided to vote for Truman.
- *Interviewer bias also contributed to the problem.* Quota sampling has an inherent problem of interviewer bias. In using this sampling procedure, interviewers have discretion to interview whomever they desire as long as they satisfy quota control requirements of the sampling procedure. As a result, working class voters are more likely to be ignored by interviewers, and in 1948, these voters were more likely to vote Democratic.
- *Changing dynamics of political party identification also contributed to the failure of the pollsters.* The Progressive Party and the Dixiecrat Party also had candidates in the race. The effect of these candidates tended to

help the Democratic Party. The Communist Party USA did not run a candidate for president, but endorsed the Progressive Party's candidate. This endorsement deflected anti-communism attacks away from the Democratic Party. Many White southerners left the Democratic Party to support the Dixiecrats. This made the Democratic Party more acceptable to Blacks, and they gave it their support.

The failure of the major polling companies to predict the winner of the 1948 U.S. presidential election motivated them to move away from quota sampling and incorporate probability sampling into their polling procedures. They joined statisticians in the federal government and academia in endorsing probability sampling. Probability sampling became the dominant sampling procedure for estimating population parameters. The major types of probability sampling are described in Chapter 5.

Up to today, sampling procedures continued to evolve. To a certain extent, as modes of collecting data changed, sampling procedures changed. During the period of the 1970s through the 1990s, there was a movement from personal interview surveys to telephone surveys. Variants of random digit dialing (RDD) sampling procedures were developed to meet challenges of telephone surveys. As research methods embraced advances in electronic technology, including the use of online surveys, fax machines, and cell phones, sampling procedures were further modified and adjusted. Today, a wide range of nonprobability and probability sampling procedures are used, making sampling choices more challenging than ever before.

MAJOR STEPS IN SELECTING A SAMPLE

One may identify six major steps in selecting a sample (see Figure 1.1):

Step 1. Prepare to make sampling choices.

Step 2. Choose between taking a census and sampling.

Step 3. Choose nonprobability, probability, or mixed-methods sample design.

Step 4. Choose the type of nonprobability, probability, or mixed-methods sample design.

Step 5. Determine the sample size.

Step 6. Select the sample.

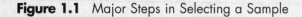

Figure 1.1 Major Steps in Selecting a Sample

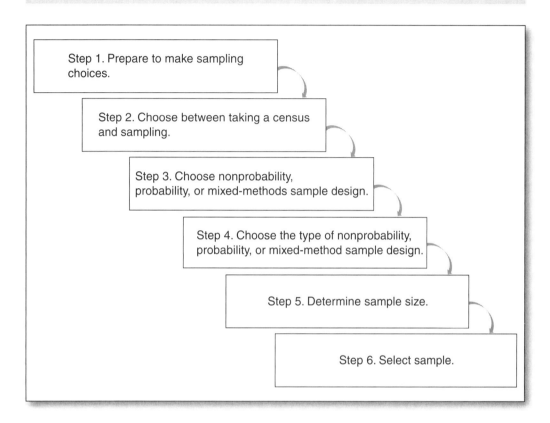

Step 1. Prepare to Make Sampling Choices

Specific preparation should be made before making sampling choices. Such preparation should include a careful review of the purpose of one's study, the nature of the population, available resources, research design considerations, and ethical and legal issues considerations. Guidelines for making these preparations are presented in the next section of this chapter.

Step 2. Choose Between Taking a Census and Sampling

The second step involves choosing between selecting the entire target population (taking a **census**) and selecting a subset of the target population (sampling). In making this choice it is important that one has a good understanding of the differences between random sampling error and systematic error. A description of these differences and guidelines for choosing between taking a census and sampling are described in Chapter 2.

Step 3. Choose Between Nonprobability, Probability, or Mixed-Methods Sample Designs

Once a decision is made to sample, the next step involves choosing between the two major types of sampling: nonprobability sampling and probability sampling. Probability sampling gives every element in the target population a known and nonzero chance of being selected. Nonprobability sampling does not. Guidelines for choosing between nonprobability sampling and probability sampling are described in Chapter 3. Guidelines for choosing mixed-methods sample designs are included in Chapter 6.

Step 4. Choose the Type of Nonprobability, Probability, or Mixed-Methods Sample Design

The next step involves choosing the specific type of nonprobability or probability sample design to be employed. One may opt to utilize a mixed-methods sample procedure combining different types of nonprobability sampling procedures, different types of probability sampling procedures, or combining nonprobability and probability sampling procedures. The major types of nonprobability sample designs are described in Chapter 4; the major types of probability sample designs are described in Chapter 5. At the end of these two chapters, guidelines are presented to assist in making a sample design choice.

Some sample designs are distinguished by the nature of their sampling units and others by the mixing of more than one sample design type. These types of designs are described in Chapter 6. Designs distinguished by the nature of their sampling units are telephone-based sampling, web-based sampling, address-based sampling, time-based sampling, and space-based sampling. In mixing different types of sample designs, one may mix different types of nonprobability sample designs, mix different types of probability sample designs, or mix nonprobability and probability sample designs. Mixed-methods sample designs are also described in Chapter 6.

Step 5. Determine the Sample Size

Having chosen a specific type of sampling design to be used to select a sample, the next step involves determining of the number of elements to be selected. Chapter 7 describes factors that should be considered in determining sample size and guidelines for doing so.

Step 6. Select the Sample

The final step in sampling involves implementing one's sampling choices. The quality of the resulting sample is dependent substantially on the first step: preparing to make sampling choices. Guidelines for preparing to make sampling choices are presented below.

GUIDELINES FOR PREPARING TO MAKE SAMPLING CHOICES

Specific preparation should be made before making sampling choices. Several guidelines may be proposed. In considering the guidelines listed below and others presented in other chapters, it should be noted that they are not equally important; nor are they absolute. In many cases, their applicability is contingent on specific conditions that may or not be present. Often, the researcher must balance competing and conflicting guidelines.

Before making sampling choices one should be able to clearly answer such questions as: What are the objectives of the study? How is the target population defined? What is the nature of the population (i.e., its size, heterogeneity, accessibility, spatial distribution, and destructibility)? What resources are available to conduct the study? What type of research design will be implemented? What ethical and legal issues should be taken into account? Considering questions such as these, guidelines for preparing to make sampling choices may be categorized as:

- Objectives of the study
- Definition of the population
- Nature of the population
- Availability of resources
- Research design considerations
- Ethical and legal considerations

Objectives of the Study

> **Guideline 1.1.** *Objectives of the study.* Prior to making sampling choices, make sure one has a good understanding of the objectives of the study, the importance of the study, and the special needs of the study, if any.

There should be a good fit between the objectives of a study and the sampling choices a researcher makes. A research study may have only one or a combination of the following objectives: exploration, description, prediction, evaluation, and explanation. **Exploratory research** targets information seeking to better understand a population, theoretical issues, or methodological issues relating to a study. A study with a descriptive objective seeks to describe the parameters of a population, differences between or among population, or relationships among variables. A study with a prediction objective seeks to predict future parameters of a population, differences between or among populations, or relationships among variables. **Evaluation research** seeks to determine the need for an intervention, how the need should be addressed, the ongoing progress of an intervention, and the outcome of an intervention. **Explanatory research** attempts to explain the patterns of population parameters and the relationships among variables.

Different objectives of a study may require different sampling choices. Typically, exploratory research does not require a rigorous sample design. A nonprobability sample with a small sample size may suffice. On the other hand, the requirements of the sample design of a descriptive study may depend on the amount of detail required, the confidence level requirements, and the homogeneity/heterogeneity of the population. The required precision of one's predictions may determine the amount of rigor in the sample design of a prediction study. In part, the sample design for an evaluation research project is dependent on the type of evaluation research one is conducting (formative evaluation, process evaluation, or outcome evaluation). A study with an explanatory research purpose may require a more rigorous sample design than a study that has one of the other purposes.

There should be a good fit between the importance of a study and the sampling choices that are made. Studies are not equally important. Highly important studies require a much more rigorous sample design than studies that are not as important. A researcher should have a clear understanding of the importance of a study before making sampling choices.

Moreover, there should be a good fit between the special needs of a study, if any, and the sampling choices that are made. The special needs of a study may require the selection of particular population elements, a particular sample size, or a particular situation. In order to ensure that the special needs of a study are met, the researcher possibly should purposefully select particular elements of the population.

Definition of the Population

Before making sampling choices, it is important that one clearly defines the **target population** (the set of elements one desires to apply the findings of the study). An ambiguously defined target population may lead to **population specification bias** (systematic bias resulting from a poor fit between the definition of the target population and the actual population studied). One should have an unambiguous definition of the target population before making sampling choices.

The definition of the target population should clearly identify inclusive and exclusive criteria for participation in the study. That is, it should clearly indicate which elements are included in the target population and which elements are not excluded in it. Inclusive and exclusive criteria should be specified. Inclusion criteria are a set of conditions that must be met for participation in a study. Exclusion criteria are a set of conditions for not allowing participation in a study. Elements may be excluded because they have health problems, their age, they possess characteristics that may confound the study's findings, they may have a language barrier, or they may create a burden for collecting data. Persons living in nursing homes, mental institutions, prisons, or jails may be excluded from the target population even though they satisfy inclusion criteria of the study.

The definition of the target population should specify:

- Nature of the elements
- Sampling units containing the elements to be selected
- Geographic location of the elements
- Time period under consideration

For example, for a study of persons with HIV who live in Washington, DC, one may define the target population as persons with HIV (nature of the elements) living in households (sampling units) in Washington, DC (geographical location), June 2008 (time period). Given this definition, persons with HIV who do not live in Washington, DC, and persons who live in Washington, DC, but reside in a hospice would not be included in the target population.

The following research note illustrates the use of inclusive and exclusive criteria in defining a target population.

> *(handwritten margin notes)*
> no adjuncts
> just PT
> Should chairs be included
> or just for teaching this
> term. No one on
> sabbatical
> Should we include
> administrators?

RESEARCH NOTE 1.1

Example of the Use of Inclusive and Exclusive Criteria in Defining a Target Population

Wingood and DiClemente (1998) described the inclusive and exclusive criteria they used in defining their target population in their study of African American women's noncondom use during sexual intercourse as follows:

Inclusion criteria consisted of being a sexually active, heterosexual African American female, 18–29 years of age, residing in the Bayview-Hunter's Point neighborhood. Exclusion criteria consisted of a history of injection drug use or crack cocaine in the past 3 months. Study participants were recruited using street outreach and media advertisements placed throughout the community. Indigenous African American female field recruiters, familiar with the Bayview-Hunter's Point neighborhood, approached and screened women at the local unemployment office, the Social Security office, public laundry facilities, beauty salons, grocery stores, health clinics, and the local (AFDC) office to identify women eligible for participation in the study.

Source: Wingood & DiClemente, 1998, p. 34. With kind permission from Springer Science+Business Media.

Nature of the Population

> **Guideline 1.2.** *Nature of the population.* Prior to making sampling choices, one should have a good understanding of the target population, including its content, size, heterogeneity/homogeneity, accessibility, spatial distribution, and destructibility.

Content of the Population

The content of the population should affect sampling choices. The elements of the population of a research study may be people, things, places, events, situations, or time. The composition of many materials that may be studied in the natural sciences may be assumed to be constant, making any sample essentially identical to any other sample. A sample of blood taken from one's finger may be considered equivalent to a sample of blood taken from one's arm. In such situations, generalizing from a single sampled element may be acceptable. However, different samples of a human population may be extremely unlike each other. Generalizing from a small sample of people may be untenable.

Size of the Population   *How many do we have?,*

The size of a population is a critical factor in making sampling choices. One should have knowledge of the size of the population before making sampling choices. More resources and a larger sample size may be necessary to study a large population than to study a small population. Costs, the amount of time needed to collect the study's data, management issues, random sampling error, and systematic error are tied to the size of the population, and thereby affect sampling choices.

Heterogeneity/Homogeneity of the Population

The homogeneity/homogeneity of a population should be considered in making sampling choices. Studies of populations that are relatively homogeneous require smaller samples than studies of populations that are relatively heterogeneous. Before making sampling choices one should determine the homogeneity/heterogeneity of the target population. In conducting a literature review and exploratory research, special attention should be paid to measures of the variability (i.e., standard deviation, variances, etc.) of one's key variables of interest. A pilot study may be in order to acquire such information.

Accessibility of the Population

Populations vary in their accessibility. The accessibility of a population will affect the ability of a researcher to successfully implement a sample design, and should be considered in making sampling choices. Segments of the population may be in remote locations, gated communities or buildings, or other inaccessible locations. Some populations are considered to be "hidden" due to the difficulty to locate them and gain their cooperation. Examples include persons at risk of HIV infection, gang-affiliated adolescents, gays and lesbians who are "in the closet," injection drug users, sex workers, and the street homeless. Elements of the target population may be inaccessible because they have neither a postal address nor an e-mail address. In preparing to make sampling choices, one should determine the accessibility of the target population. Important segments of the target population that are inaccessible may result in coverage bias.

Spatial Distribution of the Population

The spatial distribution of a population is likely to have a significant impact on the data collection costs of a study and the amount of effort necessary to get the study done. Generally, the more scattered the population, the more resources (i.e., people, time, money, etc.) are necessary to contact and collect data from the population. The sample design should take this factor into account. Acquiring information on the spatial distribution of a population is an important part of preparing to make sampling choices.

Destructibility of the Population

Total enumeration is not an option if making contact and collecting data from a population element destroys it or seriously affects its utility for use in future research. The destructibility of the population elements should be considered in making sampling choices. If destroyed or changed in a significant way, use of the population for future research may be compromised. In preparing to make sampling choices, one should assess the likelihood of the destructibility of the population.

Availability of Resources

> **Guideline 1.3.** *Availability of resources.* Prior to making sampling choices, make a comprehensive assessment of the resources available to conduct the research.

An assessment should be made of available resources to conduct a study before making sampling choices. Typical resources include money, time, personnel, authority, facilities, information sources, equipment, and sampling frame. One should determine the adequacy of availability of resources. If adequate resources are not available, one should acquire what is needed, or make appropriate adjustments to one's sampling choices.

The availability of an appropriate **sampling frame** (i.e., a listing of the target population) is critical in making sampling choices. It may determine whether one should choose nonprobability sampling or probability sampling. Examples of sampling frames include a listing of names of employees, names of customers, addresses, telephone numbers, city directory, and a map. A suitable sampling frame may not exist or may not be accessible to the researcher because of privacy regulations or other reasons. Moreover, it may be very time-consuming to develop an appropriate frame or expensive to purchase one from a vendor.

A good sampling frame would identify all members of the target population only once, and have no other entries, but also include auxiliary information that may be useful in making sampling choices. A good sampling frame would be complete, accurate, up-to-date, reliable, and convenient to use. In preparing to make sampling choices, one should determine the availability of a good sampling frame, and the resources available to create one if one does not exist. Once obtained or developed, an assessment should be made of any sampling frame bias that may exist.

Research Design Considerations

Guideline 1.4. *Research design considerations.* Prior to making sampling choices, determine the type of research design, the data collection design, and the data analysis design that will be used.

Sampling choices should be made in conjunction with other choices relating to the research design of a study. Most important are choices relating to the following:

- Type of research design
- Data collection design
- Data analysis design

Type of Research Design

There should be a good fit between the type of research design used in a study and the sampling choices that are made. One should determine the type of research design that will be employed before making sampling choices. Major types of research designs may be classified as follows:

- Qualitative versus quantitative research designs
- Nonexperimental versus experimental research designs
- Cross-sectional versus longitudinal research designs
- Mixed-methods designs

Qualitative Versus Quantitative Research Designs. Sampling choices for qualitative research tend to be different from sampling choices for quantitative research. **Qualitative research** primarily involves the collection and analysis of non-numerical data, with more attention focused on understanding the nature of the elements selected for study than to generalizing to a target population. It is characterized by in-depth inquiry; immersion into the social setting of that being studied; emphasis on the understanding of the participants' perspectives; and comprehensive description of the study's topic. Conversely, **quantitative research** primarily involves the collection and analysis of numerical data, with more attention focused on generalizing to a target population than understanding the nature of the elements selected for study.

Both probability sampling and nonprobability sampling are utilized throughout quantitative research, whereas qualitative research primarily employs nonprobability sampling. Probability sampling might not yield elements of the population that can satisfy the needs of qualitative research. Typically, the qualitative researcher is not interested in estimating population parameters, but rather interested in selecting population elements that are most useful in providing rich information about the topic of the study. These elements may have to be purposefully selected.

Typically, in quantitative research a fixed sample size is set prior to data collection. A researcher might set a target sample size so as to yield a specific margin of error or confidence interval within which is expected to include the true population value. On the other hand, in qualitative research, a sequential approach is more common. Using such an approach, a qualitative researcher would continue to sample until data saturation is reached, that is, as new elements are added to the study, no new information or understanding is forthcoming.

Nonexperimental Research Versus Experimental Research Designs. Sampling choices for experimental research tend to be different from sampling choices for nonexperimental research. In **experimental research**, a researcher controls exposure to the key independent variable of a study. The researcher creates variability in the key independent variable. On the other hand, in **nonexperimental research**, a researcher does not control exposure to the key independent variable of a study. Instead of creating variability in the key independent variable as in experimental research, the researcher measures naturally occurring variability in the variable. Although both probability sampling and nonprobability sampling are used in nonexperimental research and experimental research, the sample designs tend to be more complex and the sample sizes tend to be larger in nonexperimental research studies than in experimental research studies. The primary purpose of experimental research is to make generalizations about cause and effect relationships, and making generalizations about population parameters is of secondary importance. Experimental research attempts to achieve external validity through replication, whereas nonexperimental research attempts to achieve external validity through its sample design.

Two major subtypes of experimental design research are quasi-experimental designs and true experimental designs, such as randomized clinical trials. These designs differ in terms of the extent to which extraneous variables are controlled, and require different sample designs. In quasi-experimental designs, nonprobability sampling is used, and in true experimental designs, random sampling and random assignment to treatment modalities are used.

Cross-Sectional Versus Longitudinal Research Designs. Sampling choices for cross-sectional research tend to be different from sampling choices for longitudinal research. **Cross-sectional research designs** involve the collection of data within one time period. **Longitudinal research** designs the collection of data over multiple time periods. Cross-sectional designs are sometimes referred to as "in-time" studies, and longitudinal designs are referred to as "through-time" studies. In cross-sectional research, all measurements are made at a single point in time or over a relatively short period. There is no need to followup the participants for later data collection. Sampling requirements for cross-sectional research are generally less difficult than sampling requirements for longitudinal research.

Three major terms are used to classify different types of longitudinal designs: *trend study, cohort study,* and *panel study.* A **trend study** examines patterns of changes in variables over time. The terms **cohort study** and **panel study** are often used interchangeably as a study that tracks over time population elements that have a common experience. At times, the terms *cohort study* and *panel study* are used differently. The term *cohort study* may be used to refer to a longitudinal study in which samples are selected over time from the same sampling frame, and the term *panel study* is used to refer to a longitudinal study in which the same sample is studied over time. In this context, depending on the population size and the sample size, in using a cohort study, the same people may not be selected for each data collection event.

Longitudinal designs raise issues of bias due to repeated surveying, attrition, the burden of repeated data collection on respondents, and the proper mix of old and replacement respondents. At times a cross-sectional design is combined with a longitudinal design by systematically adding new elements from the target population to compensate for attrition. A **rotating panel design** may be used to reduce respondent burden. This involves the use of multiple panels of population elements with each being used a fixed number of times and targeting different variables of interest. Given that these designs require different sampling choices, they require different preparations to enhance their effectiveness.

Mixed-Methods Research Designs. A researcher may not limit the study he or she conducts to a single design. A combination of research designs, mixed-methods research designs, may be employed. Much of the literature on mixed-methods designs focus on the mixing of qualitative and quantitative research designs. Other options include the mixing of nonexperimental and experimental research designs, and/or the mixing of cross-sectional and longitudinal research designs. The mixing of different designs has implications for the sampling choices that are made. A mixed-methods sample design may be advisable, and a larger or smaller sample size may be required than would be required if a single-method design is used. One may mix different nonprobability sample designs, mix different probability sample designs, or mix nonprobability and probability sample designs. Mixed-methods sample designs are described in Chapter 6.

A research design has three major components or sub-designs: the selection of study participants design, the data collection design, and the data analysis design. These sub-designs must fit well together and with the purpose of a study for a study to be effective.

Data Collection Design

There should be a good fit between the data collection choices and the sampling choices that are made. The different modes of collecting data tend to have different sources of systematic error and costs. The preparation of making sampling choices includes estimating eligibility rates, unit nonresponse rates, item nonresponse rates, and data collection costs. All of these factors should be recognized and taken into account when making sampling choices.

Data Analysis Design

There should be a good fit between the data analysis choices and the sampling choices that are made. The data analysis plans of a research project might require only a few basic analyses. On the other hand, the data analysis design may require complex, multivariate procedures. Moreover, statistical procedures vary in terms of their sampling requirements. Some statistical procedures require probability sampling. Generally, the more complex the data analysis design, the larger the required sample size. Sampling choices should be made after determination of the data analysis requirements.

Ethical and Legal Considerations

> **Guideline 1.5.** *Ethical and legal considerations.* Prior to making sampling choices, identify any ethical or legal concerns relating to the research project.

There should be a good fit between the ethical and legal concerns and the sampling choices that are made. Concerns relating to informed consent, privacy, anonymity, confidentiality, and professional codes of ethics may make it impractical or impossible to implement certain sample designs. As part of the preparation in making sampling choices, one should make sure one is aware of the relevant ethical and legal regulations.

In order to acquire sufficient information to apply the above guidelines, it may be necessary to conduct formative research including a comprehensive literature review and exploratory research. Research Note 1.2 describes the formative research conducted in a study of men who have sex with other men.

RESEARCH NOTE 1.2

Example of Formative Research in Preparing to Make Sampling Choices: A Study of Men Who Have Sex With Men

In preparation for the National HIV Behavioral Surveillance (NHBS) study of men who have sex with men (MSM), MacKellar et al. (2007) conducted formative research to acquire information for planning the sample design of the study. They described the formative research conducted as follows:

Formative research was conducted to learn about the venues, times, and methods to recruit MSM. To meet these objectives, staff reviewed advertisements for MSM in online and print media, interviewed key informants, and

(Continued)

(Continued)

conducted observations at venues. Key informant interviews were conducted with MSM, MSM researchers, and knowledgeable staff of state and local health departments, prevention planning groups, community-based organizations, service providers, and commercial and social MSM venues. To help ensure that all potential venues were identified, interviews were conducted with key informants of different age groups, race/ethnicities, and sexual orientations.

For each venue identified in these interviews, staff collected information on MSM attendance during specific days and times; the estimated distribution of patrons by race, age group, and sexual orientation; safety issues; and management contact information (if applicable). Staff also asked key informants about participation motivations and disincentives, optimal referrals for prevention and health-care services, and needs for coordination with other venue-based research and prevention efforts. When applicable, staff met with venue owners or managers to solicit their approval to conduct NHBS-MSM on their property.

Finally, staff observed MSM attendance and patron flow patterns at identified venues to learn how recruitment and interview methods might be optimally applied (logistics). If initial formative research did not yield sufficient information on attendance, staff conducted 30- to 60-minute enumerations of male patrons within identified VDTs [venue-specific, day-time periods]. If the proportion of male patrons who were MSM was also unknown or thought to be low (e.g., at street locations, mixed clubs, parks), staff would approach counted men to ascertain their demographic, residence, and sexual-behavior characteristics. These data were then used to estimate the number and proportion of eligible MSM who attended VDTs. VDTs estimated to yield .75% MSM of men approached were considered MSM venues.

Source: MacKellar, Gallagher, Finlayson, Sanchez, Lansky, & Sullivan, 2007, p. 41. Reprinted with permission.

Once appropriate preparation has been made, one would then address the first major choice: whether to conduct a census or whether to sample. Guidelines relating to making this choice are presented in the next chapter.

SUMMARY

Throughout much of human history, total enumeration was considered the only valid way to study populations. Sampling was limited to straw polling, volunteer sampling, and other availability sampling procedures. Quota sampling was introduced in the early 20th century, and took off when pollsters using the technique were successful in predicting the winner of the 1936 U.S. presidential election, whereas pollsters, the *Literary Digest* in particular, utilizing haphazard polling techniques failed to predict the winner. Toward the end of the 19th century, scholars proposed the use of "scientific" sampling. As pollsters turned to quota sampling, governmental researchers and academicians turned to probability sampling in their research. Probability sampling became the preferred technique in 1948 when pollsters utilizing quota sampling failed to predict the winner of the U.S. presidential election that year.

The sampling process has six major steps:

Step 1. Prepare to make sampling choices.

Step 2. Choose between taking a census and sampling.

Step 3. Choose nonprobability, probability, or mixed-methods sample design.

Step 4. Choose the type of nonprobability, probability, or mixed-methods sample design.

Step 5. Determine the sample size.

Step 6. Select the sample.

Proper preparation should be made in the first step so that one has the necessary information to effectively carry out the subsequent steps. One should clearly understand the objectives of the study, definition of the population, content of the population, size of the population, heterogeneity of the population, accessibility of the population, spatial distribution of the population, destructibility of the population, availability of resources, type of research design to be employed, and relevant ethical and legal considerations.

REVIEW QUESTIONS

1. What are the major milestones in the history of sampling?

2. What should contemporary political pollsters learn from the problems political pollsters had in predicting the winner of the 1936 and the 1948 presidential elections?

3. What are the major steps in selecting a sample?

4. What are the major types of research objectives? Why should the objectives of a study be clarified before making sampling choices?

5. What are the characteristics of a good definition of a target population? Give examples.

6. In preparing to make sampling choices, why is it important to consider the target population's (a) content, (b) size, (c) heterogeneity, (d) accessibility, (e) spatial distribution, and (f) destructibility?

7. Prior to making sampling choices, what steps should one take in determining the availability of resources to plan and execute a sample design?

8. Suppose you were charged with developing a sample design for a study of the problems children who are homeless have in completing their school assignments. Describe in detail the formative research that you would conduct to prepare for constructing your sample design.

9. What are the major types of research designs, and how do they differ in terms of the preparation that should be done for making sampling choices?

10. How might the sampling requirements of the following pairs of research designs tend to differ from each other?

   a. Qualitative versus quantitative research
   b. Experimental versus nonexperimental research
   c. Cross-sectional versus longitudinal research

11. What ethical and legal factors should be considered in making sampling choices?

12. It is often difficult to obtain a good sampling frame for a population-based study covering a large geographical area. Would a list of driver's licenses serve as a good sampling frame? Why or why not? Once you have answered these questions, consider: Lynch, C. F. et al., "The Driver's License List as a Population-Based Sampling Frame in Iowa" (1994).

KEY TERMS

Define and give examples of the following concepts:

census	cross-sectional research design
cohort study	evaluation research
coverage bias	experimental research

explanatory research

exploratory research

longitudinal research

nonexperimental research

nonresponse bias

panel study

population specification bias

qualitative research

quantitative research

rotating panel design

sample

sampling

sampling frame

sampling frame bias

target population

trend study

REFERENCES FOR FURTHER STUDY

Bryson, M. C. (1976). The Literary Digest poll: Making of a statistical myth. *American Statistician, 30,* 184–185.

Cahalan, D. (1989). The digest poll rides again. *Public Opinion Quarterly, 53,* 129–133.

Cowles, M. (2000). Statistics in psychology: An historical perspective. Mahwah, NJ: Lawrence Erlbaum.

Crossley, A. M. (1957). Early days of public opinion research. *Public Opinion Quarterly, 21,* 159–164.

Edwin, R. (1960). Gallup polls public opinion for 25 years. *Editor & Publisher, 93,* 62–63.

Frankel, M. R., & Frankel, L. R. (1987). Fifty years of survey sampling in the United States. *Public Opinion Quarterly, 51,* S127 –S138.

Gallup, G. (1957). The changing climate for public opinion research. *Public Opinion Quarterly, 21,* 23–27.

Hansen, M. H. (1987). Some history and reminiscences on survey sampling. *Statistical Science, 2,* 180–190.

Ibo, S. E. (2006). A gold mine and a tool for democracy: George Gallup, Elmo Roper, and the business of scientific polling, 1935–1955. *Journal of the History of Behavioral Sciences, 42,* 109–134.

Katz, D., & Cantril, H. (1937). Public opinion polls. *Sociometry, 1,* 155–179.

Kish, L. (1995). The hundred year wars of survey sampling. *Statistics in Transition, 2,* 813–830.

Kruskal, W., & Mosteller, F. (1980). Representative sampling, IV: The history of the concept in statistics, 1895–1939. *International Review of Statistics, 48,* 169–195.

Link, H. C. (1947). Some milestones in public opinion research. *Journal of Applied Psychology, 313,* 225–234.

Lynch, C. F., Logsden-Sackett, N., Edwards, S. L., & Cantor, K. P. (1994). The driver's license list as a population-based sampling frame in Iowa. *American Journal of Public Health, 84,* 469–472.

Northrop, A. (1971). The rise of the polls: Bloopers amid improving aim. *National Journal, 3,* 1703.

Squire, P. (1988). Why the 1936 Literary Digest poll failed. *Public Opinion Quarterly, 52,* 125–133.

Stephan, F. F. (1948). History and uses of modern sampling procedures. *Journal of the American Statistical Association, 43*, 12–39.

Stephan, F. F. (1949). Development of election forecasting by polling methods. In F. Mosteller, H. Hyman, P. J. McCarthy, E. S. Marks, & D. B. Truman (Eds.), *The pre-election polls of 1948: Report to the Committee on Analysis of Pre-Election Polls and Forecasts, Social Science Research Council, Bulletin no 60* (pp. 8–14). New York: Social Science Research Council.

Sudman, S., & Blair, E. (1999). Sampling in the twenty-first century. *Journal of the Academy of Marketing Science, 27*, 269–277.

Wallace, H. A., &.McCamy, J. L. (1940). Straw polls and public administration. *Public Opinion Quarterly, 4*, 221–223.

Weiss, N. J. (1983). *Farewell to the party of Lincoln*. Princeton, NJ: Princeton University Press.

CHAPTER 2
CHOOSING BETWEEN TAKING A CENSUS AND SAMPLING

What you will learn in this chapter:

- The difference between random sampling error and systematic error
- Major subtypes of systematic error, their sources, how they may be minimized, and how they relate to choosing between taking a census and sampling
- Strengths and weaknesses of taking a census and sampling
- Guidelines for choosing between taking a census and sampling

INTRODUCTION

With proper preparation a researcher will be able to make informed sampling choices. The first major choice to be made is choosing between taking a census (including all of the elements in the target population) and sampling (including only a subset of the elements). This chapter reviews factors that should be considered in making this choice. It is important to understand the various sources of error in conducting research when choosing between taking a census and sampling. This chapter will describe these sources of error in research along with guidelines for choosing between taking a census and sampling.

The total error in a research study may be broken into two major categories: random error and systematic error (bias). These forms of error occur throughout the research process. Random sampling error accounts for most of a study's random error. Often the term "sampling error" is used to refer to random sampling error, and the term "nonsampling error" is used to refer to systematic error and any random errors that are not due to sampling. Although these terms may be used, we will use the terms *random sampling error* and *systematic error* in this text. A diagram of the components of total error is presented in Figure 2.1.

Figure 2.1 Components of Total Error

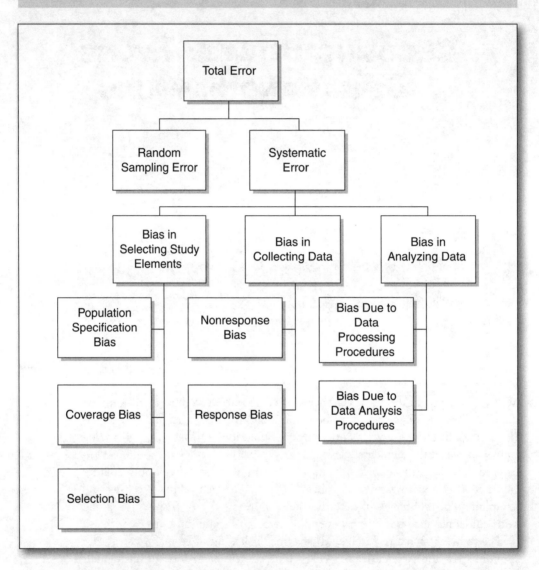

Random sampling error is the difference between a sample estimate and the true population value that is due to chance variation of multiple samples. If one selects more than one sample, it is not likely that each sample will yield exactly the same estimate. Random variation is likely to occur. This random fluctuation is random sampling error. It is measured via the calculation of the standard error of the statistics employed in analyzing the data collected (i.e., means, percentages, correlation coefficients, etc.).

A census will not have random sampling error because a sample of the population is not taken. If probability sampling is used, it may be estimated by computing the margin of error of the estimates. Random sampling error may be minimized by maximizing the sample size and sampling so as to take advantage of any homogeneity that may exist in a population. However, it should be noted that increasing the size of a sample may increase data collection costs and systematic error. Hence, there are trade-offs between precision, costs, and bias in making sampling choices.

Systematic error, or bias, is the difference between a sample estimate and the true population value that is due to factors other than random error. It tends to make one's population estimates consistently lower or higher than the true population parameter.

Random sampling error affects the precision of estimates, and systematic error affects the validity of estimates. Estimates may have a high amount of systematic error but a low amount of random sampling error, and vice versa. A depiction of the effect of random sampling error and systematic error on sample estimates is presented in Table 2.1. Depending on the combined effects of random sampling error and systematic error, an estimate may be:

- Imprecise and biased
- Imprecise and unbiased
- Precise and biased
- Precise and unbiased

Systematic error occurs throughout the research process. We may classify systematic error according to the stages of the research process. The following categories may be used: bias in selecting study elements, bias in collecting data from the selected elements, and bias in analyzing the data collected.

Table 2.1   Characteristics of Sample Estimates for Varying Levels of Random Sampling Error and Systematic Error

	Random Sampling Error	
Systematic Error	High	Low
High	Imprecise and biased	Precise and biased
Low	Imprecise and unbiased	Precise and unbiased

BIAS IN SELECTING STUDY ELEMENTS

There are three main forms of bias in the selection of study elements: population specification bias, coverage bias, and selection bias. These subcategories are described below.

Population Specification Bias

What Is Population Specification Bias?

There should be a good fit between the target population and the purposes of the proposed study. However, it is possible for a researcher to identify an inappropriate population for a study. **Population specification bias** is a poor fit between the research questions a study attempts to answer and the population that is chosen to be studied. It may be due to ambiguity in the definition of the research problem or a poor definition of the target population. It may occur in taking a census or in sampling. In a study of persons with HIV who live in Washington, DC, defining the target population so as to exclude certain types of residents of the city who are living with HIV, or include persons who live in the suburban areas of the city, would make for population specification bias. A marketing research study that targets housewives may have population specification bias for in many households the "housewife" may not be the principal decision maker regarding the product of interest.

How Can Population Specification Bias Be Minimized?

Population specification bias may be minimized by making sure one has a good understanding of the research questions of a study and by clearly defining the target population. As noted in Chapter 1, one should clearly define the population in terms of (a) the nature of the elements, (b) sampling units containing the elements to be selected, (c) geographic location of the elements, and (d) the time period under consideration.

Coverage Bias

What Is Coverage Bias?

Coverage bias is the lack of a one-to-one correspondence between the elements in the target population and the elements encompassed by the respondent selection procedures used in a study. It may occur in taking a census and in sampling.

Coverage bias is often referred to as frame error as it is often due to problems associated with the sampling frame that is used. A **sampling frame** is a listing of the target population. It may be a list frame (e.g., a listing of names, telephone numbers, addresses, time periods, or events), an area frame (e.g., a map or a diagram), or a physical manifestation of the target population. If a listing of the target population is not available, one may be able to utilize an area frame that lists geographical areas that contain elements of the target population. A study may employ a dual frame option using both a list frame and an area frame.

A good sampling frame will list individually each element of the target population (at least, every category of elements in the target population) only once, and include no elements that are not a member of the target population. Moreover, a good sampling frame would be up-to-date and consist of more than a mere listing of the target population by including auxiliary information that may be used in stratification and measuring coverage and nonresponse bias.

What Are the Subtypes of Coverage Bias?

Kish (1965) identified four basic types of sampling frame bias:

- Foreign elements: Elements listed in the frame are not members of the target population.
- Missing elements: Elements of the target population are not listed in the frame.
- Duplicate entries: Elements of the target population are listed more than once in the frame.
- Clusters of elements together in one listing. Elements of the population are listed together in aggregates or groups instead of individually.

We may label these four types of bias as: *overcoverage bias, undercoverage bias, multiple-coverage bias,* and *clustered frame bias* (see Figure 2.2). Elements that are not members of the target population may be included in the frame (overcoverage), some members of the target population may not be included in the frame (undercoverage), other members of the target population may be included more than once (multiple-coverage), and some members of the target population may be listed in aggregates of two or more elements (clustered frame bias).

Figure 2.2 Types of Coverage Bias

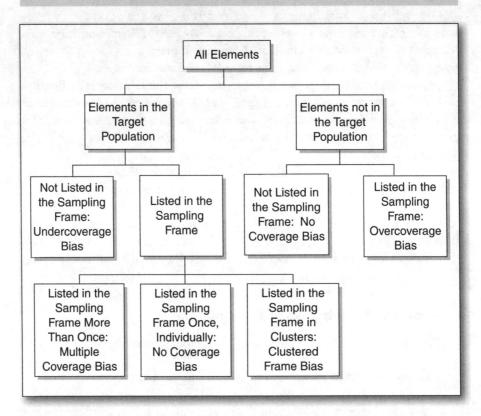

Overcoverage bias. Overcoverage bias (also referred to as "overregistration") is bias due to the use of a sampling frame that includes elements that are not members of the target population of a study. That is, "ineligible elements" or "foreign elements" are listed in the sampling frame. A sampling frame will have overcoverage to the extent it includes elements that are not in the target population. A listing of residences might include unoccupied buildings or businesses that may appear to be occupied residential housing. Overcoverage will affect the incidence rate for the study; that is, the percentage of elements on a sampling frame who qualify as members of the target population.

Undercoverage bias. Undercoverage bias (also referred to as "underregistration" and "noncoverage") is bias due to the use of a sampling frame that does not include elements that are members of the target population of a study. It may be due to:

- Mistake in listing prepared during field operations. In sampling buildings on a block, a researcher might first create a sampling frame of the building on the block. In carrying out these field operations, it is possible that a building in the rear of another building may be missed.
- Noninclusion of absent household members. In a voting behavior study, an interviewer may ask a respondent to list the persons who are registered to vote, creating a sampling frame of the household members within the target population. Undercoverage will occur if a respondent forgets to mention a household member within the target population who is infrequently at home.
- Omissions due to misunderstanding of survey concepts. A misunderstanding of the criteria for membership in the population may result in undercoverage.
- Dwelling units may be unoccupied when the sampling frame was prepared but occupied at the time of data collection. A newly constructed building may have no occupants at the time a sampling frame was prepared; however, by the time data collection commenced, the building could be fully occupied by members of the target population.
- Geographical areas may be purposely excluded because of inaccessibility.
- Population elements or groupings may be purposely excluded because of difficulty in locating them and obtaining their cooperation.
- Undercoverage may be due to the mode of a study. Web-based surveys (note that, unless specified, the term "web-based surveys" is used to refer to online surveys, email surveys, and other electronic surveys) are likely to have more undercoverage bias than telephone surveys, and telephone surveys are likely to have more undercoverage bias than personal interview surveys. A census would have undercoverage bias if elements of the population are inaccessible and are excluded from the study.

Due to this bias, one may not be able to make generalizations to the target population, and must limit one's generalizations to the accessible or available population. Moreover, undercoverage bias may lead to a decrease in the sample size, thus affecting random sampling error.

Multiple-coverage bias. Multiple-coverage bias is bias due to the use of a sampling frame that includes elements more than once. This creates a problem of multiplicity by giving some of the elements multiple chances to be included in the sample. Elements that appear more than once in the frame will have a higher probability of selection than elements that appear only once in the frame. If there is a correlation between multiplicity and the variables of interest, estimates will be biased. It is often difficult to detect such correlation and make adjustments for this problem. Multiple coverage bias may occur in taking a census or sampling.

Clustered frame bias. Clustered frame bias is due to the use a sampling frame that includes units with more than one element of the target population. For example, in a study of registered voters, clustering occurs in a sampling frame consisting of telephone numbers or addresses. These listings are likely to include more than one element in the target population. Elements that are clustered together are more likely to be similar to each other than elements that are not clustered together. Correlated observations are produced, violating the assumption of independent selection of sampled units. Whereas multiple coverage makes for overrepresentation of certain elements, clustering makes for underrepresentation of certain elements in the sample. It is almost impossible to identify clustered elements before selection, making it difficult to control the sample size. As part of data collection, one must ascertain the total number of members of the target population that is in the sampled unit.

The four types of coverage bias may be illustrated further by using an example of a telephone survey targeting the adult population of a city. Let us say a telephone book is used as a sampling frame for this study. Overcoverage bias will exist to the extent nonhousehold numbers (e.g., business numbers) are listed in the directory, especially if listed in a manner not different from household numbers. Undercoverage bias will exist to the extent that adults in the population do not have landline telephones or do not have their telephone number listed in the telephone book. Multiple-coverage bias will exist to the extent that adults in the population have more than one telephone number listed in the directory. Clustered frame bias will exist to the extent that more than one adult lives in households of the selected telephone numbers. Likewise, web-based surveys are likely to have significant coverage bias. Internet access is correlated with demographic, socioeconomic, cultural, and lifestyle differences. Significant segments of the population do not have access to or do not regularly use the Internet.

How Can Coverage Bias Be Minimized?

Overcoverage bias may be minimized by (1) thoroughly reviewing and cleaning the sampling frame and dropping all ineligibles that are discovered (e.g., screening before selection) and (2) screening respondents during data collection to ensure membership in the population (e.g., screening after selection).

However, substituting ineligibles with elements that are listed next in the sampling frame that is used is inappropriate, for that would give elements listed next to ineligibles a higher probability of selection than those elements not listed next to ineligibles. Anticipating a low incidence rate, one may increase the sample size of the study. However, these efforts may add to the cost of the study without completely eliminating overcoverage bias for all ineligibles may not be identified.

Often overcoverage bias is not discovered until the data collection phase of a study. It may introduce mode effects because it is much easier to discover and correct this type of bias in some types of research (e.g., face-to-face surveys) than in other types of research (e.g., web-based surveys). Moreover, it is often difficult to distinguish overcoverage bias from nonresponse bias. Once ineligibles are discovered, they should be dropped from the study. Indirectly, this could increase random sampling error due to the decrease in sample size. If the number of ineligibles is large, one should investigate the use of alternative or dual sampling frames. A census could have overcoverage bias if it includes elements that are not part of the population, creating population specification bias.

Undercoverage bias may be minimized via several options. One option is to utilize dual sampling frames or multiple sampling frames. More than one sampling frame may be needed to fully cover a population. One should be mindful that this may produce overcoverage bias and multiple-coverage bias. In using this option, the multiple frames should be carefully screened. Another option—comprehensive training and supervision of data collectors—might reduce undercoverage error caused by the researcher. One may also opt to ignore the omissions and/or redefine the target population to fit the frame. Redefining the population risks population specification bias as the resulting population may not be relevant to the purpose of the study. Moreover, if resources are available, one may utilize external sources to supplement the frame. Adjustments may also be made at the data analysis stage through weighting (i.e., an adjustment of the data by multiplying different categories of elements by a factor that would increase or decrease the "weight" of the value of each record in the analysis of the data collected).

The use of a dual-frame sampling design may compensate for undercoverage. In order to minimize undercoverage bias in their study, Melnik et al. (2000) utilized a dual-frame sampling design in their study of the prevalence of diabetes among Puerto Rican adults in New York City. One frame sampled telephone exchanges in proportion to the number of Puerto Rican households within New York City census tracts. The other frame sampled New York City telephone numbers with associated Hispanic surnames.

In household interview studies a "half-open interval" procedure may be used to include housing units not included in the sampling frame. Although addresses are listed in the sampling frame, the addresses are thought of as the geographical area bounded by the "property lines" of the address. Data collectors are instructed to note if new and uncovered elements appear between two elements in the sampling frame. If so, these uncovered elements are included in the sample, and data collection is sought from the uncovered element. If there are a large number of uncovered elements, a subsample is selected. This procedure is applicable when the elements of the population occur in a logical order. A major weakness of the half-open interval approach is that it makes the sample size open-ended.

Multiple-coverage bias may be minimized by thoroughly cross-checking and cleaning the sampling frame. However, this is likely to be laborious and time-consuming if the sampling frame is large and not computerized. Once discovered, duplicates should be purged. One may also select a sample, and then check to determine whether the elements selected were listed more than once in the sampling frame. All duplicated elements may be weighted by the inverse of their chance of selection.

Clustered frame bias may also be controlled via weighting. One may randomly select one of the eligible elements to participate in the study and weigh it according to the size of the cluster. Elements in large clusters will have a lower overall probability of selection than elements in small clusters. Elements in smaller clusters would be overrepresented. All clustered elements may be weighted by the inverse of their chance of selection. This may be a good option if the clusters vary widely in size; however, whereas weighting will resolve the above problems, it creates another: Elements in clustered units will have a lower probability of selection than elements in nonclustered units. Thereby, elements in nonclustered units would be overrepresented in the sample. Moreover, as all the eligible elements in the clustered unit must be identified, this solution will add to data collection time and increase the burden on the respondent.

Another approach to minimize the effects of clustered frame bias is to include all the elements within a selected clustered listing. The probability of the selection of a cluster would apply to all elements in it. This will probably create nonresponse as not every element in the selected unit is likely to agree to participate in the study. Moreover, the responses of the elements who are first to participate may influence the responses of the elements who participate later. If the clusters are of different sizes, it may be difficult to control the total sample size. Moreover, this solution would increase the effective sample size and thereby have an impact on the budget for the study.

Selection Bias

What Is Selection Bias?

Selection bias is bias due to systematic differences in the characteristics of population elements that are selected to be included in the study and population elements that are not selected. There is no selection bias when one takes a census. On the other hand, selection bias is very much a part of sampling. How much will depend upon the specific sampling procedures that are used. Non-probability sampling (e.g., availability sampling and volunteer sampling) is likely to have a great deal of selection bias. Probability sampling will also have selection bias when elements are selected with unequal probabilities and when interviewers improperly select a person to be interviewed from a household that has more than one person in the target population. If an interviewer fails to make the selection a random selection either by mistake or on purpose, selection bias will have occurred. Moreover, an interviewer creates selection bias if a randomly selected person who is not at home is substituted with someone in the household who is willing and able to respond.

How Can Selection Bias Be Minimized?

Choosing to take a census will minimize selection bias. It may also be minimized via using probability sampling with equal probability selection, effective training and supervision of data collectors, and the implementation of comprehensive quality control procedures.

BIAS IN COLLECTING DATA

Data collection bias is disparity between the true characteristics of the elements selected to be included in a study and the study's observation or measurement of those characteristics. There are two major forms of data collection bias: nonresponse bias and response bias. Both types of bias are important in deciding whether to take a census or a sample.

Nonresponse Bias

What Is Nonresponse Bias?

Nonresponse bias is bias due to systematic differences in study variables between study participants and those selected for inclusion in the study, but who did not participate. It is a form of nonobservation bias that is due to the failure to collect data from sampled elements. It should be measured, assessed, and minimized. Nonresponse affects both estimates of random sampling error, by reducing the sample size, and sampling bias to the extent that there are systematic differences between respondents and nonrespondents.

The nonresponse rate is the percentage of elements selected but not included in a study. It is often used as a measure of nonresponse bias. However, it is not a direct measure of actual nonresponse bias, but a measure of potential nonresponse bias. In spite of the nonresponse rate, if there is no difference between respondents and nonrespondents, there is no bias. If the nonresponse rate is small, nonresponse bias is likely to be small. Nonresponse bias will most likely occur when the response rate is low and the differences between responding and nonresponding cases are large.

What Are the Subtypes of Nonresponse Bias?

Nonresponse bias is multidimensional. There are two major types of nonresponse bias: unit nonresponse bias and item nonresponse bias (see Figure 2.3). Both types should be considered in choosing between taking a census and sampling.

Figure 2.3 Subtypes of Nonresponse Bias

Unit nonrespondents: Sampled elements who failed to respond

Respondents

Item nonrespondents: Sampled elements who responded, but did not respond completely to all items

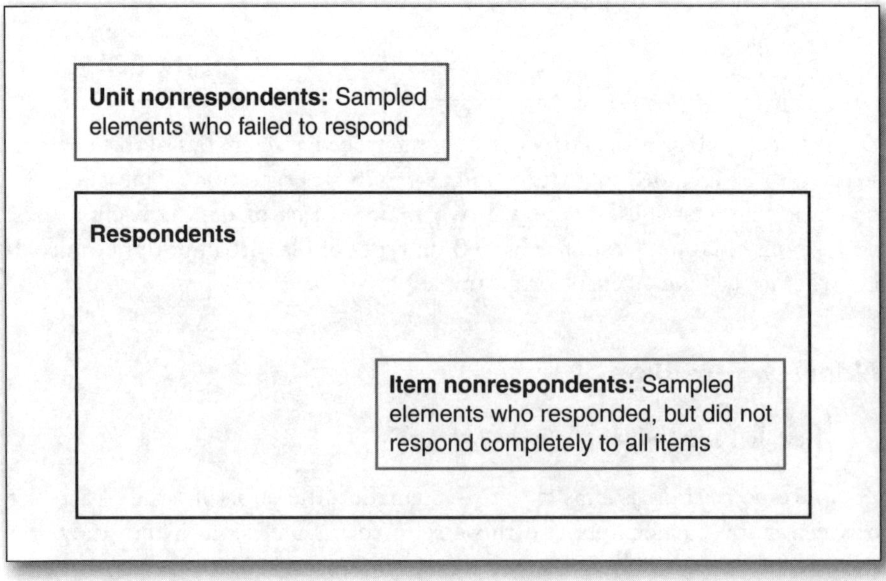

Unit nonresponse bias is bias resulting from the failure of a researcher to successfully collect any data or a sufficient amount of data from elements selected to be included in a study. Examples include unreturned mailed questionnaires or returned mail questionnaires with so little data that they are considered to be unit nonresponse.

It is important to estimate the extent of unit nonresponse. This may be estimated by using approaches, such as:

- Compare respondents and nonrespondents in terms of their responses to screener questions. These questions may reveal information on household composition, demographic characteristics, and eligibility status for the study.
- Compare respondents to nonrespondents utilizing auxiliary data in the sampling frame and/or organizational records. The value of this option depends upon the availability of auxiliary information that is related to the variables of interest in the study, and the amount of coverage bias in the sampling frame.
- Compare respondents to external data sources. Distribution of data collected in a survey may be compared to the distribution of similar variables collected in the census or benchmark surveys of the population. The value of this option depends upon the relationship between the study variables and the comparison variables, and the reliability and validity of the benchmark data.
- Conduct a follow-up study of nonrespondents ("double dipping"). A random sample of nonrespondents may be contacted using a different data collection mode. Typically a shorter data collection form is used. The follow-up study respondents would then be compared to the main study respondents. If the differences between the two sets of respondents are not statistically significant, they would then be combined into a single sample. If the differences between the two sets of respondents are statistically significant, the data in the main study may be statistically adjusted and weighted to account for the nonresponse bias that is indicated. This approach is more time-consuming and expensive when compared to other methods and assumes those who never responded to all efforts of contact are similar to those respondents who responded after the "double dipping."
- Conduct a trend analysis. Compare late responders to early responders and/or compare those easy to reach to those who were difficult to reach. One may compare respondents who responded after a few attempts to those who responded only after extensive effort. This approach does not necessarily require data from an external source or the collection of

additional data from the respondents. However, a limitation of this approach is that nonrespondents are directly measured, making hypothesized differences between respondents and nonrespondents speculative.

- For longitudinal studies, one may compare respondents who earlier indicated willingness to participate in future data requests, but failed to do so, to those who made similar commitments but participated when requested.

Item nonresponse bias is bias resulting from the failure to obtain the desired information on an item for which information is sought. Examples are unanswered questionnaire items. If the items that have missing data are the main variables in a study, item nonresponse may have the same effect as unit nonresponse. Item nonresponse impacts random sampling error by reducing the effective sample size and impacts systematic error by adding to systematic differences between the respondents and nonrespondents.

What Are the Sources of Nonresponse Bias?

Unit nonresponse and item nonresponse have overlapping causes. Factors that cause a person not to participate in a study also cause a person not to answer specific items on the data collection instrument. These overlapping causes include:

- Mistake
- Inability to contact
- Inability to respond
- Refusal to respond
- Researcher effects
- Mode effects

Mistake. A respondent may unintentionally leave an item blank. Perhaps this was a mistake that may have been indirectly caused by a faulty instrument design. The instrument may be too busy, too complicated, or too confusing. On the other hand, the respondent may be too tired, too fatigued, or too anxious to complete the instrument and move on to other things. The end result is item nonresponse, and possibly, response bias.

Inability to contact. Typically, some segments of the population are more difficult to contact than other segments. Generally, males, persons with low socioeconomic status, young persons, mobile persons, and minority group members have higher noncontact rates than females, persons with high socioeconomic status, older persons, nonmobile persons, and majority group members. Inability to contact may be due to undercoverage in the sampling frame. The reason for the inability to contact may vary by type of survey design employed. Examples of some of the reasons for noncontact include:

- Personal household surveys
  - Error in survey protocol
  - Inaccurate address
  - Moved
  - Locked apartment building
  - Gated community
  - Security guard or doormen preventing access
  - Vacant building
  - Poor or no signage on buildings or streets
  - Physical barrier to housing unit
  - Natural disaster
- Telephone surveys
  - Error in survey protocol
  - Wrong, disconnected, or nonworking telephone number
  - Use of answering machine, Caller ID
  - Phone line connected to fax machine
  - No landline telephone, "cell phone only" households
  - Use of call blocking
  - Natural disaster
  - Multiple telephone numbers
  - Unlisted telephone numbers
- Mail surveys
  - Error in survey protocol
  - Moved, no forwarding address
  - Highly mobile
  - Homeless, no address
  - Natural disaster
- Web-based surveys
  - Error in survey protocol
  - Inaccurate email address ("churn," change in Internet service provider and email address)
  - Lack of access to a computer

The lifestyle of the persons selected may affect the amount of noncontact bias. Given the lifestyle of persons with young children and the lifestyle of the elderly, they are easier to contact than young persons with no children. Employed persons are more difficult to contact than unemployed persons. Employed persons who work irregular hours or have jobs that involve a great deal of travel are more difficult to contact than other employed persons. Persons who live in urban areas are more difficult to contact than persons who live in rural areas. Renters are more difficult to contact than homeowners.

Inability to respond. Successfully contacting a sampled member of the target population does not guarantee one will be able to collect the information needed. The selected and contacted member of the target population may be unable to respond. A number of factors may prevent a selected element from responding. For example, the selected person may be ill, either physically or mentally. In an organizational study, the population element contacted may not have the authority to respond. The selected and contacted element may have a hearing or speaking disability, or some other disability that would make responding difficult. Perhaps most common, there may a language barrier. The language used by the researcher may be different from the language used by the selected element.

Refusal to respond. Although a population element may be contacted and has the ability to respond, unit nonresponse may still occur. The selected and contacted element that is capable to respond may refuse to participate in a study. Moreover, what is thought to be a unit nonresponse due to noncontact or inability to respond may be a "hidden refusal," "soft refusal," or a "passive refusal." Respondents who repeatedly request callbacks; those who do not answer the door although it is evident they are at home; those who report that they had already responded although they had not; and those who use answering machines to screen calls fall into these categories. Examples of factors associated with refusal to participate in research include:

- Apathy, lack of interest
- Organizational policy (individual in organization contacted may not have the authority, capacity, or motive to respond; requirement for approval at different levels of the bureaucracy)
- Sponsor of the survey (government versus academic versus commercial)
- Prior negative experience with the sponsor of the survey
- Feeling of being inundated by survey requests

- Fear of invasion of privacy
- Negative past research experiences
- Salience of topic
- Respondent time constraints
- Low sense of civic responsibility
- Concerns about safety, fraud, and misrepresentation
- Characteristics of the researcher such as age, gender, dress, and race
- Perceived time required to complete instrument
- Human subjects requirements
- Participation burden (e.g., length of questionnaire or interview)
- Demographic characteristics of the respondent and the data collector
- For longitudinal studies, the length of time between data collection efforts
- Nonmotivating title and/or introduction
- Initial questions are dull, sensitive, or threatening

The respondent may also intentionally refuse to answer specific items in the data collection instrument. It is not unusual for respondents to refuse to provide information considered to be sensitive or threatening (e.g., information on income, religion, age, drug use, or HIV status). The more sensitive the information requested, the greater the potential for embarrassment on the part of the respondent; and the greater the lack of trust between the respondent and the researcher, the greater the refusal rate.

As there may be hidden or passive refusals for unit nonresponse, there may be hidden or passive refusals for item nonresponse. Hidden item nonresponse takes the form of selecting the "neutral" or "midpoint" options in scales, responding "don't know," and responding to skip or filter questions in such a way that permits one to skip questions that follow. The respondent may provide whatever answers necessary to complete the data collection as quickly as possible.

Moreover, item nonresponse may be an unintended result of refusal conversions and decreasing unit nonresponse. Reluctant respondents who participate only after intensive efforts to reduce unit nonresponse may be more inclined to refuse to answer questions than nonreluctant respondents (Mason, Lesser, & Traugott, 2002).

Researcher effects. Researcher effects are most prevalent in interview studies. Interviewers may skip dwelling units selected to be part of the sample of a study because they feel uncomfortable in approaching the buildings. Moreover, interviewers may fail to ask questions because they may feel uncomfortable in doing so or because they may want to quickly terminate an interview.

Mode effects. Bias due to limitations of the type of research design used to conduct a study represents mode effects. As noted earlier, the mode of the research may influence nonresponse due to inability to contact. Mode differences continue to exist after contact is made. For example, survey research designs utilizing interviewers, especially face-to-face interview surveys, tend to have higher response rates than the response rates in other types of surveys (e.g., mail surveys and web-based surveys). Interviewers may use their persuasive skills and training to encourage persons to participate in the study. It is not unusual for people to refuse to participate in telephone and face-to-face interview surveys before they are aware of the purpose of the study. On the other hand, mail surveys may have greater unit nonresponse bias than other surveys because the respondents are able to preview the instrument before responding. Caller ID, caller blocking, and the Do Not Call registry (although it does not apply to researchers) are among the factors accounting for nonresponse in telephone surveys.

Electronic surveys tend to have lower response rates than paper surveys. Factors accounting for this difference include the use of multiple email accounts; infrequent use of email and the Internet; the blocking of emails; concern about anonymity, confidentiality, junk mail, and viruses; changes of email addresses; and the lack of understanding as to how to respond.

Different modes of carrying out a study have different effects on item nonresponse bias. Item nonresponse is likely to be greater in studies using self-administered instruments than in studies using interviewers. In interview surveys, if an item is not understood by a respondent the interviewer is there to explain it. In other types of studies, the respondent may leave the item blank. Moreover, studies using computer-assisted data collection (computer-assisted telephone interviewing, computer-assisted personal interviewing, web-based surveys, and computer-assisted self-administered questionnaires) may program the data collection process so as to force the respondent to answer an item in order to proceed.

How Can Nonresponse Bias Be Minimized?

Once the data are collected, statistical adjustments may be made to minimize the effects of unit nonresponse. Weighting is often used to adjust for nonresponse. Weight variables may be generated to compensate for differential nonresponse across subgroupings of the target population. The weighting factor for each grouping could be the inverse of the response rate of the grouping. For example, in a survey of males and females in a target population, if the response rate for males was 83%, and the response rate for females was 75%, the nonresponse weighting factor for males would be 1.20 and the nonresponse weighting factor for females would be 1.33. The data collected for males and females would be adjusted using these weighting factors. The weighting for nonresponse may be combined with the weighting for other aspects of the study (i.e., post-stratification adjustment, noncoverage, unequal selection probabilities, etc.). If population benchmarks are known, poststratification procedures may include raking (rim raking), an iterative process that creates weights for adjusting the sample data to population parameters (see Berry, Flatt, & Pierce, 1996; Groves, et al., 2001; Groves & Couper, 1998; Holt & Elliot, 1991; Little & Wu, 1991; Skinner, 1991).

Adjustments may be made for item nonresponse. These include:

- Drop the cases with missing data from the database. If there are 20 variables in one's database and a record has missing data for any one of these variables, it would be deleted from the database. This will reduce sample size and is not recommended if one has a great deal of missing data.
- Use listwise deletion (or case deletion) of missing cases. Delete all cases that have missing data for any variable that is under analysis. If one desires to compute the correlation that 6 of the 20 variables in one's database have with each other, cases would be deleted from all of the correlations calculated. This will also reduce the sample size.
- Use pairwise deletion of missing cases. If the calculation of bivariate statistics is used in the analysis, delete only those cases that have missing data for the specific bivariate analysis that is calculated. If one desires to compute the correlation that 6 of the 20 variables have with each other, cases would be deleted only for those correlation analyses for which data are missing for one of the two variables being correlated.
- Conduct imputation. There are three major types of imputation: mean imputation, "hot deck" imputation, and regression imputation. Mean imputation involves substitution of the mean of all cases or the mean of a subgroup of the sample for the missing data. "Hot deck" imputation involves the substitution of the data collected from a similar respondent for the missing data. Regression imputation involves the use of regression analysis to predict the missing data using variables highly correlated with the variable that has missing data as predictors.

For a more detailed discussion of the above procedures see Tanguma (2000) and Allison (2001). In spite of the weighting and imputations, nonresponse bias may yet exist. Nonresponse bias would exist to the extent to which there are differences between respondents and nonrespondents. Statistical adjustments would not necessarily account for these differences. Other efforts should be made to minimize the need to make statistical adjustments to the data collected. These efforts should be tailored to the factors causing the bias.

Procedures that may be used to minimize mistakes include:

- Improved training and supervision
- Application of quality design principles in preparation of instrument and instructions
- Extensive data-cleaning procedures to detect and correct mistakes

Procedures that may be used to minimize inability to contact bias include:

- Repeating callbacks at different times and different days. Extending the data collection period to allow more time to contact study element. Once contact is made, one may use that opportunity to inquire as to the reason for the initial nonresponse.
- Improving the scheduling and protocols of data collection attempts.
- Using the most current sampling frame possible and updating where necessary.
- Using mixed-methods to contact elements. Once contact is made via a different mode from the initial mode, the researcher may inquire as to the respondent's use of and availability of contact via the initial mode.
- Replacing nonrespondents in the current study with nonrespondents from an earlier study. The replacement nonrespondents should come from a similar study conducted about the same time.
- Substituting nonrespondents with other elements of the population. Substitution should be carefully used. It adds to the costs, effort, and, possibly, the bias in a study, especially if based on convenience. Probabilities of selection of potential substitutes may be affected. In a household survey, if nonrespondents are substituted with their neighbors, persons living in households close to nonrespondents would have a higher probability of selection than persons living in household close to respondents. If possible, substitutes should be similar to particular nonrespondents but dissimilar to respondents already in the sample. Nonresponse bias would not be reduced if the substitutes are similar to respondents already in the sample.

Inability to respond bias may be minimized by extending the data collection period, using modes to accommodate persons with various disabilities, using multiple language versions of the data collection instrument, and using translators. It is also noted that translation problems may lead to response bias.

Mode effects may be minimized by using mixed-methods research designs (e.g., a design that includes web-based surveys, personal interview surveys, and telephone surveys). Using mixed-methods designs, the disadvantages of one may be offset by the advantages of others.

Various theoretical frameworks have been used as guides in developing procedures to minimize refusals to participate in research. These theoretical approaches identify factors related to response propensity (the theoretical probability that a sampled unit will cooperate with a participation request), and suggest procedures that may be used in increasing response rates (Groves, 2006). They include utility theory, social exchange theory, and leverage-saliency theory (Dillman, 1978; Dillman, Gallegos, & Frey, 1976; Groves, Cialdini & Couper, 1992; Groves, Singer, & Corning, 2000; Morton-Williams, 1993).

Utility theory provides the basis for explaining response propensity. It implies that individuals use cost-benefit calculations in deciding whether to participate in a research project. If the expected costs are greater than the expected benefits, nonresponse is likely to occur (Groves & Couper, 1998). Perceived costs might include such factors as the following:

- Opportunity costs, things that would not be done because of the time it takes to participate in the study
- Amount of time required
- Effort required
- Potential embarrassment

Perceived benefits might include such factors as the following:

- Money
- Pride in making a civic contribution, helping the organization, etc.
- Satisfaction of personal interests

Social exchange theory extended standard utility theory by incorporating the concept of trust (Dillman, 1978, 2007). Part of the equation in determining whether to participate in a research project is the extent to which the participant trusts the researcher to deliver the expected benefits. Hence, the researcher has the task of minimizing perceived costs and maximizing perceived benefits and trust. Dillman (2007) described social exchange theory as follows:

Social exchange is a theory of human behavior used to explain the development and continuation of human interaction. The theory asserts that actions of individuals are motivated by the return these actions are expected to bring, and in fact usually do bring, from others (Blau, 1964; Dillman, 1978; Goyder, 1987). Three elements are critical for predicting a particular action: rewards, costs, and trust. Simply stated, rewards are what one expects to gain from a particular activity, costs are what one gives up or spends to obtain the rewards, and trust is the expectation that in the long run the rewards of doing something will outweigh the costs. The theory of social exchange implies three questions about the design of a questionnaire and the implementation process: How can we increase rewards for responding? How can perceived costs be reduced? How can trust be established so that the ultimate rewards will outweigh the costs of responding? (p. 14)

Leverage-saliency theory developed by Groves, Singer, and Corning (2000) extends social exchange theory. It holds that the salient features of a research project have different "leverage" in the decision of the intended respondents whether or not to participate in the study. The salient features may include the topic, purpose, and sponsorship of the study; how the findings will be used; and the expected length of the data collection process. Considering this theory, it is important that the researcher make salient features of the study that have high leveraging value for the intended respondent. Whether or not a person responds in a survey would depend upon the leveraging of the perceived salient features of the study (Groves, Presser, & Dipko, 2004).

Using the above theoretical frameworks as guidelines, specific activities that have been used to minimize refusal rates include:

- Repeated callbacks at different times and different days
- Prenotification
- Follow-up reminders
- Assurance of confidentiality and anonymity
- Short introduction justifying the study
- Emphasis on the study's purpose and sponsor
- Use of "cooling off period" for callbacks with more experienced data collectors
- Placement of dull, sensitive, and threatening items at the end of the data collection instrument
- Leaving messages on voice mail, answering machines, etc.
- Effective refusal conversion training of data collectors
- Assigning specially trained refusal conversion data collectors to specific cases
- Matching data collector's observable attributes (e.g., age, gender, and race) with the characteristics of respondents

- Appeals to altruism
- Holding community meetings to discuss the purposes of the research
- Use of short instrument and placing emphasis on this fact
- Including return postage and return envelope
- Personalization
- Incentives, especially prepayment monetary incentives versus post-payment monetary incentives and nonmonetary incentives
- Improved training and supervision of data collectors

Efforts to reduce nonresponse may have an unintended effect of increasing response bias. Including reluctant respondents might reduce the quality of the data by increasing response bias. The quality of the data collected from reluctant respondents may be much less than the quality of the data collected from nonreluctant respondents. Response bias is reviewed in the following section.

In personal interview studies, often multiple callbacks must be made to secure a completed interview. Included in Research Note 2.1 is a description of the use of callbacks in a study of smoking behavior of Vietnamese men living in California.

RESEARCH NOTE 2.1

Example of Research Utilizing Multiple Callbacks to Minimize Nonresponse: Study of Smoking Behavior of Vietnamese Men Living in California

Often multiple callbacks must be made to obtain a completed interview. Rahman et al. (2005) described their procedures efforts to obtain completed interviews in their telephone survey of smoking behavior of Vietnamese men living in California as follows:

> Once a household was reached, all persons living in the household aged 18 years or older were eligible to participate in the study. The average number of adults was three per household. If more than one member of the household was eligible, they were enumerated and randomly selected using a computer-generated random selection process. If the selected person was not available, an appointment was made to conduct an interview at another

(Continued)

(Continued)

time or day. When a respondent was selected, no other household member could be selected, even if an interview could not be completed. Respondents who refused to participate were not eliminated immediately. In an effort to persuade them to participate, a second call was made after a cooling-off period of 2–5 days. If a second refusal came from a household member other than the respondent, or if the interviewer believed that the respondent might change his or her mind, a third call was made to the household a day or two after the second refusal. A potential respondent was eliminated if the second call resulted in a refusal and the telephone number was assigned a final disposition of "refused." Telephones that rang with no answer, gave a busy signal, or were picked up by an answering machine were eliminated after six attempts, with at least one call each during an evening, weekend, and day shift.

Source: Rahman et al., 2005, p. 104. Reprinted by permission of Oxford University Press.

Response Bias

What Is Response Bias?

Response bias is bias due to the collection of invalid or inappropriate data from sampled elements. It is a form of observation error, information bias, and measurement error. It is to be anticipated in taking a census and in sampling, and should be minimized.

What Are the Sources of Response Bias?

There are four major sources of response bias:

- Respondent effects
- Researcher effects
- Data collection instrument effects
- Mode effects

Respondent effects. Response bias may be the result of a respondent's lack of understanding of the question (e.g., the respondent misinterpreted the time frame referred to in a question), deliberate error (e.g., reporting false information on one's income, age, drug use, or HIV status), and unconscious error (e.g., error due to fatigue, boredom, or misinterpretation). There may be fluctuations in interests, attitudes, memory, mood, and motivation.

Persons being observed, participants in focus group research, or respondents in a survey may intentionally or unintentionally provide erroneous information. Persons being observed may experience the guinea pig effect by feeling uneasy about being observed, and modify their normal behavior. Focus group participants may tune in or tune out of the discussion because of the actions of other participants. Survey research respondents may adjust their response in order to maximize their projected image to the researcher.

Respondents tend to have different psychological orientations toward responding to different item formats. Such tendencies may lead to response bias. Various forms of response bias due to the respondents have been identified. Examples include:

- *Acquiescence bias*: Tendency to agree or concur with any stated position
- *Extremity bias*: Tendency to select extreme positions
- *Central tendency bias*: Reluctance to give extreme scores
- *Social desirability (prestige) bias*: Tendency to give socially desirable response
- *Leniency bias*: Tendency to rate something too high or too low
- *Proximity bias*: Tendency to give similar responses to items that occur close to one another
- *Recall bias*: Tendency not to remember correctly

Careful attention to data collection procedures may limit such bias. Typically, sampling would permit more resources for limiting such bias than is the case for taking a census.

Researcher effects. The researcher may be the source of the response bias. The researcher may commit questioning errors or recording errors, or may purposely fail to follow instructions. The following may happen in a research study:

- The moderator of a focus group may cause some of the participants not to express themselves openly.
- The researcher conducting participant observation may overlook critical behavior and nuances.
- An interviewer's behavior may cause a respondent not to trust his/her promise that the information collected would be confidential.
- An interviewer may read a question with inappropriate emphasis or intonation.

- An interviewer may be too friendly or too cold.
- An experimental researcher's behavior may cause participants in the experiment to believe that they are receiving a placebo and not the medication that is being tested.
- A data collector collects data from the wrong respondent, does not ask questions as written, or in some other way deviates from the required protocol.

Such problems may cause study participants to provide inaccurate responses. These problems may be due to the data collectors' inadequate training, poor supervision, recording error, cheating, misinterpretation of respondents' remarks, carelessness, not asking questions as written, not probing when circumstances indicate that they should, and poor questioning technique. These problems may be compounded by instrument effects.

Data collection instrument effects. The data collection instrument may be the source of response bias. Such bias may be due to **surrogate information error** (discrepancy between the information required for a study to achieve its objectives and the information sought by the researcher), the wording of the items in the instrument, sequence of the items, formatting of the items and the instrument, and bias associated with nonverbal materials. Leading questions, double-barreled questions, and the use of ambiguous words and phrases all lead to response bias. Careful instrument design and pretesting may minimize this type of bias.

Mode effects. Different modes of carrying out a study have different effects on response bias. In face-to-face surveys the interviewer is able to control who responds when more than one person in a household is eligible to participate in the survey. On the other hand, a researcher has no such control in mail surveys and Internet surveys. The person who elects to respond may be different from the household members who are reluctant to respond.

Moreover, the mode of the survey may determine the amount of response bias due to primacy effects and recency effects. Primacy effects are bias due to a tendency of respondents to pay more attention at the beginning than at the end of a list of responses. Recency effects are bias due to a tendency of respondents to pay more attention at the end of a list of responses. Middle items in a list are likely to be missed. When questions are presented in writing, primacy effects are more likely to occur. When questions are presented orally, recency effects are more likely to occur.

The different modes of conducting research tend to take place in different environments, and thereby have different situational and environmental effects on response behavior. Experimental research and observational studies may take place in the field or in a laboratory and be subject to various demand effects of the environment. Web-based survey questionnaires and mail questionnaires may be completed in an office, a home, an Internet café, or other places wired for Internet access.

The quality of responses may vary by the research design mode. Face-to-face interviews tend to yield longer and more detailed open-ended responses than mail, telephone, and web-based surveys. Moreover, in face-to-face interview studies nonverbal communication may yield significant information relating to the study. Interview studies permit probing by the interviewer to ensure that relevant and on-point data are collected. Telephone surveys tend to have greater time pressure than other surveys. As the minutes tick away, respondents become more and more anxious to terminate the interview. Such pressure may affect the quality of their responses.

Bias due to the psychological orientation of the respondent may vary by mode of the research design. For example, social desirability bias is more likely to be a factor in personal interview surveys than web-based surveys or mail surveys.

How Can Response Bias Be Minimized?

Response bias may be minimized by:

- Designing data collection procedures and instruments via a respondent-centered approach
- Comprehensive training of data collectors
- Incorporating a quality control system during data collection
- Extensive data cleaning including validity checking and reliability checking
- Using external data sources to detect and correct error once identified

BIAS IN ANALYZING DATA

Bias in analyzing data is disparity between actual population parameters and sample estimates that are due to the data analysis procedures that are used. Typically, data analysis proceeds in two stages: data processing and data analysis. Data processing involves the preparation of the data collected for analysis. Data analysis involves the application of various statistical procedures to satisfy the objectives of the study. Error may occur in carrying out these procedures. The subtypes of data analysis bias relate to the two stages in analyzing the data collected in a research study: the data processing errors and the data analysis errors.

Data processing may involve the following activities:

- Editing completed questionnaires or interview schedules
- Coding the data collected
- Keying the data into an electronic format if they are not in that format already
- Detecting and correcting respondent, interviewer, coder, and data entry errors
- Determining the extent of bias (e.g., coverage bias, nonresponse bias, response bias), and make adjustments (e.g., weighting and imputation) wherever possible
- Checking the validity and reliability of measures
- Modifying the data to make them more suitable for analysis and creating indices and composite measures

Errors may be made in all of these activities. Yet, even though they may be detected, there may be errors in the procedures used to correct them. With effective training and implementing comprehensive quality control procedures, data processing errors may be minimized.

Errors may also occur in the analysis of the data collected. The assumptions of the statistical procedures employed may not be satisfied. Errors may occur in the use of various imputation procedures in adjusting for missing data. The decision whether to weight the data or not, and the calculation of the weights if weighting is used may be flawed. Extraneous and confounding variables may not be properly controlled. Variance estimates may be calculated using formulas that do not reflect the sample design that was used. For example, one may employ a complex sample design, such as a multistage cluster sample design that requires special formulas, but use in one's analyses formulas designed for a basic sample design such as simple random sampling. Such applications may result in biased findings.

Data analysis bias might be minimized by utilizing redundant quality control procedures. The work of editors, coders, and data entry personnel should be checked and double-checked. Detected errors should be corrected. Care should be taken to make sure that assumptions relating to the statistical procedures that are used—in particular assumptions that relate to level of measurement, type of sampling used, and sample size—are satisfied.

STRENGTHS AND WEAKNESSES OF TAKING A CENSUS AND SAMPLING

Considering random sampling error, systematic error, costs, purpose of the research, and other factors, the strengths and weaknesses of taking a census and sampling may be compared. Although intuitively, one might assume that a census will always have less error than sampling, this is not necessarily the case. A census will not have random sampling error because it does not involve sampling. However, a census may have a great deal of systematic error. Next, guidelines are presented for choosing between taking a census and sampling.

The strengths and weaknesses of taking a census versus sampling primarily revolve around their ability to minimize random sampling error and systematic errors and the availability of resources to conduct the research. These strengths and weaknesses are summarized in Table 2.2.

Table 2.2 Strengths and Weaknesses of Taking a Census and Sampling in Addressing Selected Contingencies

Contingencies	Taking a Census	Sampling
Objectives:		
Research has an exploratory purpose	Weakness	Strength
Requirement of total enumeration	Strength	Weakness
Need for quick decision	Weakness	Strength
Need to regularly collect up-to-date information	Weakness	Strength
Need for a great deal of in-depth information	Weakness	Strength
Need to target specific elements of the population	Weakness	Strength
Need for representation of a very small segment of the population	Strength	Weakness
Important study	Strength	Weakness
Importance to minimize publicity of the study	Weakness	Strength

(Continued)

Table 2.2 (Continued)

Contingencies	Taking a Census	Sampling
Nature of the population:		
Large population size	Weakness	Strength
Heterogeneous population	Strength	Weakness
Difficult to gain access or locate population elements	Strength	Weakness
Population is highly scattered	Weakness	Strength
High destructibility of population	Weakness	Strength
Continuous manufacturing production of population	Weakness	Strength
Availability of resources:		
Limited time, money, personnel, etc.	Weakness	Strength
Research design considerations:		
Important to minimize sampling error	Strength	Weakness
Likelihood of extremely high nonresponse rate	Strength	Weakness
Important to minimize response bias	Weakness	Strength
Important to use easy operational procedures	Weakness	Strength
Detailed data analysis requirements	Strength	Weakness
Ethical and legal restrictions on use of control groups	Strength	Weakness

Considering the major strengths of taking a census compared to sampling, taking a census would be the better choice in the following situations:

- Requirement of total enumeration
- Need to include very small categories of the population in the study
- Importance of having credible results

- Heterogeneous population
- Difficult to gain access or locate population elements
- Important to minimize sampling error
- Likelihood of extremely high nonresponse rate
- Detailed data analysis requirements
- Ethical and legal restrictions on use of control groups

Considering the major strengths of sampling compared to taking a census, sampling would be the better choice in the following situations:

- Research has an exploratory purpose
- Need for quick decision
- Need to regularly collect up-to-date information
- Need for a great deal of in-depth information
- Need to target specific elements of the population
- Importance of minimizing publicity of study
- Large population size
- Population is highly scattered
- High destructibility of population
- Continuous manufacturing and production of population
- Resources (i.e., time, money, personnel, etc.) are limited
- Important to minimize response bias
- Important to use easy operational procedures

GUIDELINES FOR CHOOSING BETWEEN TAKING A CENSUS AND SAMPLING

Considering the factors described above, a number of guidelines may be proposed for choosing between taking a census and sampling. The guidelines listed below are not equally important. Some will matter only if specific conditions are met. They are proposed assuming all other factors are held constant. The topics of the guidelines include:

- Objectives of the study
- Nature of the population
- Availability of resources
- Research design considerations
- Ethical and legal requirements

Objectives of the Study

In order to satisfy the objectives of a study, it may be more favorable to take a census rather than sampling. One should consider the following factors that relate to the purposes of a study:

- Exploratory/nonexploratory purpose
- Requirement for total enumeration
- Need for a great deal of in-depth information
- Need to make a quick decision
- Need to regularly collect up-to-date information
- Need to target specific elements of a population
- Need to include rare or very small segments of the population in the study
- Importance of the study
- Need to minimize publicity of the study
- Importance of minimizing total error

Guideline 2.1. *Exploratory/nonexploratory purpose.* If the research has an exploratory purpose, it is more favorable to choose sampling.

It is not necessary to include every element in a target population for studies that have an exploratory purpose. In most cases, sampling will suffice. Moreover, using the entire population in an exploratory study could bias the main study. If one is at the stage of a research project of conducting a pilot study or pretest of instruments, sampling is preferred to taking a census.

Guideline 2.2. *Requirement for total enumeration.* If the objectives of the study require enumeration of all the elements in the target population, it is necessary to take a census.

Some research projects require the inclusion of every member of the population. The United States Constitution requires the taking of a census every 10 years. The data collected are used to reapportion congressional seats to states and to make decisions regarding the distribution of federal services and funds to local, state, and tribal governments each year. Other governmental units and private organizations may have information needs that require inclusion of all members of a target population in a study.

Guideline 2.3. *Need for a great deal of in-depth information.* If a large amount of in-depth information is needed to satisfy the objectives of a study, it is more favorable to choose sampling.

This guideline depends much on the size of the population and the resources available for the research. Sampling provides the researcher more time and resources to obtain in-depth information from the participants in a study. Resources that would have gone into obtaining more participants can be used to acquire more detailed and better quality information from those who participate in a study. If the population is large, it may not be practical to collect a great deal of in-depth information. On the other hand, collection of such data may be feasible for small populations.

Guideline 2.4. *Need to make a quick decision.* If it is necessary to make a quick decision on the basis of the findings of a study, it is more favorable to choose sampling.

This guideline is also dependent on the population size. Typically, taking a census is more time-consuming than sampling. If there is a need to make a quick decision based on the data to be collected, it is more favorable to sample than to take a census. Taking a census may be too time-consuming. Once data collection is finished, the data collected may not be relevant to the decisions that must be made.

Guideline 2.5. *Need to regularly collect up-to-date information.* If it is necessary to regularly collect up-to-date information, it is more favorable to choose sampling.

Generally, the larger the study, the more time it takes to process the data collected and produce appropriate reports. Therefore, the application of this guideline depends upon the size of the population and the available resources. The U.S. government conducts a census every 10 years. It takes several years of planning and several years before most of the data collected are published. This process is not practical for up-to-date informational needs of the government. In order to satisfy these needs, governmental agencies regularly conduct sample surveys.

Guideline 2.6. *Need to target specific elements of a population.* If it is necessary to target specific elements of a population, it is more favorable to choose sampling.

If a research project were specifically focused on particular individuals, events, or settings, sampling is the immediate choice.

Guideline 2.7. *Need to include small segments of the population in the study.* If it is necessary that small subpopulations or geographical areas be represented in the study, it is more favorable to choose to take a census.

The objectives of the study may require the inclusion of small subpopulations and/or geographical areas in the study. It is possible to miss these elements if sampling is used (especially if a sampling procedure such as simple random sampling is used). A census may be the better choice.

> **Guideline 2.8.** *Importance of the study.* The more important a study, the more favorable it is to choose to take a census.

Users of research findings are more likely to attribute credibility of findings based on a census than findings based on sampling. Random sampling error would be avoided. On the other hand, the larger the population, the greater the need to have quality control procedures in place to minimize systematic errors.

> **Guideline 2.9.** *Need to minimize publicity of the study.* If a research project focuses on products or concepts for which publicity must be minimized, the more favorable it is to choose sampling.

Particularly in business and marketing research, it may be in the best interest of a researcher to control exposure to information included in a study. The study may concern a product or concept that an organization desires to limit exposure. Sampling would minimize the number of persons exposed to the product or concept.

Nature of the Population

Several characteristics of a target population are important factors in choosing whether to take a census or to sample. These include:

- Size of the population
- Heterogeneity/homogeneity of the population
- Accessibility of the population
- Spatial distribution of the population
- Destructibility of the population
- Continuous production of the population

> **Guideline 2.10.** *Size of the population.* The larger the population, the more favorable it is to choose sampling; the smaller the population, the more favorable it is to choose to take a census.

A direct relationship exists between the number of elements included in a study and systematic error, project management problems, costs, and the resources necessary to conduct the study. Although the factors may be manageable for relatively small populations, say populations of 200 elements or less, a carefully designed sample often yields better results than a census. A medical researcher might take a census of all known cases of a rare medical problem but probably will not take a census of all known cases of high blood pressure. If the population is infinite (or for all practical purposes, the population is so large that it may be regarded as infinite, for example, the number of trees in a forest), taking a census is not a realistic option.

Guideline 2.11. *Heterogeneity/homogeneity of the population.* The more heterogeneous the population, the more favorable it is to choose to take a census; the more homogeneous the population, the more favorable it is to choose sampling.

If there is only a small amount of variability among the elements of a population in terms of the study variables, it is not necessary to include a large segment of the population in a study to represent the population. The rule of homogeneity holds that the more homogeneous a population in terms of the characteristics that are most relevant to the research problem, the more representative the sample is likely to be in terms of those characteristics. The more homogeneous the population, the fewer the number of elements are necessary to represent the population. A small number of population elements may suffice. Increasing the number of elements in the study would reduce sampling error, but it would not necessarily reduce sampling bias. If all the elements in a target population are exactly alike in terms of your study variables, only one element is necessary to properly represent the population.

On the other hand, if a population is very heterogeneous, it may be necessary to include a large segment of the population in order to properly represent the population. The rule of heterogeneity holds that the more heterogeneous the population, the greater the chance is that certain characteristics of the population will not be represented in the sample. Therefore, the more heterogeneous the population, the greater the number of elements are necessary to represent the population. In some cases, it may be best to include the entire population in the study.

Guideline 2.12. *Accessibility of the population.* The more difficult it is to gain access or locate elements of the target population, the more favorable it is to choose to take a census.

At times it is difficult to identify, locate, or gain access to a target population. "Hard-to-reach" populations include rare and hidden populations. One may consider a segment of the population that represents less than 2% of the population as a rare population. Hidden populations are segments of the population for whom there is limited official information, and they prefer to keep it that way due to their behaviors or conditions. Examples include sex workers, criminals, youth gang members, drug users, homosexuals, and illegal immigrants. Total enumeration might be necessary to ensure their inclusion in a study. This may be a reasonable choice if the population is small and one has sufficient resources. On the other hand, if the population is large, the choice of a census may be too expensive and not practical. Considering available resources, sampling may be the only option.

Guideline 2.13. *Spatial distribution of the population.* The more scattered a population, the more favorable it is to choose sampling.

The spatial distribution of a population significantly affects the data collection costs of a study. Considering this relationship, the spatial distribution of the population is an important factor in choosing between taking a census and sampling. If the geographical area and the size of a population are small, it may be feasible to take a census. There is a direct relationship between the size and spatial distribution of a population and the costs of collecting data from the population. As a result, it is generally more practical to sample if the population is widely scattered.

Guideline 2.14. *Destructibility of the population.* The greater the likelihood a study would contaminate or make impossible future research on a population, the more favorable it is to choose sampling.

Due to the nature of the subject matter studied and the measurement procedures used, research may involve the destruction, contamination, or consumption of the subject matter of a study. In the case of destructive testing, the sample elements or units must be destroyed or must be consumed to obtain necessary measurements. As a result, there will be contaminated elements or nothing left after the research is completed. If it is likely that a study would contaminate or destroy a population thus affecting future research, sampling may be preferred to taking a census. It would not be economical for General Motors to perform crash tests on every automobile leaving the production line. There would be no cars left to sell. A cook need not taste the whole pot of soup to determine whether it has a desired taste; if he or she were to do so, there would be nothing left to eat later.

Guideline 2.15. *Continuous production of the population.* If the population comprises elements that are continually produced by a manufacturing or other production process, the more favorable it is to choose sampling.

Sampling every widget that is produced in a manufacturing or other production process would be impractical and noneconomical. Sampling would be more appropriate.

Availability of Resources

Guideline 2.16. *Availability of resources.* The more limited one's resources (e.g., personnel, money, time), the more favorable it is to choose sampling.

Available financial, logistical, material, and human resources will greatly influence one's choice between taking a census and taking a sample. Often due to limited money, time, and personnel, one does not have the resources to conduct a census. This is especially the case if the target population is large and scattered. Information that is sought may require the use of specialized equipment (e.g., x-ray machines) and/or staff (e.g., physicians), making it impossible or unreasonable to take a census. It probably would not be practical to subject all members of a population to a medical examination to collect information on the prevalence of swine flu or some other medical problem. Considering such factors, it may be impossible, impracticable, or unreasonable to conduct a census.

Research Design Considerations

Several factors relating to the research design of a study should be considered in choosing between taking a census and sampling. These include considerations relating to:

- Random sampling error
- Selection bias
- Nonresponse bias
- Response bias
- Ease of operational procedures
- Data analysis requirements

Guideline 2.17. *Random sampling error.* Considering the minimization of random sampling error, it is more favorable to choose to take a census.

With total enumeration, a census will not have random sampling error. If sampling is chosen, random sampling error may be minimized with a large sample size.

> **Guideline 2.18.** *Selection bias.* Considering the minimization of selection bias, it is more favorable to choose to take a census.

The fact that all elements of the target population are selected in taking a census means there will be no selection bias.

> **Guideline 2.19.** *Nonresponse bias.* The larger the anticipated unit nonresponse bias and item nonresponse bias, the more favorable it is to choose to take a census.

High nonresponse rates might result in too few elements to conduct a credible study. A survey may have a unit response rate that is less than 5%. In such situations, taking a census may be a better choice than taking sampling.

> **Guideline 2.20.** *Response bias.* The greater the need to maximize response quality, the more favorable it is to choose sampling.

The smaller the project, the more attention can be devoted to quality control. The greater the quality control, the fewer uncorrected errors and invalid responses. Sampling permits one to maximize the quality of the training and supervision of data collectors.

> **Guideline 2.21.** *Ease of operational procedures.* The greater the need to utilize efficient operational procedures, the more favorable it is to choose sampling.

It is likely that taking a census will require more complex operational procedures than taking a sample, especially if the target population is large and geographically dispersed. The smaller the number of elements in a study, the less likely it will require complex data collection operational procedures.

> **Guideline 2.22.** *Data analysis requirements.* Unless the population is extremely large, the larger the number of variables in a study, and the complexity of the data analysis plan, the more favorable it is to choose to take a census.

Generally, the more variables used in a study, the more cases one needs to have in order to satisfy the assumptions of the statistical procedures used. Moreover, the more complex one's analysis design, the greater the number of cases one would need to properly carry out the analyses. If a population is relatively small, it may be necessary to include the entire population in a study in order to have enough cases to properly carry out the analyses. Some studies involve the comparison of subgroups of a population. The more subgroups that are compared, the more cases you need to properly carry out the analyses.

Ethical and Legal Requirements

Guideline 2.23. *Ethical and legal requirements.* Ethical and legal requirements may prohibit the selection of some population elements for participation in the study and the exclusion of others, thus requiring the taking of a census.

Although an effective research design may require the use of a control group, ethical principles may consider refraining from administering a needed benefit to a control group as unethical. It may be unethical to exclude segments of the population from a study. A solution may be to include the entire population in the study.

The above guidelines provide a framework for choosing between taking a census and sampling. Applying the above guidelines, one may choose to take a census, sample, or combine taking a census and sampling in a mixed-methods design. If sampling is chosen, the next step is choosing between probability sampling and nonprobability sampling. The next chapter describes guidelines for making these choices.

SUMMARY

The total error in a study may be broken into two major categories: random sampling error and systematic error. An understanding of the differences between random sampling error and systematic error is important in choosing procedures for selecting study participants. Random sampling error is the difference between a sample estimate and the true population value that is due to chance variation of multiple samples. It may be minimized by selecting a large sample size and by implementing a stratified sample design rather than an unstratified sample design. Systematic error is the difference between a sample estimate and the true population value that is due to factors other than random error.

Systematic error is error due to the sampling procedures that produce estimates that systematically differ from the actual characteristics of the population. It has three major subtypes: population specification bias, coverage bias, and selection bias. Population specification bias occurs when there is a poor fit between the research questions a study attempts to answer and the population chosen to be studied. It may be minimized by clearly defining the target population. Coverage bias occurs when there is no one-to-one correspondence between the elements in the target population and the elements encompassed by the selection procedures used. Coverage bias has four subcategories: overcoverage, undercoverage, multiple-coverage, and clustered frame bias.

Overcoverage bias occurs when elements that are not members of the target population are listed in the sampling frame and selected for inclusion in the sample of the study. It may be minimized by thoroughly reviewing and cleaning the sampling frame and dropping all ineligibles that are discovered and by screening respondents during data collection to ensure membership in the population. Undercoverage bias occurs when members of the target population are not identified or accessible by the procedures employed by the researcher. It may be minimized by utilizing multiple frames, redefining the target population to fit the frame, utilizing external sources to supplement the frame, and using the "half-open interval" procedure. Multiple-coverage bias occurs when elements of the population are counted more than once. It may be minimized by thoroughly cross-checking and cleaning the sampling frame. Clustered frame bias occurs when units in the sampling frame include more than one element of the target population. It may be minimized by including all the elements within a selected clustered listing or randomly selecting one of the eligible elements to participate in the study and weighing it according to the size of the cluster.

The two major forms of data collection bias are nonresponse bias and response bias. Nonresponse bias is a form of nonobservation bias and occurs when there is a failure to collect data from sampled elements. The two major types of nonresponse bias are unit nonresponse bias and item nonresponse bias.

Unit nonresponse bias occurs when a researcher is unsuccessful in collecting any data or a sufficient amount of data from a sampled element. There are four major sources of unit nonresponse: the researcher's inability to make contact with the sampled elements, inability of the contacted element to respond, refusal by the contacted element to respond, and mode effects.

Item nonresponse bias occurs when there is a failure to obtain the desired information on an item for which information is sought. There are four major sources of item nonresponse: mistake, inability to respond, refusal to respond, and mode effects. Utility theory, social exchange theory, and leverage-saliency theory have been proposed to explain response propensity and suggest procedures that may be effective in reducing nonresponse. A number of procedures are recommended to minimize unit nonresponse and item nonresponse.

Response bias is a form of observation bias and occurs when one is able to collect data from sampled elements; however, the data collected are inaccurate or inappropriate. Response bias may be attributed to the respondent, the researcher, the data collection instrument, or the mode of conducting the research. Response bias may be minimized through designing data collection procedures and instruments via a respondent-centered approach; comprehensive training of data collectors; incorporating a quality control system during data collection; extensive data cleaning, including validity checking and reliability checking; and using external data sources to detect and correct error once identified.

There are two major types of data analysis bias: bias caused by data processing errors and bias caused by data analysis errors. These errors may be minimized by effective training, implementing comprehensive quality control procedures, and taking care to satisfy the assumptions of the statistical procedures used.

Considering the relative strengths and weaknesses of taking a census and sampling, guidelines are presented for choosing between these two procedures. The guidelines relate to the objectives of the study, importance of the study, importance of minimizing publicity of study, nature of the population (including its size, heterogeneity/homogeneity, accessibility, spatial distribution, destructibility, and continuous production), availability of resources, research design considerations (including random sampling error, selection bias, nonresponse bias, and response bias), ease of operational procedures, data analysis procedures, and ethical and legal requirements.

REVIEW QUESTIONS

1. What is the difference between random sampling error and systematic error?

2. What are the major subtypes of systematic error?

3. Distinguish the following types of systematic error, give examples, and describe how they might be minimized.

   a. Clustered frame bias

   b. Data processing bias

   c. Item nonresponse bias

   d. Multiple-coverage bias

   e. Overcoverage bias

   f. Population specification bias

   g. Response bias

   h. Selection bias

   i. Undercoverage bias

   j. Unit nonresponse bias

4. In what circumstances would it be preferable to sample instead of taking a census?

5. What do you consider to be the most critical guidelines for choosing between taking a census and sampling? Why?

6. Which types of systematic error are likely to have the most devastating effect on a study? Why?

7. What is the relationship between nonresponse bias and the nonresponse rate? Can a study have a high level of nonresponse bias, but a low nonresponse rate? Why?

8. Compare and contrast procedures for estimating unit nonresponse.

9. How do mode effects influence the choice of taking a census or sampling?

10. What relevance do the rule of homogeneity and the rule of heterogeneity have to sampling?

11. The U.S. Bureau of the Census is charged to carry out the enumeration of the population of the United States every 10 years that is required by the U.S. Constitution. It is extremely expensive and time-consuming to count every single person. Should the Bureau of the Census focus on making a complete count or on carrying out supplemental sampling that may be used to make statistical adjustments to problems of undercounting and overcounting that are likely to occur? Consider the following sources:

Brown, L.D., et al. (1999). *Statistical controversies in Census 2000* (Technical Report 537). Department of Statistics, University of California, Berkeley. Available at http://www.stat.berkeley.edu/~census/537.pdf

Nguyen, P. (2004). Some notes on biased statistics and African Americans. *Journal of Black Studies, 34,* 514–531.

Prewitt, K. (1999). Census 2000: Science meets politics. *Science, 283,* 935.

Wright, T. (1998). Sampling and Census 2000: The concepts. *American Scientist, 86,* 245.

KEY TERMS

Define and give examples of the following concepts:

clustered frame bias	response bias
coverage bias	sampling frame
item nonresponse bias	selection bias
multiple-coverage bias	surrogate information error
nonresponse bias	systematic error
overcoverage bias	undercoverage bias
population specification bias	unit nonresponse bias
random sampling error	

REFERENCES FOR FURTHER STUDY

Assael, H., & Deon, J. (1982). Nonsampling vs. sampling errors in survey research. *Journal of Marketing, 46*, 114–123.

Biemer, P. P., & Lyberg, L. E. (2003). *Introduction to survey quality*. New York: Wiley & Sons.

Biemer, P., Groves, P., Lyberg, L., & Mathiowetz, N. (2004). *Measurement errors in surveys*. New York: Wiley & Sons.

Brick, J. M., & Kalton, G. (1996). Handling missing data in survey research. *Statistical Methods in Medical Research, 5*, 530–535.

Cox, B. G., & Cohen, S. B. (1985). *Methodological issues for health care surveys*. New York: Marcel Dekker, Inc.

Daniel, W. W. (1975). Nonresponse in sociological surveys: A review of some methods for handling the problem. *Sociological Methods & Research, 3*, 291–307.

DeMaio, T. (1980). Refusals: Who, where, and why. *Public Opinion Quarterly, 44*, 223–233.

Dillman, D., Gallegos, J., & Frey, J. (1976). Reducing refusals rates for telephone interviews. *Public Opinion Quarterly, 40*, 66–78.

Efron, B. (1994). Missing data, imputation and the bootstrap. *Journal of the American Statistical Association, 89*, 463–479.

Fox, R. J., Crask, M. R., & Kim, J. (1988). Mail survey response rates: a meta-analysis of selected techniques for inducing response. *Public Opinion Quarterly, 52*, 467–491.

Goyder, J. C. (1987). *The silent minority: Nonrespondents on sample surveys*. Boulder, CO: Westview Press.

Groves, R. M. (1989). Survey error and survey costs. New York: Wiley & Sons.

Groves, R. M. (2006). Nonresponse rates and nonresponse bias in household surveys. *Public Opinion Quarterly, 70*, 646–675.

Groves, R. M., & Couper, M. P. (1998). *Nonresponse in household interview surveys*. New York: Wiley & Sons.

Groves, R. M., Dillman, D. A., Eltinge, J. L., & Little, R. J. A. (2001). *Survey nonresponse*. New York: Wiley & Sons.

Groves, R. M., & Peytcheva, E. (2008). The impact of nonresponse rates on nonresponse bias: A meta-analysis. *Public Opinion Quarterly, 72*, 187–189.

Holt, D., & Elliot, D. (1991). Methods of weighting for unit non-response. *The Statistician, 40*, 333–342.

Lessler, J. T., & Kalsbeek, W. D. (1992). *Nonsampling error in surveys*. New York: Wiley & Sons.

Mandell, L. (1975). When to weight: Determining nonresponse bias in survey data. *Public Opinion Quarterly, 38*, 247–252.

Singer, E. (2006). Nonresponse bias in household surveys. *Public Opinion Quarterly, 70*, 637–645.

Weisberg, H. F. (2005). *The total survey error approach: A guide to the new science of survey research*. Chicago: The University of Chicago Press.

CHAPTER 3

CHOOSING BETWEEN NONPROBABILITY SAMPLING AND PROBABILITY SAMPLING

What you will learn in this chapter:

- Differences between probability sampling and nonprobability sampling
- Strengths and weaknesses of probability sampling and nonprobability sampling
- Guidelines for choosing between probability sampling and nonprobability sampling

INTRODUCTION

After choosing to sample instead of taking a census, the next major decision is whether to select a probability sample design or a nonprobability sample design. **Probability sampling** is a sampling procedure that gives every element in the target population a known and nonzero probability of being selected. If this condition is not satisfied, the sampling procedure is a nonprobability sampling procedure. **Nonprobability sampling** is a sampling procedure that does not give some elements in the population a chance to be in the sample.

The "known" term in the definition of a probability sample design implies that the size of the population was known at the time that the sample was selected, and the probability of any element of the population being selected into the sample could be calculated. The "nonzero" term in the definition implies that at the time that the sample was selected, every element in the population had a chance to be selected. Every element in the target population need not have an equal probability of selection. However, every element must have a chance to be selected.

This chapter presents a description of factors that should be considered in choosing between probability and nonprobability sampling. First, the strengths and weaknesses of nonprobability sampling and probability sampling are presented, followed by guidelines for making this choice. Another choice researchers have is to choose to combine nonprobability sampling procedures and probability sampling procedures and use a mixed-methods sample design. Mixed-methods sample designs are described in Chapter 6.

STRENGTHS AND WEAKNESSES OF NONPROBABILITY SAMPLING AND PROBABILITY SAMPLING

The strengths and weaknesses of probability sampling and nonprobability sampling should be considered in choosing between these sampling procedures. A summary of these strengths and weaknesses is presented in Table 3.1. In probability sampling, the selection of elements for the sample is independent of the

Table 3.1 Strengths and Weaknesses of Nonprobability Sampling and Probability Sampling in Addressing Selected Contingencies

Contingencies	Nonprobability Sampling	Probability Sampling
Objectives:		
Research has an exploratory purpose	Strength	Weakness
Need for quick decision	Strength	Weakness
Need to target specific elements of the population	Strength	Weakness
Need for a representative sample	Weakness	Strength
Need to make statistical inferences from the sample	Weakness	Strength
Need to minimize selection bias	Weakness	Strength

(Continued)

Table 3.1 (Continued)

Contingencies	Nonprobability Sampling	Probability Sampling
Important study	Weakness	Strength
Purpose of the sampling is to provide illustrative example	Strength	Weakness
Nature of the population:		
Heterogeneous population	Weakness	Strength
Difficult to gain access or locate population elements	Strength	Weakness
Population is highly scattered	Strength	Weakness
Availability of resources:		
Limited time, money, etc.	Strength	Weakness
Skilled and highly trained personnel	Strength	Weakness
Sampling frame is not available	Strength	Weakness
Research design considerations:		
Qualitative research design used	Strength	Weakness
Important to use easy operational procedures	Strength	Weakness
Very small sample size targeted	Strength	Weakness

feelings of the researcher; however, in nonprobability sampling, the selection of the elements for the sample is dependent on the feelings of the researcher. Probability selection may be detrimental to the research project. Subjective selection may be an essential aspect of a study. In some studies, the researcher might be interested in only certain members of the population. Giving all elements in the population a chance to be included in the sample may be wasteful and inconsistent with the purposes of the study. It may be more appropriate for the researcher to use his or her personal judgment or the judgment of "experts" in selecting elements from the population. Purposive sampling, a nonprobability sampling procedure, may be most appropriate.

Considering the major strengths of nonprobability sampling compared to probability sampling, it is likely that nonprobability sampling would be the better choice in the following situations:

- Research has an exploratory purpose
- Need for a quick decision
- Need to target specific elements of the population
- There is no need for a representative sample
- There is no need to make statistical inferences from the sample
- Research project is not highly important
- There is no need to minimize selection bias
- The purpose of the sampling is to provide an illustrative example
- Homogeneous population
- Difficult to gain access or locate population elements
- Population is highly scattered
- Resources (i.e., time, money, personnel, etc.) are extremely limited
- Low skill level of personnel
- Sampling frame is not available
- Qualitative research design is used
- Important to use easy operational procedures
- Extremely small sample size targeted

However, the greatest weakness of nonprobability sampling is the inability to estimate its sampling error. Nonprobability sampling lacks a mathematical basis for estimating the margin of error of estimates generated via the sample. Considering the major strengths of probability sampling compared to nonprobability sampling, probability sampling would be the better choice in the following situations:

- Research has a nonexploratory purpose
- There is no need for a quick decision
- Specific elements of the population are not targeted
- Heterogeneous population
- Target population is not a "hidden" population
- Population is not highly scattered
- Resources (i.e., time, money, personnel, etc.) are not extremely limited
- Personnel with sufficient expertise
- Sampling frame available
- Quantitative research design
- Not essential to use easy operational procedures

- Extremely small sample size not targeted
- Need for a representative sample
- Need to make statistical inferences from the sample
- Research project is highly important
- Need to minimize selection bias

Considering the above factors, probability sampling is generally the preferred choice. However, for some research it is not a practical choice, and nonprobability sampling becomes a viable alternative. This was the case for the research described in Research Note 3.1 below.

RESEARCH NOTE 3.1

Explanation for Choosing Nonprobability Sampling Instead of Probability Sampling in a Study of Gay and Lesbian Domestic Violence

Burke, Jordan, and Owen (2002) described their decision to use nonprobability sampling in their study of gay and lesbian domestic violence as follows:

> First, the results of this research should be considered carefully in light of its nonrandom sampling. Only respondents willing to self-identify as gay or lesbian completed the survey used in this study. Random sampling of the gay and lesbian population is not possible (Turell, 2000) due to the fact that participants had to self-identify and report being gay or lesbian (Burke, Owen, & Jordan, 2001; Turell, 2000). Unlike other types of research in which random samples can be drawn (i.e., from an enumerated sampling frame), "there is no 'master list' of gay individuals" (Burke, et al., 2001, p. 4). Accordingly, the nonrandom sample in this study may not speak to the experiences of all gays and lesbians.

Source: Burke, Jordan, & Owen, 2002, p. 240. Reprinted with permission.

GUIDELINES FOR CHOOSING BETWEEN NONPROBABILITY SAMPLING AND PROBABILITY SAMPLING

Considering the strengths and weaknesses of probability sampling and nonprobability sampling described above, a number of guidelines may be proposed for choosing between these two forms of sampling. These guidelines relate to the following factors:

- Objectives of the study
- Nature of the population
- Availability of resources
- Research design considerations

Objectives of the Study

Several of the strengths and weaknesses of probability sampling and nonprobability sampling relate to the objectives of the study. In choosing between these two sampling procedures, it is important to consider:

- Exploratory/nonexploratory purpose
- Need to make a quick decision
- Need to target specific elements of a population
- Need for a representative sample
- Need to make statistical inferences from the sample
- Need to minimize selection bias
- Importance of the study
- Purpose of the sampling is to provide illustrative examples

Guideline 3.1. *Exploratory/nonexploratory purpose.* If the research has an exploratory purpose, it is more favorable to choose nonprobability sampling.

The objectives of some studies dictate that a nonprobability sample would be more appropriate than a probability sample, and the objectives of other studies dictate that a probability sample would be more appropriate than a nonprobability sample. The intent of exploratory research is not to make generalizations to a larger population. Instead, the purpose of the research might be to obtain a general idea about the nature of the problem of the topic to be investigated, generate hypotheses and theories, test methodological procedures, and identify potential problems of later research activity. Moreover, if the purpose of the research is to demonstrate that a particular characteristic is present, then one needs only a single instance of the characteristic. The choice of nonprobability sampling would be reasonable for such purposes. Probability sampling, on the other hand, is likely to be the better choice for conclusive research with description, prediction, explanation, and evaluation purposes.

Abbassi and Singh's (2006) exploratory study of marital relationships among Asian Indians provides an example of the use of nonprobability sampling in exploratory research. The sampling procedures that they used are described in Research Note 3.2.

RESEARCH NOTE 3.2

Using Nonprobability Sampling for Exploratory Research: Study of Marital Relationships Among Asian Indians

Abbassi and Singh (2006) used a nonprobability sample design in their exploratory study of assertiveness in marital relationships among Asian Indians. They described their sampling procedures as follows:

> A sample of Asian Indians residing in a metropolitan area in the southwestern region of the United States was systematically selected. We do not claim, however, that we had a representative sample of all Asian Indian families in that region. Nonprobability samples in exploratory research, such as the one reported here, are justified in cross-cultural studies where complete listings of all members of a particular population are not fully available (Ihinger-Tallman, 1986).
>
> The sampling procedures employed in the study are as follows. First, we secured a membership list of addresses and phone numbers from a local association of the Asian Indians. Second, 402 persons in households in that list were contacted by telephone to determine whether (a) adults living in the household were first-generation immigrants from India who were currently married and (b) either the husband or the wife in each household would be willing to be interviewed in person.

Source: Abbassi & Singh, 2006, p. 394. Reprinted with permission.

Guideline 3.2. *Need to make a quick decision.* If it is necessary to make a quick decision on the basis of findings of a study, it is more favorable to choose nonprobability sampling.

At times, decision makers need to make quick decisions. Typically, nonprobability sampling is much less time-consuming than probability sampling. In fact, once the data collected via probability sampling are made available, they may be out-of-date and have decreased utility for the purposes of the study.

It may take up to 3 years for the findings of a large study utilizing probability sampling to be made available. If there is a need to make a quick decision based on the data to be collected, it may be more favorable to employ nonprobability sampling than probability sampling.

> **Guideline 3.3.** *Need to target specific elements of a population.* If there is a need to target specific elements of a population, it is more favorable to choose nonprobability sampling.

Probability sampling cannot ensure that specific elements of the population will be selected for a study. If a research project were specifically focused on particular individuals, events, or settings, it is possible that probability sampling would be an inappropriate sampling choice. On the other hand, the ability to target specific elements of a population is a strength of nonprobability sampling. For instance, if one were interested in studying the psychological effects of being trapped in a coal mine disaster, a nonprobability sample design may be more appropriate than a probability sample design for selecting study participants.

> **Guideline 3.4.** *Need for a representative sample.* If there is a need for a sample to be representative of a target population, it is more favorable to choose probability sampling.

A sample is considered to be representative of a population to the extent that there is no difference between the sample and the population in terms of the variables of interest. A probability sample is not necessarily representative of the population from which it was selected. Nor is a nonprobability sample necessarily unrepresentative of the population from which it was selected. A probability sample can be quite different from a target population, and a nonprobability sample can have much smaller differences. However, probability samples have a greater likelihood than nonprobability samples to be representative samples. Moreover, considering the variability of the variable of interests in the population and the sample size, the degree of random sampling error may be estimated if probability sampling is used.

> **Guideline 3.5.** *Need to make statistical inferences from the sample.* If there is a need to make statistical inferences from the sample, it is more favorable to choose probability sampling.

If there is a need to make inferences to the population from which the sample was drawn, probability sampling should be used. Nonprobability sampling does not permit the calculation of the margin of error of population estimates. The findings of a study utilizing nonprobability sampling procedures are limited to the elements sampled. This may be sufficient for such research as exploratory research, concept mapping, and packaging and name tests in marketing research. On the other hand, for conclusive research in which the making of statistical inferences from the sample is central to the research, probability sampling should be used.

Guideline 3.6. *Need to minimize selection bias.* If the minimization of selection bias is critical to a study, it is more favorable to choose probability sampling.

Selection bias is a major component of the total error of a study. It occurs when elements of the population selected to participate in a study are different from those not selected. Probability sampling minimizes selection bias by eliminating the subjective biases of the researcher from the selection process. Nonprobability sampling, especially availability sampling, is likely to have a great deal of selection bias.

Guideline 3.7. *Importance of the study.* The more important the research problem, the more favorable it is to choose probability sampling.

If a study is not important, nonprobability sampling may suffice. Resources will be saved, and the amount of effort needed to select the sample will be minimized. Although nonprobability sampling has serious limitations and weaknesses, if a study is of little importance, nonprobability sampling may suffice. On the other hand, if a study is highly important, probability sampling should be used.

Guideline 3.8. *Purpose of the sampling is to provide illustrative examples.* If the purpose of the sampling is to provide illustrative examples, the more favorable it is to choose nonprobability sampling.

If one is attempting to describe an illustrative example, a probability selection might not yield the best example for one's purposes. A nonprobability selection would be more appropriate.

Nature of the Population

Several characteristics of a target population are critical in choosing between probability sampling and nonprobability sampling. These include:

- Size of the population
- Homogeneity/heterogeneity of the population
- Accessibility of the population
- Spatial distribution of the population

Guideline 3.9. *Size of the population.* If the population is extremely small, it may be more favorable to choose nonprobability sampling.

If the population is extremely small, say, less than 30, if a census is not undertaken, it may be most appropriate to use a nonprobability sampling procedure such as purposive sampling.

Guideline 3.10. *Homogeneity/heterogeneity of the population.* The more heterogeneous the population with respect to the variables of interests, the more favorable it is to choose probability sampling; the more homogeneous the population with respect to the variables of interests, the more favorable it is to choose nonprobability sampling.

At the extreme, if a population is totally homogeneous in terms of the variables of interest, it would not matter if one chooses probability sampling or nonprobability sampling. Either way, one would select a representative sample. However, most populations studied in the social and behavioral sciences are not homogeneous in terms of the study variables. Nonprobability sampling would be less likely than probability sampling to capture the variability that exists. If a population is heterogeneous, probability sampling is more likely to result in a representative sample of the population.

Guideline 3.11. *Accessibility of the population.* The more difficult it is to gain access or locate important segments of the target population; the more favorable it is to choose nonprobability sampling.

Hard-to-reach and hidden populations are likely to require a great deal of resources and effort to identify, contact, and obtain their participation in research. For studying these populations, nonprobability sampling, in particular, respondent-assisted sampling, may be more cost-effective.

Guideline 3.12. *Spatial distribution of the population.* Taking into account data collection costs, the more scattered a population, the more favorable it is to choose nonprobability sampling.

Probability sampling could be very expensive if the population is widely scattered. Although much will depend on the type of probability design, the mode of collecting the data (e.g., personal interview versus web-based data collection), with a very limited budget, nonprobability sampling may be the better option.

Availability of Resources

Nonprobability sampling makes much less demand on resources than probability sampling. Key resources that relate to the choice of using nonprobability sampling or probability sampling include:

- Availability of money, time, etc.
- Availability of staff with requisite training and skill level in sampling
- Availability of sampling frame

Guideline 3.13. *Availability of money, time, etc.* The more limited one's resources, such as money and time, the more favorable it is to choose nonprobability sampling.

It takes more time and effort to plan and execute a probability sample design than it takes to plan and execute a nonprobability sample design. In most cases, the greater time and effort requirements translate into higher financial requirements.

Guideline 3.14. *Availability of trained and skilled staff.* If the study personnel have little or no training, understanding, and skills in constructing and implementing probability sample designs, the more favorable it is to choose nonprobability sampling.

Basic to advanced skills in constructing and implementing probability sample designs are required in order to properly execute such designs. This is not the case for nonprobability sampling. The planning and implementation of most nonprobability sample designs require little or no special training or skills.

Guideline 3.15. *Availability of sampling frame.* If a sampling frame is not available and one cannot be economically constructed, it is more favorable to choose nonprobability sampling.

As noted above, a sampling frame is typically required for selecting a probability sample. However, often a sampling frame for the target population does not exist, and it is not practical to construct one. Locating, generating, and cleaning a sampling frame may be very time consuming and expensive. However, a sampling frame is not required for nonprobability sampling. If a suitable sampling frame is not available and one does not have the resources to develop one, nonprobability sampling may be one's only option.

Research Design Considerations

The type of sample design used should have a good fit with other components of the research design of a study. Some of the research design considerations relevant to choosing between probability and nonprobability sampling are:

- Qualitative versus quantitative research designs
- Anticipated systematic errors
- Ease of operational procedures
- Size of the sample

> **Guideline 3.16.** *Qualitative versus quantitative research designs.* For qualitative research, it is generally more favorable to choose nonprobability sampling; on the other hand, for quantitative research, it is generally more favorable to choose probability sampling.

Qualitative research tends to have different objectives than quantitative research. Sampling in qualitative research is designed to facilitate the collection of "rich" information that enhances understanding of the problem under study. On the other hand, sampling in quantitative research is designed to facilitate the description of population parameters and the testing of hypotheses. Statistical estimation of population parameters is more important. It is likely that nonprobability sampling would be more appropriate for such qualitative research methods as focus group research, case studies, observational studies, and ethnographic research; and probability sampling would be more appropriate for such quantitative research as survey research and content analysis.

> **Guideline 3.17.** *Anticipated systematic errors.* The greater the likelihood of systematic errors, such as coverage bias and selection bias, the more favorable it is to choose probability sampling.

Depending on the specific sampling procedure that is used, it is likely that probability sampling will have less coverage bias and systematic bias than nonprobability sampling.

> **Guideline 3.18.** *Ease of operational procedures.* The more important it is to implement simple and easy-to-carry-out operational procedures of a study, the more favorable it is to choose nonprobability sampling.

The operational procedures of probability sampling are much more involved than the operational procedures of nonprobability sampling. Some probability sample designs are highly complex and require specialized training. Quality training and effective quality control procedures may minimize some of these problems. On the other hand, for the most part, the operational procedures of nonprobability sampling are straightforward and easy to implement.

> **Guideline 3.19.** *Size of the sample.* The smaller the projected sample size, the more favorable it is to choose nonprobability sampling.

Often, given the objectives of a study, nature of the research project, available resources, and other factors, the sample size is limited to a very small number of elements (say, fewer than 20 elements). The statistical benefits of probability sampling are lessened with small sample sizes. A nonprobability sample design, for example, purposive sampling, will be the favorable choice.

The above guidelines should assist in choosing between nonprobability sampling and probability sampling. If nonprobability sampling is chosen, the next step is to choose the type of nonprobability sampling procedure one would use. Likewise, if probability sampling is chosen, the next step is to choose the type of probability sampling procedure one would use. The next chapter describes guidelines for choosing among the various types of nonprobability sampling procedures. Then, Chapter 5 provides guidelines for choosing among the various types of probability sampling procedures.

SUMMARY

Probability sampling is a sampling procedure that gives every element in the target population a known and nonzero probability of being selected. If this condition is not satisfied, the sampling procedure is a nonprobability sampling procedure.

Considering the major strengths of nonprobability sampling compared to probability sampling, nonprobability sampling would be the better choice in the following situations:

- Research has an exploratory purpose
- Need for a quick decision
- Need to target specific elements of the population
- Population is homogeneous
- Difficulty in gaining access or locating population elements
- Population is highly scattered
- Resources are limited (i.e., time, money, personnel, etc.)
- Requires a low skill level of personnel
- Sampling frame is not available

- Qualitative research design is used
- Important to use easy operational procedures
- Targets a very small sample size

Considering the major strengths of probability sampling compared to nonprobability sampling, guidelines are presented for choosing between these two procedures. These guidelines relate to the following factors:

- Objectives of the study (including whether the purpose is exploratory or nonexploratory, the need to make a quick decision, the need to target specific elements of a population, the need for a representative sample, the need to make statistical inferences from the sample, the need to minimize selection bias, and the importance of the study)
- Nature of the population (including the homogeneity/heterogeneity of the population, accessibility of the population, and the spatial distribution of the population)
- Availability of resources (including availability of money, time, etc.; availability of staff with requisite training and skill level in sampling; and availability of sampling frame)
- Research design considerations (including whether the research design is qualitative or quantitative, the ease of operational procedures, and the size of the sample)

REVIEW QUESTIONS

1. What is the difference between nonprobability sampling and probability sampling?

2. Provide examples of research questions for which (a) nonprobability sampling would be a better fit than probability sampling, (b) probability sampling would be a better fit than nonprobability sampling, and (c) either nonprobability sampling or probability sampling would be a good fit.

3. What do you consider to be the most critical guidelines for choosing between nonprobability sampling and probability sampling? Why?

4. Berenson, Elifson, and Tollerson (1976) used nonprobability sampling in their study of political activism among Black ministers in Nashville, Tennessee. They were successful in getting participation from 154 of the 184 ministers in the city. Since the sample constituted 84% of the population, the authors felt justified in generalizing from the sample to the entire population of Black ministers in Nashville. What do you think? Do you agree with the authors? Why? Why not?

5. In order to maximize population generalizability, it is important to utilize representative samples. However, it is often difficult to obtain participation from certain segments of the population. Field, Pruchno, Bewley, Lemay, and Levinsky (2006) compare probability

and nonprobability sampling in reaching hard-to-reach participants for health-related research. What is your assessment of their findings? What additional factors should be considered in assessing the differences between probability and nonprobability sampling in health-related research? Are the authors' findings applicable to other areas of research, such as education, criminology, marketing, and so on?

6. Let us assume you desire to study demographic and psychological characteristics of the elderly. If you are to use probability sampling, how will your findings differ from the findings you might obtain if you were to use nonprobabiity sampling? What are the reasons for your answer? Once you have answered these questions, consider Hultsch et al.'s "Sampling and Generalizability in Developmental Research: Comparison of Random and Convenience Samples of Older Adults" (2002).

KEY TERMS

Define and give examples of the following concepts:

nonprobability sampling

probability sampling

REFERENCES FOR FURTHER STUDY

Field, L., Pruchno, R. A., Bewley, J., Lemay, E. P., Jr., & Levinsky., N. G. (2006). Using probability vs. nonprobability sampling to identify hard-to-access participants for health-related research: Costs and contrasts. *Journal of Aging and Health, 18*, 565–583.

Henry, G. T. (1990). *Practical sampling.* Thousand Oaks, CA: Sage.

Hultsch, D. F., MacDonald, S. W. S., Hunter, A., Maitland, S. B., & Dixon, R. A. (2002). Sampling and generalizability in developmental research: Comparison of random and convenience samples of older adults. *International Journal of Behavioral Development, 26*, 345-359.

Kuzel, A. (1999). Sampling in qualitative inquiry. In B. Crabtree & W. Miller (Eds.), *Doing qualitative research* (pp. 33–45). Thousand Oaks, CA: Sage.

Levy, P. S., & Lemeshow, S. (2008). *Sampling of populations: Methods and applications.* New York: Wiley & Sons.

CHAPTER 4

CHOOSING THE TYPE OF NONPROBABILITY SAMPLING

What you will learn in this chapter:

- Framework for classifying types of nonprobability sample designs
- Major types of nonprobability sampling and how they differ from each other
- Steps in carrying out the major types of nonprobability sample designs
- Strengths and weaknesses of the various types of nonprobability sampling
- Guidelines for choosing a nonprobability sample design

INTRODUCTION

Once a choice is made to use a nonprobability sample design, one must choose the type of nonprobability sampling to use. This chapter includes descriptions of the major types of nonprobability sampling and their subtypes, steps involved in their administration, and their weaknesses and strengths. Moreover, considering the strengths and weaknesses of the various methods, guidelines are presented for choosing among them.

There are four major types of nonprobability sample designs: availability sampling, purposive sampling, quota sampling, and respondent-assisted sampling (see Figure 4.1). Availability sampling is an unstructured sampling procedure. In using this type of sampling procedure the researcher primarily uses convenience and availability in determining whom he or she selects for participation in the research being conducted. No attempt is made to select particular population elements. Purposive sampling, quota sampling, and respondent-assisted sampling are structured sampling procedures.

Figure 4.1 Major Types of Nonprobability Sampling

```
                    ┌─────────────────┐
                    │  Nonprobability  │
                    │     Sample       │
                    │    Designs       │
                    └────────┬────────┘
         ┌──────────────┬────┴──────┬──────────────┐
  ┌────────────┐ ┌────────────┐ ┌──────────┐ ┌──────────────┐
  │Availability│ │ Purposive  │ │  Quota   │ │  Respondent- │
  │  Sampling  │ │  Sampling  │ │ Sampling │ │   Assisted   │
  │            │ │            │ │          │ │   Sampling   │
  └────────────┘ └────────────┘ └──────────┘ └──────────────┘
```

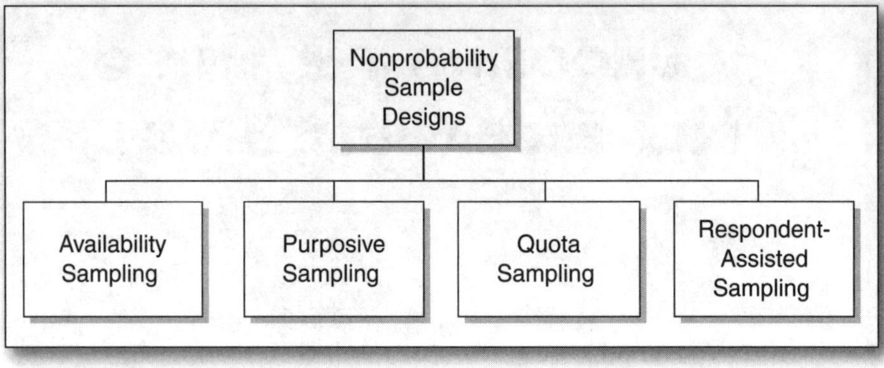

In employing these procedures, the researcher attempts to select particular elements of the target population.

AVAILABILITY SAMPLING

What Is Availability Sampling?

Availability sampling is a nonprobability sampling procedure in which elements are selected from the target population on the basis of their availability, convenience of the researcher, and/or their self-selection. A radio talk show host invites members of his audience to call in to vote on a community issue. A psychology instructor asks her students to complete a questionnaire as part of a study of issues relating to attitude formation. A market researcher studying buying behavior intercepts and interviews shoppers at a local mall. A researcher asks her friends and co-workers to complete a questionnaire to pretest the instrument she plans to use in a major study. A doctor asks his patients to participate in a clinical trial of the effects of a new medication. A pollster interviews persons as they leave a polling place. A TV reporter interviews people on the street gathering around a house where five family members were killed. A person using the Internet responds to a pop-up invitation to click on a link and complete a questionnaire on visitors to the website. All of these sampling procedures have one thing in common: They are examples of availability sampling.

What Are the Steps in Selecting an Availability Sample?

There are four major steps in selecting an availability sample:

1. Define the target population.

2. Identify convenient ways to recruit and select available elements in the target population.

3. Determine the sample size.

4. Select the targeted number of population elements.

This plan involves selecting elements on the basis of their availability. A wide range of recruitment procedures are used. These include mass media advertising, street canvassing, mailing campaigns, emails, bulletin boards, community outreach efforts, telephone canvassing, and the distribution of flyers. Typically, the recruitment of study participants continues until the targeted sample size is satisfied or the resources necessary to continue sampling are exhausted.

What Are the Subtypes of Availability Sampling?

There are several subtypes of availability sampling. They include: convenience sampling, haphazard sampling, accidental sampling, chunk sampling, grab sampling, opportunistic sampling, fortuitous sampling, incidental sampling, straw polling, volunteer sampling, nonprobability systematic sampling, and nonprobability web-based sampling.

These different forms of availability sampling provide easy-to-use options for such research as predicting the results of an election. As these names imply, voters may be selected haphazardly, based on the convenience of the researcher and/or the respondent, or seemingly by accident. A researcher may select whomever happens to be on the street at the time data collection commences. In a study of documents or records, a researcher may take a "chunk" of records in a filing cabinet. The researcher may be seen as "grabbing" persons off the streets or in the mall for inclusion in the study, or seizing the "opportunity" to include elements in the sample that "fortuitously" or "incidentally" happen to be available at the time of the data collection activity. Straw polling may be done with persons who are available at a meeting, or contacted via advertisements placed on bulletin boards, web sites, or in newspapers requesting persons to volunteer to participate in a study. The researcher may also stand near a polling place and haphazardly ask persons leaving the polling place to consent to be interviewed. The sample for a study may be whoever made themselves available by volunteering, such as responding to a pop-up invitation on a web site.

What Are the Strengths and Weaknesses of Availability Sampling?

The strengths and weaknesses of nonprobability availability sampling are typical of those of nonprobability sampling in general. However, there are some differences (see Table 4.1).

Availability sampling is the most frequently used sampling procedure in research. This is because it is the least time-consuming, least expensive, and the least complicated sampling procedure. An availability sample design is not necessarily easy to implement. However, overall the operational procedures of availability sampling are simplest and easiest to implement. It can be done very quickly, making the data collected timely. Given that only persons who are available, able, and willing to participate are selected to participate in the

Table 4.1 Strengths and Weaknesses of Availability Sampling Compared to Other Nonprobability Sampling Procedures

Strengths	Weaknesses
Least resources requirements: time, money, personnel	Cannot satisfy a need to target specific elements of the population
Simplest operational procedures	Least reliable
Least effort required	Overrepresentation of population elements that are the most readily accessible, articulate, and visible
Least sampling skills required	Does not take advantage of knowledge of the population that the researcher might have
	Underrepresentation of population elements that are not readily accessible, uncooperative, and hidden
	Most likely to underestimate the variability in the population

study, availability sampling tends to have high response rates. As availability sampling procedures are rather straightforward and uncomplicated, they may be easily understood by others. Moreover, as in the case with other nonprobability sample designs, availability sampling does not require a sampling frame.

Availability sampling has serious weaknesses, however. An implied assumption of availability sampling is that the target population is homogeneous in terms of the study variables. This assumption is often untenable. Persons who are selected tend not to be similar to those who were not selected. As other nonprobability sampling procedures, availability samples tend not to be representative of the population from which they are selected. Elements in the population that are more easily accessible tend to be overrepresented in the sample, and elements in the population that are more inaccessible tend to be underrepresented in the sample. One cannot assume that persons who participate in Internet surveys utilizing nonprobability sampling procedures are representative of all Internet users, nor representative of all persons in the larger population of Internet users and non-Internet users. One cannot assume that persons who are readily available to participate in a study are representative of the target population. One cannot assume that persons who volunteer for participation in research are representative of persons who do not volunteer. As a result, availability sampling has low external validity. Moreover, as extreme cases and hard-to-reach elements of the population are often not likely to be selected, availability sampling tends to underestimate the variability in the population.

As is the case with other nonprobability sampling procedures, availability sampling does not permit the use of inferential statistics for the calculation of the margin of error of its estimates. However, although a strength of some nonprobability sampling procedures is the ability to target specific elements of the population, this is not the case for availability sampling. No attempt is made to target specific elements of the population; whoever agrees to participate in the study is included in the study. No attempt is made to maintain documentation on those who refuse to participate in the study or are unable to participate in the study. Moreover, although availability sampling is used often in exploratory research and pretesting instruments, one cannot generalize the findings of such research to the target population.

The research notes below describe examples of availability sample. Research Note 4.1 describes the sampling procedure used in a study of partner violence among gay men who are HIV positive. Research Note 4.2 describes an availability sampling procedure used in a study of battered women. Research Note 4.3 describes an availability sampling procedure used in a study of women in post-Katrina New Orleans.

RESEARCH NOTE 4.1

Example of Availability Sampling: Study of Partner Violence Among Gay Men Who Are HIV Positive

Craft and Serovich (2005) used availability sampling in their study of partner violence among gay men who are HIV positive. They described their sampling procedure as follows:

A nonprobability, convenience sampling technique was used to solicit men for the current study. Eligible participants were men who were HIV positive and older than the age of 18 years, currently engaged in an intimate relationship with another man, or in an intimate relationship with another man within the past year. For the purpose of the current study, an intimate relationship was defined as one in which the participant shared emotional and physical experiences and affection and sexual activity. Men were recruited in four ways. They were approached when they attended regularly scheduled visits to a longitudinal research study conducted by the second author, in an AIDS Clinical Trials Unit (ACTU) at a large midwestern university, during an HIV educational forum, and at a regional HIV conference. Participants were paid $5 for completing the survey. Because of the variety of means required to recruit this sample, the number of men who did not consent to participate in the study was not counted, thus the calculation of a refusal rate was not possible.

Source: Craft & Serovich, 2005, p. 782. Reprinted with permission.

RESEARCH NOTE 4.2

Example of Availability Sampling: Study of Battered Women

Campbell and Soeken (1999) used a volunteer sample in their longitudinal study of battered women. Their study participants were interviewed more than 3 times over 3½ years. They described their sampling procedures as follows:

Participants were recruited by newspaper advertisements and bulletin board postings in the metropolitan area of a major Midwestern city. Women who were having "serious problems in an intimate relationship with a man for at least a year" were asked to participate in the research study. A $15 stipend was offered in return for participating in the original interview, with a total of $50 for all three interviews. When the women called the number in the advertisement, they were screened for battering.

Source: Campbell & Soeken, 1999, p. 25. Reprinted with permission.

RESEARCH NOTE 4.3

Example of Availability Sampling: Study of Perinatal Mood and Alternative Therapies Among Women Living in New Orleans, Post–Hurricane Katrina

Savage et al. (2010) used availability sampling in their exploratory study of perinatal mood and the use of alternative therapies among childbearing women living in New Orleans, post–Hurricane Katrina. They described their sampling procedures as follows:

> A convenience sample of 199 pregnant and postpartum women in the Greater New Orleans area participated in the study. They were recruited from hospital-based prenatal classes, postpartum units, and a postpartum database of women who had given birth at a private, not-for-profit community hospital in New Orleans the first year after Katrina. Participant inclusion criteria were (a) 18 years of age or older, (b) medically uncomplicated pregnancy or birth within the last calendar year, (c) and ability to understand English. Age restriction correlated with the greatest range of pregnancy incidence.

Source: Savage et al., 2010, p. 125. Reprinted with permission.

PURPOSIVE SAMPLING

What Is Purposive Sampling?

Purposive sampling is a nonprobability sampling procedure in which elements are selected from the target population on the basis of their fit with the purposes of the study and specific inclusion and exclusion criteria. It is also referred to as *purposeful sampling*. Unlike availability sampling, in purposive sampling elements are not selected simply on the basis of their availability, convenience, or self-selection. Instead, the researcher purposely selects the elements because they satisfy specific inclusion and exclusion criteria for participation in the study. After verifying that an element satisfies the criteria, its participation in the study is solicited.

What Are the Steps in Selecting a Purposive Sample?

There are five major steps in selecting a purposive sample:

1. Define the target population.

2. Identify inclusion and exclusion criteria for sample.

3. Create a plan to recruit and select population elements that satisfy the inclusion and exclusion criteria.

4. Determine the sample size.

5. Select the targeted number of population elements.

What Are the Subtypes of Purposive Sampling?

Purposive sampling may be classified into several major subtypes according to the type of criteria used for including or excluding elements of the population. These criteria for inclusion and exclusion tend to fall into four major categories:

- Criteria based on central tendency
- Criteria based on variability
- Criteria based on theory/model development
- Criteria based on judgment and reputation

An outline of purposive sampling procedures per these criteria is presented in Figure 4.2, and a description of the procedures is presented below.

Types Based on Central Tendency

Population elements may be selected because they are considered to be average or typical; or the opposite, because they are rare or extreme and not average at all.

Figure 4.2 Major Types of Purposive Sampling

Major Types of Purposive Sampling

Selection criteria: Elements' fit or lack of fit with central tendency

Typical case sampling
Modal instance sampling

Deviant case sampling
Rare element sampling
Outlier sampling
Extreme case sampling
Intense case sampling

Selection criteria: Variability of elements

Homogeneous sampling

Diversity sampling
Heterogeneity sampling
Maximum variation sampling

Selection criteria: Theory, model development, and hypothesis testing

Confirmatory sampling
Disconfirming sampling
Negative case sampling
Theoretical sampling
Critical case sampling
Matched sampling
Case control sampling
Consecutive sampling
Targeted sampling

Selection criteria: Judgment, reputation, or specialized knowledge

Judgment sampling
Subjective sampling
Bellwether case sampling
Reputational sampling
Politically important cases
Expert sampling
Informant sampling

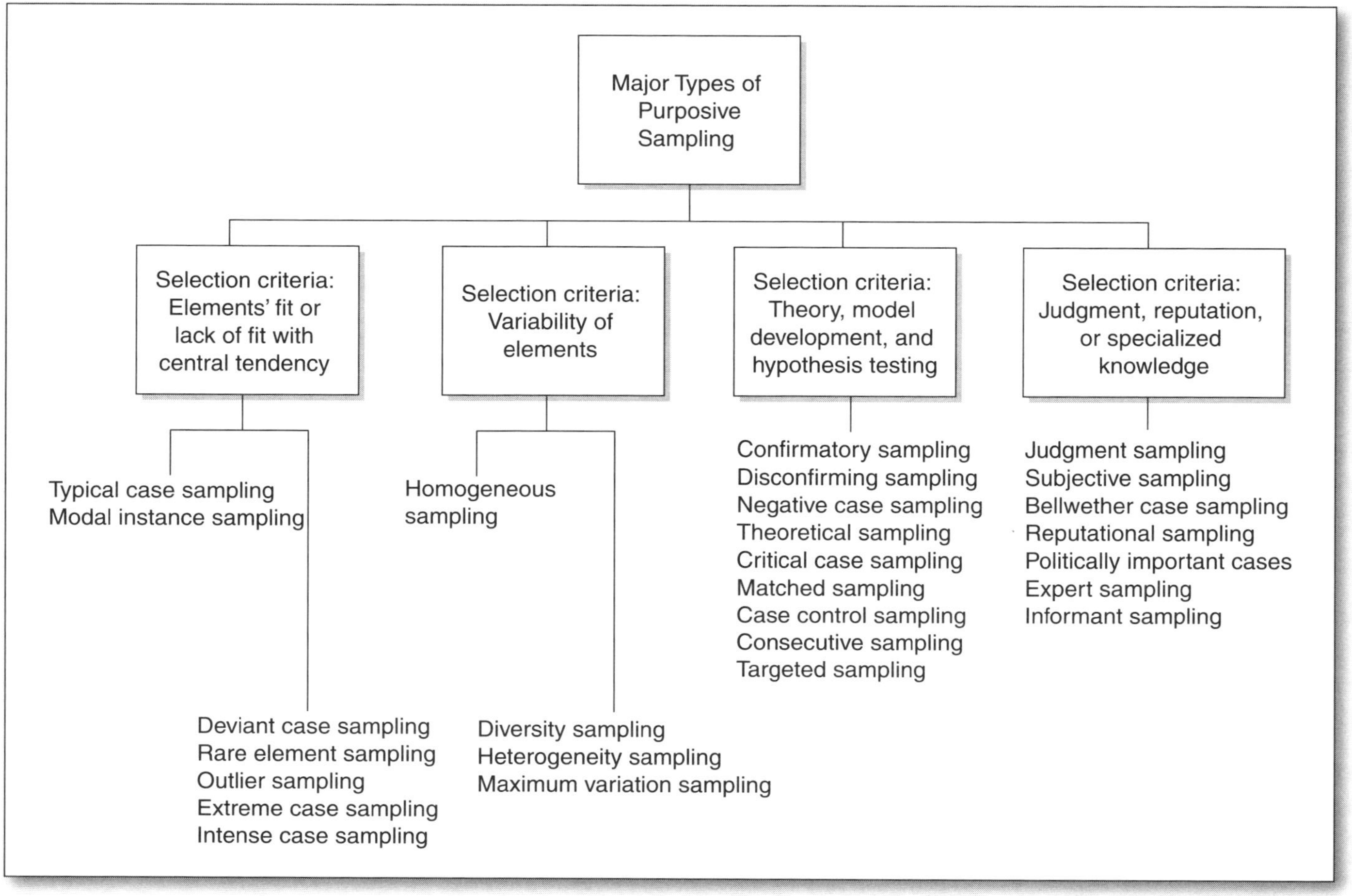

In **typical case sampling** and **modal instance sampling** the researcher attempts to select elements that may be considered "average," typical, or have the highest frequency of occurrence. In selecting a city to test market a product, a researcher might not want to randomly select a city, but to select a city that has characteristics similar to national averages.

On the other hand, instead of selecting elements considered to be "average" or "typical," a researcher may select elements because they are unique or extreme. Such sampling procedures are referred to as **deviant case sampling**, **rare element sampling**, **outlier sampling**, **extreme case sampling**, and **intensity case sampling** Elements are selected because they are unusual, unique, atypical, deviant, rare, or extreme. At times elements that are less than extreme, but have an intense level of a variable of interest, are selected.

Types Based on Variability

Purposive sampling may also be classified in terms of whether the inclusion and exclusion criteria focused on minimizing the variability of the sample or maximizing the variability of a sample. The researcher may either attempt to achieve a homogeneous sample (**homogeneous sampling**) or sample in such a way so as to maximize variability (heterogeneous sampling, **diversity sampling** and **maximum variation sampling**). In using these types of purposive sampling, the researcher attempts to either select a sample that controls for extraneous variables (homogeneous sample) or covers a wide range of elements in the population (diversity sampling, **heterogeneity sampling**, and maximum variation sampling). The proportion of population at the different levels of diversity is typically not the focus of the study. On the other hand, a wide variety of elements may be selected so as to identify important common patterns that cut across the variations. The researcher must first identify a variable(s) whose variation is important to have represented in the sample, and then select elements of different subcategories of the variable(s).

Types Based on Theory, Model Development, and Hypothesis Testing

Elements may be selected because they are prime candidates to either confirm (**confirmatory sampling**) or disconfirm (**disconfirming sampling** and **negative case sampling**) a hypothesis. **Theoretical sampling** incorporates both confirmatory sampling and disconfirming sampling. In this procedure the researcher selects population elements that are most likely to inform a theory of interest. Elements are useful for the study and are selected on the basis of their value in developing or illustrating the theory relating to the study. Data are interpreted in terms of a theory and generalized to a theory, rather than to a population. Glaser (1978) indicated that in using theoretical sampling "the analyst jointly collects, codes, and analyzes his data and decides what to collect next and where to find them, in order to develop his theory as it emerges" (p. 36).

Elements likely to provide highly strategic information in assessing a theory or hypothesis may be selected (**critical case sampling**). In order to facilitate hypothesis testing, elements may be selected on the basis of their similarities or differences to a comparison group (systematic matching sampling and case control sampling). These sampling procedures are often used in medical research, psychological research, and public health research. In systematic matching and **case control sampling**, persons who have a characteristic of interest are matched on the basis of correlated factors with those who do have the characteristics. A sample selected from a panel of respondents recruited using opt-in web-based sampling may be selected by matching them on a case-by-case basis with characteristics of respondents in a probability sample of the target population. In employing **consecutive sampling**, every person who meets the inclusion and exclusion criteria of a sample design within a defined time frame is included in the sample. Such a sample design might be used in a hospital-based or clinic-based medical research study. Targeted sampling is a mixed-methods sample design that involves an initial formative research and ethnographic mapping of the geographical area frequented by members of the target population. Once rapport is established with the target population, the sample is selected utilizing availability sampling, quota sampling, respondent-assisted sampling, and other sampling procedures.

Types Based on Judgment, Reputation, and Specialized Knowledge

Sample elements may be selected on the basis of a judgment or subjective belief that certain elements in the population should be selected for a study (**judgment sampling** and **subjective sampling**). The elements may be selected because of political expediency (sampling of politically important elements), because of their reputation of having an association with various variables of interest (**reputational sampling**), or because of their history of being particularly representative of the population, such as political precincts that have historically voted for the winner of elections (**bellwether case sampling**). Members of the population may be selected on the basis of their expertise (**expert sampling**) or because of their special knowledge of the population under study (**informant sampling**).

What Are the Strengths and Weaknesses of Purposive Sampling?

With a few exceptions, the strengths and weaknesses of purposive sampling are typical of the strengths and weaknesses of other forms of nonprobability sampling. However, purposive sampling has several strengths and weaknesses that are not typical of other forms of nonprobability sampling (see Table 4.2). These factors should be considered in choosing a nonprobability sample design to use. Purposive sampling provides more control over who is selected to be included in a sample than availability sampling, and, as particular elements of the population are purposely selected, it is more appropriate than

Table 4.2 Strengths and Weaknesses of Purposive Sampling Compared to Other Nonprobability Sampling Procedures

Strengths	Weaknesses
Compared to availability sampling:	Compared to availability sampling:
Provides more control over who is selected to be included in a sample	Requires greater resources: time, money, etc.
More appropriate for research focused on particular segments of a target population	Requires more recent and up-to-date information and knowledge about the population, the sites, and the conditions of the research
Findings more generalizable	Requires greater effort
Less selection bias likely	If judgment or expert sampling is used, there may be bias to that person's beliefs
Consecutive sampling provides less opportunity for intentional or unintentional manipulation by data collectors	Consecutive sampling may not pick up temporal or seasonal variation
If maximum variation sampling is used, it is made certain that the widest variety of subjects are represented	Compared to respondent-assisted sampling, more likely to underestimate hidden populations
Homogeneous sampling and matching may control for extraneous variables, thereby increasing internal validity	Researcher must be knowledgeable about the population, the sites, and the conditions of the research
Less bias due to underrepresentation and overrepresentation	

availability sampling for research focused on particular segments of a target population. As a nonprobability sampling procedure, purposive sampling limits the ability of a researcher to make valid generalizations beyond the elements included in the sample. However, due to its targeting of specific elements, it may be more appropriate for a particular study than availability sampling. Selection bias may be less in purposive sampling than availability sampling since the selection of elements are not purely made on the basis of availability. Moreover, via employing homogeneous sampling, the internal validity of purposive sampling tends to be higher than the internal validity of availability sampling. Homogeneous sampling, and matching, in particular, provides a means of controlling for the effects of extraneous variables in analyzing relationships among study variables.

On the other hand, in order to demonstrate the effect of an independent variable, maximum variation sampling, heterogeneity sampling, or extreme case sampling may be appropriate. An independent variable must vary in order to demonstrate its effect. Extreme case sampling provides a basic sampling procedure for such research. However, one can only make conclusions about the extremes. Elements at intermediate levels may behave differently than those at the extremes. If a relationship is curvilinear, only comparing extremes may yield erroneous results. Sampling across levels of the independent variable via diversity sampling or maximum variation sampling may resolve this issue.

Although purposive sampling requires fewer resources and effort than most probability sampling procedures, it tends to require more resources than availability sampling. Compared to availability sampling, purposive sampling requires more resources such as time, money, and personnel. Moreover, purposive sampling takes much more effort and requires more recent and up-to-date information than that required for availability sampling. If expert sampling and informant sampling are used, there may be bias due to the erroneous information provided by the experts and informants.

The research notes below provide illustrations of some of the subtypes of purposive sampling. Research Note 4.4 describes the deviant case sampling procedures that were used in a study of violence against women in Nicaragua. In order to clearly identify differences in the moral reasoning abilities of juvenile sexual and nonsexual offenders, extreme case sampling was used in the study described in Research Note 4.5. Homogeneous sampling was used in the study of the Black community described in Research Note 4.6. The next three research notes provide examples of maximum variation sampling. Research Note 4.7 concerns older women who experienced domestic violence.

Research Note 4.8 is a study of patients living with pacemakers. Research Note 4.9 is a study of the hip hop and electronic dance music nightclub scenes in Philadelphia. The next two research notes, Research Note 4.10 and Research Note 4.11, describe variants of targeted sampling procedures used to study the subculture of sex workers. An example of consecutive sampling is described in Research Note 4.12. This study examined the use of a hospital emergency department by low-income Hispanic and African American patients with type 2 diabetes. Expert sampling was used in a study of police officers' assessment of specialized training to handle youth-related incidents described in Research Note 4.13.

RESEARCH NOTE 4.4

Example of Deviant Case Sampling: Study of Cultural Beliefs in Nicaragua Relating to Violence Against Women

Ellsberg and Heise (2005) described the following study utilizing deviant case sampling in their guide for researching violence against women:

[R]esearchers with the Nicaraguan organization Puntos de Encuentro embarked on a project to collect information useful for designing a national media campaign that called on men to renounce violence in their intimate relationships. They wanted to understand the beliefs and attitudes that existed in Nicaraguan culture that supported violent behavior toward women. More importantly, they wanted to know if there were any "benefits" of nonviolence that could be promoted to encourage men to reconsider their behavior. . . . Rather than concentrating on collecting information on the norms and attitudes of "typical" Nicaraguan men, the researchers decided to use "deviant case" sampling and concentrate on interviewing men who had already had a reputation for being nonviolent and renouncing machism. They were interested in finding out from these men what benefits, if any, they perceived from this choice, and what life-course events, influences, or individuals pushed them in this direction. The goal was to investigate what aspirations and life experiences help create "healthy" intimate partnerships. The findings were used to design an information campaign aimed at recruiting more men to a nonviolent lifestyle.

Source: Ellsberg & Heise, 2005, pp. 106–107. Reprinted with permission.

RESEARCH NOTE 4.5

Example of Extreme Case Sampling:
Study Comparing Moral Reasoning Abilities of
Juvenile Sexual and Nonsexual Offenders

Ashkar and Kenny (2007) used extreme case sampling in their study of moral reasoning abilities of juvenile sexual and nonsexual offenders. They described their sampling procedures as follows:

> Potential participants were screened for suitability via a departmental information database. Extreme case sampling was employed to identify serious and/or repeat offenders, and purposeful sampling was employed to identify sexual and nonsexual offenders. Detention center clinical staff were presented with a list of possible participants for the study and asked to identify those most appropriate on the basis of the following exclusion criteria: (a) untreated psychosis, (b) substance withdrawal (excluding nicotine and cannabis), and (c) recent history of self-harming or suicidal behaviour. A total of 19 candidates were approached. All but 1 expressed interest in participating in the study.

Source: Ashkar & Kenny, 2007, p. 111. Reprinted with permission.

RESEARCH NOTE 4.6

Example of Homogeneous Sampling:
Study of Black Perceptions of the Black Community

Grayman (2009) used homogeneous sampling in an exploratory study of the meaning Blacks attached to the concept "Black community." Grayman described the sampling procedures that were used as follows:

> Specifically, purposeful homogeneous sampling was used with regard to participant race and region of recruitment. All participants recruited for this study were Black, determined by phenotypic features (i.e., dark skin, curly hair, facial features), and all were recruited from urban areas within the

(Continued)

(Continued)

mid-Atlantic region of the United States (Brooklyn, New York; Wilmington, Delaware; and Washington, D.C.). Black participants were chosen because it was hypothesized that the meaning of "the Black community" has the greatest potential mental health policy and program implications for members of this group given the differential social capital associated with race in the United States. In this respect, the Black race has always been associated with disadvantaged social, economic, and political positions in the United States that have instigated the marginalization of truth according to those labeled "Black." Thus, it was important that voices from this group be privileged in this examination. These particular urban areas within the mid-Atlantic region of the United States were selected because of their Black population density (U.S. Census Bureau, 2000), because they represent the endpoints and midpoint of the mid-Atlantic continuum, and because of their accessibility to the principal investigator. Additionally, we used purposeful stratified sampling along the lines of gender and generational affiliation, such that approximately equal numbers of men and women within each of the three primary adult generational positions (i.e., young adulthood, middle adulthood, and older adulthood) were recruited from each city within the region.

Source: Grayman, 2009, p. 436. Reprinted with permission.

RESEARCH NOTE 4.7

Example of Maximum Variation Sampling: Focus Group Study of Older Women Who Experienced Domestic Violence

Beaulaurier, Seff, Newman, and Dunlop (2007) utilized maximum variation sampling in their focus group research on domestic violence experienced by older women. They described their sampling procedures as follows:

The sampling strategy (i.e., maximum variation sampling) emphasized obtaining a respondent pool that was diverse enough to capture as much of the deviation in the population as possible. . . . However, open discussion in focus groups is facilitated by assigning study participants to groups with others like themselves with regard to age, ethnicity, race, and income. Therefore, individual group composition was selected to allow for relatively broad differences between focus groups, while maintaining enough similarity between respondents within focus groups to enhance the comfort of the members.

Source: Beaulaurier, Seff, Newman, & Dunlop, 2007, p. 748. Reprinted with permission.

RESEARCH NOTE 4.8

Example of Maximum Variation Sampling: Study of Patients Living With Pacemakers

Malm and Hallberg (2006) wanted to describe the broad range of experiences of patients living with pacemakers. They used maximum variation sampling to achieve this objective. They described their sampling procedures as follows:

The study was carried out using patients with pacemakers in a health care area in southern Sweden. A total of 13 informants (7 women) with pacemakers were interviewed, all of who had had the pacemaker implanted at the same county hospital. The participants were selected according to maximum variation sampling technique (Strauss & Corbin, 1990), using the variables age, sex, number of years with a pacemaker and pacemaker mode in order to get as broad a range as possible of patient experiences.

Source: Malm & Hallberg, 2006, p. 789. Reprinted with permission.

RESEARCH NOTE 4.9

Example of Maximum Variation Sampling: Study of the Hip Hop and Electronic Dance Music Nightclub Scenes in Philadelphia

Anderson, Daly, and Rapp (2009) used maximum variation sampling in their exploratory study of the relationship between masculinities and crime within the hip-hop and electronic dance music nightclub scenes in Philadelphia. They described their sampling procedures as follows:

An ethnographic mapping/maximum variation sampling approach was used to recruit members of each nightclub scene (Strauss & Corbin, 1990; Watters

(Continued)

(Continued)

& Biernacki, 1989). Respondents were recruited in a variety of ways. Recruitment began at a local Philadelphia record store, a small independent venue specializing in EDM. Early on, two store staff members were hired as key informants to assist in participant recruitment. Although efficient, relying on this recruitment strategy alone could have introduced bias into our study as early contacts were situated within the same social networks. We ran into some of this bias, as our sample overrepresents people with long-standing ties to the scenes we studied and who were also linked to the record-store employees. Live recruitment during direct observation was an alternative recruitment strategy, one that permitted us quick access to unrelated respondents. It helped reduce selection bias by discovering new or opening up networks of respondents. Live recruitment at nightclub events produced some respondents, but they were fewer than predicted. To address this, two more key informants were hired: (a) an Asian male DJ working at the record store and (b) a White female HH enthusiast who worked at another record store frequented almost exclusively by HH fans.

The sampling strategy was designed to recruit comparable groups of people in each scene. The original goal was to sample equal numbers of respondents across the major race groups, with respect to how they were represented in each scene. For difficulty in recruiting populations (e.g., Hispanics), the research team adopted a more targeted strategy, approaching specific race group members at events once saturation was reached for other racial categories.

Source: Anderson, Daly, & Rapp, 2009, p. 308. Reprinted with permission.

RESEARCH NOTE 4.10

Example of Targeted Sampling: Study of the Subculture of Violence Encompassing Female Street Sex Workers in Miami, Florida

Surratt, Inciardi, Kurtz, and Kiley (2004) examined the subculture of violence encompassing female sex workers in Miami, Florida. They described the sample design for their study as follows:

Participants in the study were located and recruited through traditional targeted sampling strategies (Watters & Biernacki, 1989), which are especially useful for studying drug-involved women in the sex industry. Because it is impossible to achieve a random sample of active sex workers, a purposive, targeted sampling plan was constructed that would best reflect what is typical of the larger population. Such a strategy has been used successfully in recent years in studies of injection and other out-of-treatment drug users (Braunstein, 1993; Carlson, Wang, Siegal, Falck, & Guo, 1994; Coyle, Boruch, & Turner, 1991). Targeted sampling has been referred to as a purposeful, systematic method by which specified populations within geographical districts are identified, and detailed plans are designed to recruit adequate numbers of cases within each of the target areas (Watters & Biernacki, 1989). Several elements are necessary for this approach, including the systematic mapping of the geographical areas in which the target population is clustered, the examination of official indicator data (such as police arrest reports), information from professional and indigenous informants, and direct observations of various neighborhoods for signs of sexual solicitation.

Periodic updates of these are necessary should the locations of the strolls temporarily shift as the result of urban renewal or police activity. Because the authors of this article have been conducting street studies in Miami for a number of years, numerous contacts have been built up with drug users and dealers, sex workers, police officers, HIV prevention specialists, and treatment professionals. A number of these informants were contacted prior to the onset of the research to elicit information about where the highest concentrations of active sex workers might be found. In addition, through focus groups with current and former sex workers, the downtown Miami strolls most heavily traveled in the sex industry were specifically described, identified, and subsequently located.

Source: Surratt, Inciardi, Kurtz, & Kiley, 2004, p. 47. Reprinted with permission.

RESEARCH NOTE 4.11

Example of Targeted Sampling Enhanced With Scroll Sampling: Study of Sex Workers in San Francisco and Montreal

Shaver (2005) and her colleagues addressed challenges in selecting a representative sample of sex workers. They described these challenges and their solution as follows:

[C]hallenges arise when conducting research on the sexual service industry. First, the size and boundaries of the population are unknown, so it is extremely

(Continued)

(Continued)

difficult to get a representative sample. The traditional methods of sampling such populations—snowball sampling, key informant sampling, and targeted sampling—do not solve this problem. Snowballing samples, for example, tend to be biased toward the more cooperative participants. Data from key informants (social service agencies, health care workers, and police) generally reflect their interactions with clients who are in crisis. Consequently, the stories of those less interested in participating and those not in crisis are rarely reported. Targeted sampling, although widely used, is only as good as one's ability to penetrate the local networks of the stigmatized population. In addition, bias can be introduced during targeted sampling when the most visible participants (such as street workers) are oversampled and the least visible (those who work inside) undersampled. . . . Our general approach to these challenges was to adopt techniques allowing us to (a) identify appropriate sites and penetrate local networks while preserving representativeness, (b) legitimate our role as researchers in ways that would encourage cooperation and veracity, and (c) build on strategic comparisons. . . . Our field strategies were grounded in a participant-centered approach. They varied slightly from city to city but generally involved three stages: gaining entry, working the stroll, and leaving the field. The first, gaining entry, entailed 2 to 4 weeks of introductions and public relations activities that served to legitimate both the study and our role as researchers. We worked in pairs during the regular operating hours of the stroll, introducing. . . . As we came to know the regulars by name, we had many opportunities to discuss their work, and our work, informally with them. We made it clear by our actions that we were guests in their territory; that we were not police, press, outreach or social workers; and that we were able to do research without putting them at risk or alarming the johns. We also made it clear during these conversations that participation was voluntary and that we would take no for an answer and move on politely. In doing so, however, we also pointed out that although it was their right to say no to an interview, it was our job to keep on trying. . . . To preserve the representativeness of the stroll samples and the integrity of the database, we only interviewed people we had seen working on several different occasions (the regulars) and who were not under the influence of drugs at the time. We also took care to ensure that the distinguishing characteristics of those interviewed reflected the characteristics of the stroll population in question as much as possible. Full stroll counts were conducted on a regular basis during our field observations, and with the help of the women, men, and transgender workers, we were able to create lists of the regular workers by their street names. . . . We walked the stroll in pairs hailing and chatting to those we knew and introducing ourselves to others. A good time to ask for an interview was when business was slow or when it was clear that a worker was returning from a date. Because we had observed who was involved in the sex trade, no mistakes were made (e.g., asking non-sex-workers), and because we had become well known on the street, there were very few refusals.

Source: Shaver, 2005, pp. 296–304. Reprinted with permission.

RESEARCH NOTE 4.12

Example of Consecutive Sampling: Study of African American Adolescents With Type 2 Diabetes

Auslander, Sterzing, Zayas, and White (2010) used consecutive sampling in their study of African American adolescents with type 2 diabetes. They described their sampling procedures as follows:

African American adolescents (n = 10) with type 2 diabetes who received health care at the pediatric clinic of the Department of Pediatrics at Washington University in St. Louis and St. Louis Children's Hospital and their mothers (n = 10) were recruited for the present study after approval by the Human Research Protection Office at Washington University. The clinic serves approximately 1200 pediatric diabetes patients of which about 10% are diagnosed with type 2 diabetes. Eligibility criteria for the study included African American ethnicity, adolescent (14–19 years of age) with a diagnosis of type 2 diabetes mellitus, minimum of 1 year since initial diagnosis, participation of the parent or legal guardian of the eligible adolescent, and no diagnosis of mental illness. We utilized a consecutive sampling strategy commonly used in qualitative inquiry because there was a relatively small number of identified cases at the clinic that met the eligibility criteria. Recruitment of subjects was more difficult than anticipated because of a high rate of missed clinic appointments among eligible subjects. Of those subjects who were recruited during their clinic visit, 3 missed their interview appointments. Each of the participants received a stipend of $35 and $9 worth of meal vouchers to compensate for their time and effort in the study.

Source: Auslander, Sterzing, Zayas, & White, 2010, p. 615. Reprinted with permission.

RESEARCH NOTE 4.13

Example of Expert Sampling: Study of Police Officers' Assessment of Specialized Training to Handle Youth-Related Incidents

Schulenberg and Warren (2009) incorporated expert sampling in their study of police officers' assessment of specialized police training to handle youth-related incidents. They described their sampling procedures as follows:

> The current research uses interview data from police officers in Canada origi-
> nally conducted in March through August 2002. . . . The agencies were
> selected based on the principles of representativeness of the regions of Canada,
> of communities of different sizes, communities inside and outside of Census
> Metropolitan Areas, and the different modes of police service delivery (indepen-
> dent municipal, provincial, RCMP municipal and provincial contract, Ontario
> Provincial police municipal contract, and First Nations self-policing). . . . The
> number of officers interviewed per police agency varied between one and seven,
> depending on the size of the agency, the availability of interviewees, or
> through officer referrals. In the case of police services with specialized youth
> officers, these were specifically targeted for inclusion in the interview
> sample. . . . Purposive sampling assembles a sample of persons with known or
> demonstrable experience and expertise, which in this case is handling youth-
> related incidents or developing relevant organizational policies and operating
> procedures. In the original sample and the current subsample, sampling for
> proportionality was not a primary concern making expert sampling (a subtype
> of purposive sampling) the most appropriate sampling technique. For the current
> research sample, purposive sampling was chosen to select those interviewees
> that represented the duty and rank differentiations of trainer, administrator,
> and practitioner who were trained at specific academies.

Source: Schulenberg & Warren, 2009, p. 462. Reprinted with permission.

QUOTA SAMPLING

What Is Quota Sampling?

Quota sampling is a nonprobability sampling procedure in which the population is divided into mutually exclusive subcategories, and interviewers or other

data collectors solicit participation in the study from members of the subcategories until a target number of elements to be sampled from the subcategories have been met. Quota sampling is also referred to as "accidental quota sampling," "purposive quota sampling," "stratified purposive sampling," "demographic balancing," and "purposive heterogeneity sampling with quotas."

In a sense quota sampling combines availability sampling and purposive sampling by targeting specific numbers of elements that have specific characteristics. In conducting quota sampling, a researcher gives data collectors a specific number (quota) of elements to be selected according to whether they fit certain criteria (quota controls). Data collectors then use availability sampling in selecting elements that satisfy their quota controls.

What Are the Steps in Selecting a Quota Sample?

There are six major steps in selecting a quota sample:

1. Define the target population.

2. Identify inclusion and exclusion criteria for the sample.

3. Determine the quota controls (variables) to be used. The quota controls should be related to the variables of interest, easy for respondents to provide a response, easy for interviewers to classify. Moreover, only a small number of quota controls should be used so as to make the process manageable by the interviewers.

4. Determine the sample size.

5. Determine the number of elements each data collector should select for each quota control category and whether to use noninterlocking quotas or interlocking quotas. Noninterlocking quotas consider each quota separately. For instance, let us say an interviewer was required to interview 40 persons. For the quota controls of gender and ethnicity, each field representative would be required to satisfy the quotas of 20 males, 20 females. Moreover, 10 of the persons interviewed must be Hispanic, 10 must be non-Hispanic White, 10 must be non-Hispanic Black, and 10 of other ethnicity. Interlocking quotas consider each quota jointly. For instance, using same general study requirements described above, each field representative would be required to satisfy the quotas of 5 males within each of the four ethnic categories, and 5 females within each of the four ethnic categories.

6. Select the targeted number of population elements per the quota controls utilizing availability or purposive sampling.

Quota controls may be demographic characteristics (e.g., age, race, ethnicity, occupational group, gender, and income), attitudinal characteristics (e.g., whether dissatisfied or satisfied, whether likely to vote or not likely to vote, whether likely to buy a specific product or not likely to buy a specific product), or behavioral characteristics (e.g., whether voted or did not vote, whether never used a specific product or regularly use the specific product, whether regularly watch a particular TV program or seldom watch the TV program). In order to make the project manageable, only a small number of quota controls should be used. Typically, a project would not use more than three quota controls.

What Are the Subtypes of Quota Sampling?

There are two major subtypes of quota sampling: proportional quota sampling and nonproportional quota sampling. They differ in terms of the criteria used in the allocation of the number of elements to be selected within each quota category of the population (see description below).

Proportional Quota Sampling

In **proportional quota sampling**, the allocation of the number of elements to be selected for each quota category is based on their proportions in the target population. It is used when the researcher desires to ensure that the proportional distribution of certain characteristics of the sample is equal to their proportional distribution in the target population. If the percentage of males and females in the total population are 46% and 54%, respectively, quotas are set for data collectors to ensure that the same percentage of males and females are in the sample. At times, the proportional distribution of the characteristics in the population is unknown and must be estimated.

One of the applications of proportional quota sampling is the use of the selection of a quota sample from panels of respondents generated via web-based sampling. Web users are invited to join a survey panel and complete a form providing demographic and other general information. In selecting respondents for a specific study, a proportional quota sampling is selected from the panel so as to match the characteristics of the population or the characteristics of a randomly selected "target sample."

Often proportional quota sampling is misused. Having matched the proportional distribution of the quota control variables in the sample to their proportional distribution in the population, often a researcher would declare the sample to be a representative sample. Such a declaration is inappropriate, especially for interview studies. It ignores interviewer selection bias and other forms of bias typical of nonprobability sample designs.

Nonproportional Quota Sampling

In **nonproportional quota sampling,** the allocation of the number of elements to be selected for each quota category is not based on their proportions in the target population but some other criterion. The goal of nonproportional quota sampling is not to produce a representative sample. On the other hand, the researcher may desire to conduct detailed analyses of relatively small groups in the population or possibly desire to compare categories of the population to each other. It may be necessary to target sample sizes to make sure that a minimum number of elements is in each category, regardless of its proportion in the target population. In order to achieve such purposes it may be necessary for the proportion of some categories in the sample to be larger or smaller than their proportion in the target population

Dimensional sampling is a special case of nonproportional quota sampling. In using this procedure the researcher selects elements so that there will be at least one element in the sample representing each possible combination of dimensions of the variables targeted in the study.

What Are the Strengths and Weaknesses of Quota Sampling?

Quota sampling has the major strengths and weaknesses of other forms of nonprobability sampling. As availability sampling is used in its final steps, it shares the selection bias that is typical of availability sampling. However, it also has special features that distinguish it from other forms of nonprobability sampling (see Table 4.3). These factors should be considered in choosing a nonprobability sample design to use.

One of the most important differences between availability sampling and quota sampling is the inclusion of stratification features in quota sampling thereby enhancing the representation of the sample and the ability to compare subgroups in the population. Compared to availability sampling, quota sampling ensures the inclusion of members of different subpopulations; introduces stratification of population into the sampling process; and, due to the quota controls, has less data collector error.

Given that the proportional distribution of subgroups in the sample in terms of the quota controls is equal to their proportional distribution in the population,

Table 4.3 Strengths and Weaknesses of Quota Sampling Compared to Other Nonprobability Sampling Procedures

Strengths	Weaknesses
Compared to availability sampling:	**Compared to availability sampling:**
Guarantees the inclusion of members of different subpopulations	Greater resources required: More time, money, personnel, and effort
Introduces a degree of stratification of the sample into the process	Control of fieldwork more difficult
Less data collector error	**Compared to purposive sampling:**
Proportional quota samples tend to be more representative of the population; attempt made to represent population's views proportionately	Overrepresentation of population elements that are most readily accessible, cooperative, articulate, and visible
Nonproportional quota sampling facilitates the comparison of subgroups, especially subgroups of relatively small size	Requires more recent and up-to-date information on the population; must know in advance the characteristics of groups, and their representation in the population
	Underrepresentation of population elements that are not readily accessible and uncooperative
	Compared to respondent-assisted sampling, more likely to underestimate hidden populations

it is more likely to represent the targeted population than availability sampling. Yet, as a nonprobability sampling procedure, one cannot make statistical estimates from the sample to the target population.

More so than availability sampling, nonproportional quota sampling facilitates the comparison of subpopulations to each other. Unlike availability sampling, nonproportional quota sampling can increase the likelihood that small subgroups of the population are represented in the sample in sufficient numbers for analysis. Yet quota sampling has weaknesses that other nonprobability sampling procedures do not have. For instance, quota sampling requires more resources, and it is more time-consuming than most of the other types of nonprobability sampling. The researcher must have up-to-date and accurate information about the distribution of the quota controls in the population in order to properly utilize proportional quota sampling. Often, only information on the demographic characteristics of the population is available. These demographic characteristics may not necessarily correlate with the variables of interest of the study. In such situations, quota sampling may not be much better than availability sampling in representing the population.

Quota sampling requires greater supervision of data collectors than that required using other nonprobability sampling procedures. Some data collectors might relax guidelines in order to meet their quotas. Strictly controlling fieldworkers may be extremely difficult.

Presented below are two illustrations of quota sampling. In Research Note 4.14, the researcher wanted to test a scale measuring willingness to care for persons living with AIDS across the range of caregivers providing such services. He elected to use proportional quota sampling. On the other hand, for the research described in Research Note 4.15, the researchers desired to compare two populations to each other, White professional women and Black professional women, in their perceptions of racism and sexism. They used nonproportional quota sampling, selecting 100 persons for each category.

RESEARCH NOTE 4.14

Example of Proportional Quota Sampling: Study of the Development of a Scale Measuring Willingness to Care for Persons Living With AIDS

Abell (2001) used a proportional quota sample design to develop and validate a scale for measuring the willingness to care for persons living with AIDS. He described his sampling procedures as follows:

> With the support of the Medicaid Managed Health Care offices in Florida, AIDS service organizations were identified for potential participation. Criteria for selection included prior receptivity to research involvement, agencies' blend of rural and urban foci, and the degree to which caseloads of Project AIDS Care (PAC or Medicaid waiver-eligible) clients reflected diversity in race, gender, and routes of viral acquisition. Seven sites from around the state were ultimately recruited.
>
> Accessing potential subjects for the study was complicated by the heightened demands of confidentiality associated with HIV disease. Caregivers,

(Continued)

(Continued)

the primary targets for the study, were not technically clients of the participating agencies. The PLAs for whom they cared, although formally associated with the agencies, were not (and could not be) known to the investigators. Consequently, a two-step proportional quota sampling process was employed to protect the confidentiality of potential subjects and attempt the desired sampling goals.

First, case managers, working from goals reflecting statewide AIDS surveillance demographics (i.e., proportional representations by race), identified potential clients (PLAs) for recruitment. This step was designed as a nonprobability strategy for achieving racial proportionality similar to that which might ideally have been attained had random sampling been an option. Clients agreeing to participate signed consent forms permitting investigators to access case management information from their personal files and to contact their caregivers to determine their willingness to participate in the study. Second, caregivers, who also could not have been otherwise known to the investigators, were contacted and asked to consent to a brief structured interview to be held, according to their preference, at agency offices or the location (i.e., home, restaurant, etc.) of their choice. Subjects were offered $10 for their time.

Source: Abell, 2001, pp. 121–122. Reprinted with permission.

RESEARCH NOTE 4.15

Example of Nonproportional Quota Sampling: Study of the Differences Between Black and White Professional Women in Their Perception of Racism and Sexism

Weber and Higginbotham (1997) used a nonproportional quota sample design in their comparative study of Black and White professional/managerial women's perceptions of racism and sexism in the workplace. They described his sampling procedures as follows:

Interview data from a quota sample of 200 full-time employed women professionals, managers, & administrators (100 black & 100 white) in the Memphis, TN, metropolitan area indicate that the majority perceived differential treatment due to sex in their workplaces. Although a majority of the

> black women also perceived differential treatment due to race, this was less
> often the case with the white women, & while many of these black & white
> women recognized group discrimination, they were less likely to see personal
> disadvantage in their work settings.
>
> *Source:* Weber & Higginbotham, 1997, p. 155. Reprinted with permission.

Compared to purposive sampling, quota sampling may yet yield samples that overrepresent population elements that are most readily accessible, cooperative, articulate, and visible, and underrepresent population elements that are not readily accessible and uncooperative. Respondent-assisted sampling is more likely to include representation of hard-to-reach and hidden populations in the sample than quota sampling. Respondent-assisted sampling is described below.

RESPONDENT-ASSISTED SAMPLING

What Is Respondent-Assisted Sampling?

Respondent-assisted sampling is a nonprobability sampling procedure in which elements are selected from a target population with the assistance of previously selected population elements. As certain population elements with characteristics that fit the purposes of a study are sought, this type of sampling may be viewed as an extension of purposive sampling.

As the sampling procedure is based on referrals, respondent-assisted sampling is often used in studying social networks, rare populations, and hidden populations. Hidden populations are populations that are inaccessible or hard to find due to their low numbers in the target population and/or the illegality or sensitivity of their behavior. Such hidden populations include:

- Drug dealers and users
- Commercial sex workers
- Criminals
- Undocumented workers
- Persons with AIDS
- Gay, bisexual persons, lesbian, and transgendered persons
- Men on the "down-low"
- Homeless persons
- Women who had an illegal abortion
- Runaway youths
- Persons with eating disorders
- Migrant workers
- Illegal immigrants
- Artists
- Victims of sexual harassment, rape, or spousal abuse

These populations are often missed using other sampling procedures. Respondent-assisted sampling makes the assumption that members of these populations have social, spatial, and organizational linkages, and can identify others who share their attributes.

What Are the Steps in Selecting a Respondent-Assisted Sample?

Although there may be some variability depending on the purpose of the study and the nature of the population, there are seven major steps in selecting a respondent-assisted sample:

1. Define the target population.

2. Identify inclusion and exclusion criteria for sample.

3. Recruit and select initial "seeds," the first wave of the sampling design. Diverse seeds (e.g., seeds that are heterogeneous in terms of age, gender, and geographical location) may be recruited via social service agencies, stores, social organizations, bars, and sex clubs using outreach workers and ethnographic methods.

4. Interview those selected.

5. As part of the interviewing process, after rapport and trust have been established, ask the interviewees for referrals. This initiates a referral chain, with each referral representing a link in the chain. In order to maintain confidentiality and anonymity, respondents may be asked to distribute questionnaires via email or other means to others who fall in the target population of the study with a request that they send the completed questionnaires directly to the researcher. This step assumes that the elements of the population know each other and are willing to provide information on each other.

6. Contact those referred.

7. Repeat Step 5 and Step 6 with new referrals until targeted sample size or saturation (no new referrals are forthcoming) is achieved.

Critical questions that should be addressed in carrying out respondent-assisted sampling include:

- How many chains should be initiated?
- How many links in each chain should be targeted?
- Should the study have a lot of chains with a few number of links, or a smaller number of chains with a relatively large number of links?

The ideal number of links in a referral chain depends upon the purpose of the study, the nature of the network, and the expected size of the network. The more links, the greater the likelihood of theoretical saturation and the identification of isolates. On the other hand, the more links in a referral chain, the more likely the sample is to be homogeneous and not reflective of the heterogeneity of the population. However, isolates that are not connected to any networks will not be identified.

What Are the Subtypes of Respondent-Assisted Sampling?

Subtypes of this form of sampling include **snowball sampling, chain-referral sampling, referral sampling,** nominated sampling, **multiplicity sampling, network sampling,** and **respondent-driven sampling.** Snowball sampling is the most popular. This terminology reflects that as the number of links in a chain increases, a "snowball effect" emerges as the sample size systematically increases. Respondent-driven sampling (RDS) is a new, emerging subtype of respondent-assisted sampling (Heckathorn, 1997).

Respondent-driven sampling has the premise that the peers of members of hidden populations are better able than outreach workers and researchers to locate and gain participation of other members of the target population. Moreover, by limiting the number of referrals from a single respondent and utilizing information on the size of the participants' networks, it is argued that reasonable estimates of population characteristics and the variances of the estimations may be calculated (Heckathorn, 2002; Salganik, 2006; Volz & Heckathorn, 2008). Respondent-driven sampling differs from the other respondent-assisted sampling procedures such as snowball sampling as follows:

- Instead of asking interviewees for contact information on additional members of the target population, in respondent-driven sampling, respondents are asked to recruit additional respondents from among the members of the target population they associate with. Typically, respondents are limited to two to three referrals in order to control the overrepresentation of large personal networks. As a result, the sample is not dependent on the initial seeds.
- Respondents travel to a project office site to be interviewed rather than the researcher traveling to the respondent.
- A dual incentive system is used to encourage participation. Respondents are given a cash payment for each person referred who is interviewed, and each referral is given a cash payment for being interviewed. Coupons are given to respondents to be given to those they recruit. Those recruited

will then report to a project office, redeem the coupon for its cash value, and be interviewed. The coupons have a unique serial number, and are used to track who recruited whom, and identify social networks.

- Information on personal network size are gathered, recorded, and used in estimating population characteristics.
- At least four to six chains (waves) of recruitment are employed in order to enhance network penetration.
- The relationship between recruiters and recruits is documented so that recruitment biases can be assessed.
- An interview site accessible to the members of the target population must be utilized.

What Are the Strengths and Weaknesses of Respondent-Assisted Sampling?

Respondent-assisted sampling has the major strengths and weaknesses of other forms of nonprobability sampling. However, it also has special features that distinguish it from other forms of nonprobability sampling (see Table 4.4).

Table 4.4 Strengths and Weaknesses of Respondent-Assisted Sampling Compared to Other Nonprobability Sampling Procedures

Strengths	Weaknesses
Compared to other nonprobability sampling:	Compared to other nonprobability sample designs:
More effective in sampling rare and hard-to-reach populations	Likely to underestimate the variability in the population; similar elements are likely to be sampled
More appropriate for studying social networks	May require more resources: time, money, effort, etc.
Compared to snowball sampling and other respondent-assisted sampling, respondent-driven sampling:	Nonindependence of observations; a selection is dependent on ties to those previous selected
Does not have ethical problems of snowball sampling: Persons referred may not want to be known, nor participate in the research project	"Gatekeepers," such as teachers, nurses, and others who are charged with the protection of the privacy of those under their care, may prevent participation in the study

Strengths	Weaknesses
Unlike snowball sampling and other nonprobability sampling procedures, the network data collected in respondent-driven sampling makes possible the estimates of population parameters	Some respondents may recruit more effectively than others, especially in respondent-driven sampling, and as a result, the characteristics of the recruits of the best recruiters may be overrepresented in the sample
	Extremely socially isolated persons are less likely to be sampled; extremely social persons are more likely to be sampled
	The recruiters used in respondent-driven sampling may contaminate the responses of those they recruit
	The size of the population must be stable during the time frame of the study
	Masking, the protection of others by not referring them, may occur
	Geographical spread of the population may deter participants

Compared to other nonprobability sample designs, respondent-assisted sampling is more effective in sampling rare, low-incidence, and hard-to-reach populations and studying social networks. If a population is relatively small, its members know each other, and they are willing to provide the names of each other, respondent-assisted sampling can yield useful results.

However, the success of respondent-assisted sampling depends much on (a) the extent to which members of the target population know each other; and (b) the researcher's ability to gain their trust, overcome their resistance to participate in research on a topic typically perceived as very private and sensitive, and obtain their assistance in recruiting others for the study.

Respondent-driven sampling has strengths that other respondent-assisted sampling procedures do not have. RDS does not have the ethical problems of snowball sampling. In snowball sampling, typically names and contact information are given to the researcher without the prior consent of those whose names and contact information are given. Persons referred may not want to be known nor participate in a research project. As a result of the referral, they have a researcher contacting them. On the other hand, the names and contact information are not needed in respondent-driven sampling, and those recruited technically agree to participate prior to contacting the researcher.

Yet, respondent-driven sampling shares the selection bias of other respondent-assisted sampling procedures in that the selection of elements for the sample is determined by the subjective choice of respondents previously selected.

Compared to other nonprobability sample designs, respondent-assisted sampling may require more resources requirements: time, money, and effort. Some members of hidden populations may take a great deal of effort to locate. It should be noted, on the other hand, that this is not a problem with respondent-driven sampling since the recruited population members go to the site of the researcher.

Respondent-assisted sampling usually underestimates the variability in the population as it is likely that similar elements will be sampled. However, this problem is minimized in respondent-driven sampling by limiting the number of recruits per respondent.

The selections of elements sampled in respondent-assisted sampling are not independent of each other. The selection of a member of the population is dependent on ties to those previously interviewed.

It is also possible that some respondents may recruit more effectively than others, and as a result, the characteristics of the recruits of the best recruiters may be overrepresented in the sample. Extremely socially isolated persons are less likely to be sampled; extremely social persons are more likely to be sampled. Moreover, it is possible that recruiters may contaminate the responses of those they recruited by discussing the project and the questions to be asked. Moreover, masking may occur; that is, recruiters may purposefully not refer certain persons for participation in the research.

Many rare and hidden populations are protected by "gatekeepers," creating an undercoverage problem for respondent-assisted sampling as in other forms of sampling. Legal, ethical, and informed consent restrictions may apply in gaining access to the population. Gatekeepers, such as teachers, nurses, social workers, doctors, psychiatrists, prison administrators, and others who are charged with the protection of the privacy of those under their care may prevent participation in the study.

The size of the population must be stable during the time frame of the study. If the population is unstable, mobile, and changing, it may be difficult to contact those referred, and those sampled may not be representative of the current population. Moreover, if the population is highly dispersed, the cost of data collection when using snowball sampling increases, and respondent-driven sampling recruits may be less likely to participate in the study.

The following research notes provide examples of respondent-assistant sampling. Both are studies of drug use in New York City. Research Note 4.16 describes a study that used snowball sampling, and Research Note 4.17 describes a study that used respondent-driven sampling.

RESEARCH NOTE 4.16

Example of Respondent-Assisted Sampling: Study of Violence and the Distribution of Crack Cocaine in New York City Using Snowball Sampling

Fagan and Chin (2006) utilized snowball sampling in their study of violence and the distribution of crack cocaine in New York City. They described their sampling procedures as follows:

> Samples were constructed from two northern Manhattan neighborhoods with high concentrations of crack use and selling: Washington Heights and West Harlem. Samples included individuals from the study neighborhoods who had been arrested for drug possession or sales, residents of the study neighborhoods who matched the arrested populations but who had avoided legal or social intervention for drug use or selling, and participants in residential drug treatment programs. Within each group, subjects included crack users or sellers, cocaine HCl users or sellers who were not involved with crack, heroin users or sellers, and polydrug (primarily marijuana) users.
>
> Samples were recruited through chain referral or "snowball" sampling procedures (Biemacki and Waldorf 1981). Since the research was part of a larger study of crack, crack users and sellers were oversampled. Crack arrestees were recruited from drug arrestees who were awaiting initial court appearances in the Manhattan central booking facility. They were identified from special charge flags recorded by arresting officers on booking slips. The arrest flags have been used by the NYPD since 1986 to identify crack offenses, since charge categories do not distinguish various types of controlled substances. Residential neighborhood was determined from the addresses and corresponding zip codes provided by arrestees to the interviewers.
>
> Referrals for interviews were made by pretrial services interviewers during routine interviews to determine eligibility for release on their own recognizance. Arrestees released at arraignment were interviewed shortly after release. (Those arrestees detained were interviewed in the detention facility.) Arrestees who indicated their willingness to participate in a research study were given cards that told them where and how to arrange for an interview. Their names also were given to the interview team who, in some cases, sought them out.
>
> Other subjects also were recruited through chain referral procedures: non-crack drug arrestees; nonarrested neighborhood samples who were matched

(Continued)

(Continued)

to the arrested samples on age, gender, and ethnicity; and participants in two residential treatment programs in Manhattan. Several types of chain referral methods were used. Arrestees were asked to nominate potential respondents who were "like them in many ways but who have avoided arrest." Interviewers then sought out the nominees, or the nominees were referred to the field office by friends. Chains also were developed among drug users and sellers who were known to the interviewers. Interviewers were members of a street research unit that maintained ethnographic contact and did reconnaissance on drug scenes throughout the New York metropolitan area.

Source: Fagan & Chin, 2006, pp. 13–14. Reprinted with permission.

RESEARCH NOTE 4.17

Example of Respondent-Assisted Sampling: Study of Drug Users in New York City Using Respondent-Driven Sampling

McKnight et al. (2006) utilized respondent-driven sampling in their study of drug users in New York City. They described their sampling procedures as follows:

In April 2004, Beth Israel Medical Center staff recruited eight seeds from a syringe exchange in Lower Manhattan. Each seed was screened for eligibility before being given a coupon to come back for an interview. The seeds were asked about their drug use, including mode of use and drug preparation techniques. Those who claimed to be an injection drug user (IDU) were also asked to show track marks. Although not a requirement of RDS, the seeds were recruited to resemble the race and gender profile of drug users in Lower Manhattan. They were asked to come to a research storefront in Lower Manhattan the following day to complete a computer-assisted interviewer-administered personal interview (CAPI) and to have their blood drawn for an HIV test. Each seed, and subsequent study subject, received $20 compensation for their time.

When subjects arrived at the storefront, they were questioned by the study screener to ensure eligibility. Once they were deemed eligible by the screener, each subject was assigned a unique code to serve as their study identification. This code included the following information: the first two letters of the last name, first letter of mother's first name, the last two digits of the birth year, one letter for the person's race, and one letter for gender. This code was used to identify blood work and questionnaires and could be regenerated if the subject forgot it. No names or other identifying information were asked.

After being assigned a study code, subjects met with an interviewer to be consented and interviewed. The interview had three parts, an hour-long questionnaire, administered by the interviewer, HIV pre-test counseling and a blood draw for an HIV test. The interview consisted of a structured questionnaire which took approximately 1 h and asked about drug-use frequency, drug and sexual risk behavior, syringe acquisition, and knowledge of HIV and hepatitis B and C. After the interview, HIV counseling, and blood collection, each subject was given three coupons to recruit three other drug users into the study. The subjects were briefly trained on how to recruit others, with specific emphasis on the recruitment of friends and acquaintances who use drugs. Eligible respondents had to have done the following: injected, smoked, or snorted an illicit drug in the past 6 months (those who smoked only marijuana were not eligible for the study); turned age 18 years or older by the time of the interview; been able to speak English adequately to consent to the study and complete the questionnaire; and lived, bought, and/or used drugs on the Lower East Side of Manhattan. Subjects could have, however, lived in the larger New York metropolitan area, as long as they bought or used their drugs on the Lower East Side of Manhattan.

Coupons contained the time that the storefront opened (9:00 a.m.) and a unique number (to make each one distinct). To make them difficult to duplicate, coupons were printed on thick cardstock paper with color images. To track the coupons and payment for each respondent, we used custom-developed software for RDS called IRIS Plus. Information such as respondent's unique code, physical traits, coupon number, and the numbers of the coupons each respondent distributed were all recorded in IRIS Plus. This information enabled us to link coupons together, determine when respondents should be paid and who gave coupons to whom. This software also helped to prevent the redemption of duplicated coupons because the database would not accept duplicate coupon numbers. When respondents came in to make an appointment, the coupon was checked in the IRIS Plus database

(Continued)

(Continued)

to verify that it had not been used previously. Additionally, each person's code was checked in IRIS Plus after being screened to determine whether a person with that code had previously been enrolled in the study. If another study subject had that code, the screener looked at the physical traits listed for that person for verification. Additionally, if the screener felt that a person looked familiar, she would search for the person's physical traits in IRIS Plus to see if another person with similar characteristics was previously enrolled.

On July 2, 2004, we ceased coupon distribution to give potential subjects 2 weeks to redeem remaining coupons. On July 16, 2004, we concluded data collection, and the study officially concluded on July 30, 2004. The last 2 weeks of July were set aside to allow the remainder of subjects to come in for their HIV test results.

Source: McKnight et al., 2006, pp. 55–57. Reprinted with kind permission from Springer Science+ Business Media.

GUIDELINES FOR CHOOSING THE TYPE OF NONPROBABILITY SAMPLE DESIGN

Considering the features and the strengths and weaknesses of the sample designs described above, the following guidelines may be offered:

Guideline 4.1. *Sampling with minimum resources.* Consider choosing availability sampling if one's resources (i.e., time, money, personnel, etc.) are extremely limited, the purpose of one's study is exploratory, and one's variable of interest is physiological.

Although availability samplings have serious limitations, especially for research attempting to estimate population parameters, it requires minimal resources.

Guideline 4.2. *Sampling of typical cases.* Consider choosing typical case sampling or modal instance sampling if it is necessary to obtain a general view of the typical or modal case.

It may be useful for the researcher to select elements that are considered to be typical of the target population or, at the other extreme, atypical of most of the elements in the target population.

> **Guideline 4.3.** *Sampling of atypical cases.* Consider choosing extreme case sampling, deviant case sampling, rare element sampling, and/or intensity sampling if one's objective is to study unusual or special elements of a population.

It may be useful for the researcher to select elements that are homogeneous as to certain variables in the study (e.g., extraneous variables) or to select elements to make for a heterogeneous sample.

> **Guideline 4.4.** *Sampling to create homogeneity.* Consider choosing homogeneous sampling if it is desired to conduct in-depth analyses controlling for extraneous variables and/or one is employing a focus group research design.

Homogeneous provides a means of controlling for extraneous variables via the sampling procedure that is used. It may be useful in qualitative research and exploratory studies.

> **Guideline 4.5.** *Sampling to create heterogeneity.* Consider choosing among deviant case sampling, rare element sampling, extreme case sampling, intensity sampling, maximum variation sampling, and diversity sampling if one desires to conduct comparative analyses of differences within a population, or if one desires to maximize the variation of the characteristic of interest in a study, conduct brainstorming, and/or nominal group processes.

Heterogeneity provides a means of testing the generality of hypotheses and the applicability of findings across cases, situations, and conditions. Sampling to create heterogeneity enhances one's ability to detect differences and identify conflicts or potential conflicts.

> **Guideline 4.6.** *Sampling for theory testing, model development, and hypothesis testing.* Consider choosing confirmatory sampling, disconfirming sampling, negative case sampling, theoretical sampling, critical case sampling, case control sampling, and/or consecutive sampling if a one's objective is to test a specific theory or hypothesis.

Although nonprobability sampling limits one's use of inferential statistical procedures for testing hypotheses, these sampling procedures provide a means of testing theories, models, and hypotheses.

> **Guideline 4.7.** *Sampling based on personal judgment, reputations, and specialized knowledge.* Consider choosing judgment sampling, subjective sampling, bellwether case sampling, reputational case sampling, politically important case sampling, expert sampling, and/or informant sampling to take advantage of historical knowledge, patterns, trends, and reputations in selecting a sample.

These procedures may provide a "quick and dirty" procedure for identifying elements in a population most likely to provide useful information for a study.

> **Guideline 4.8.** *Proportional quota sampling.* Consider choosing proportional quota sampling if one has low resources and one's objective is to describe the characteristics of a population.

Proportional quota sampling is most likely among the nonprobability sampling procedures to yield a sample that provides proportional representation of demographic and other categories of the population. If the proportional distribution of the target population across categories of interest is known, this may be a preferred option.

> **Guideline 4.9.** *Nonproportional quota sampling.* Consider choosing nonproportional quota sampling if one has low resources and one's objective is to compare subgroups of a population.

Nonproportional quota sampling is most likely among the nonprobability sampling procedures to yield a sample that provides a sufficient number of cases within small categories of the target population for comparative research purposes.

> **Guideline 4.10.** *Respondent-assisted sampling.* Consider choosing respondent-assisted sampling if one's objective is to study a rare or hidden population that is well networked but is difficult to approach directly.

Respondent-assisted sampling provides a means of obtaining assistance from members of hard-to-reach populations in identifying, contacting, and collecting information from other members of the population.

SUMMARY

There are four major choices of nonprobability sample designs: availability sampling, purposive sampling, quota sampling, and respondent-assisted sampling. The strengths and weaknesses of the above sample designs are compared, and guidelines are presented for their selection.

Availability sampling is an unstructured sampling procedure. In using this type of sampling procedure, the researcher selects study units as they become available. It is the least time-consuming, least expensive, and least complicated sampling procedure. On the other hand, availability sampling has low external validity and is not likely to include extreme cases and hard-to-reach elements of the population. As such, this sampling procedure tends to underestimate the variability in the population.

Purposive sampling is a nonprobability sampling procedure in which elements are selected from the target population on the basis of their fit with the purposes of the study and specific inclusion and exclusion criteria. Considering the criteria that are used, the various types of purposive sampling tend to fall into four categories: selection criteria based on central tendency (including typical case sampling, modal instance sampling, deviant case sampling, rare element sampling, extreme case sampling, intensity case sampling, and outlier sampling); selection criteria based on variability (including homogeneous sampling, maximum variation sampling, heterogeneity sampling and diversity sampling); selection criteria based on theory/model development (including confirmatory sampling, disconfirming sampling, negative case sampling, theoretical sampling, critical case sampling, systematic matching sampling, case control sampling, and consecutive sampling); and selection criteria based on judgment and reputation (including judgment sampling, subjective sampling, bellwether case sampling, reputational sampling, politically important sampling, expert sampling, and informant sampling).

Quota sampling is a nonprobability sampling procedure in which the population is divided into mutually exclusive subcategories, and interviewers or other data collectors solicit participation in the study from members of the subcategories until a target number of elements to be sampled from the subcategories have been met.

There are two major subtypes of quota sampling: proportional quota sampling and nonproportional quota sampling. In proportional quota sampling, the allocation of the number of elements to be selected for each quota category is based on their proportions in the target population. In nonproportional quota sampling, the goal is not to produce a representative sample. On the other hand, the researcher may desire to conduct detailed analyses of relatively small groups in the population or possibly desire to compare categories of the population to each other.

Respondent-assisted sampling is a nonprobability sampling procedure in which elements are selected from a target population with the assistance of previously selected population elements. Subtypes of this form of sampling include snowball sampling, chain-referral sampling, referral sampling, network sampling, and respondent-driven sampling.

REVIEW QUESTIONS

1. What are the four major types of nonprobability sample designs, and how do they differ from one another?

2. What are the key features of availability sampling? What accounts for the popularity of this sample procedure?

3. What are the steps in selecting an availability sample?

4. What are the strengths and weaknesses of availability sampling?

5. Given the strengths and weaknesses of availability sampling, provide examples of research questions for which this sampling procedure would be most appropriate, and research questions for which this sampling procedure would be least appropriate.

6. What are the key features of the various types of purposive sampling?

7. What are the steps in selecting a purposive sample?

8. What are the major types of purposive sampling, and how do they differ from one another?

9. What are the strengths and weaknesses of the various types of purposive sampling?

10. Given the strengths and weaknesses of the various types of purposive sampling, provide examples of research questions for which these sampling procedures would be most appropriate, and research questions for which these sampling procedures would be least appropriate.

11. What are the key features of quota sampling?

12. What are the steps in selecting a quota sample?

13. What are the strengths and weaknesses of quota sampling?

14. Given the strengths and weaknesses of quota sampling, provide examples of research questions for which this sampling procedure would be most appropriate, and research questions for which this sampling procedure would be least appropriate.

15. What is the difference between proportional quota sampling and nonproportional quota sampling, and when is it preferable to use one instead of the other?

16. What are the key features of respondent-assisted sampling?

17. What are the strengths and weaknesses of respondent-assisted sampling?

18. How does respondent-driven sampling differ from other forms of respondent-assisted sampling?

19. Given the strengths and weaknesses of respondent-assisted sampling, provide examples of research questions for which this sampling procedure would be most appropriate, and research questions for which this sampling procedure would be least appropriate.

20. What alternative sample designs would you propose for the sample designs described in the research notes in this chapter?

KEY TERMS

Describe and give examples of the following terms:

availability sampling	maximum variation sampling
bellwether case sampling	modal instance sampling
case control sampling	multiplicity sampling
chain-referral sampling	negative case sampling
confirmatory sampling	network sampling
consecutive sampling	nonproportional quota sampling
critical case sampling	outlier sampling
deviant case sampling	proportional quota sampling
dimensional sampling	purposive sampling
disconfirming case sampling	quota sampling
diversity sampling	rare element sampling
expert sampling	referral sampling
extreme case sampling	reputational sampling
heterogeneity sampling	respondent-assisted sampling
homogeneous sampling	respondent-driven sampling
informant sampling	snowball sampling
intensity case sampling	subjective sampling
judgment sampling	theoretical sampling
matched sampling	typical case sampling

REFERENCES FOR FURTHER STUDY

Draucker, C. B., Martsolf, D. S., Ross, R., & Rusk, T. B. (2007). Theoretical sampling and category development in grounded theory. *Qualitative Health Research, 17,* 176–188.

Gile, K. J., & Handcock, M. S. (2010). Respondent-driven sampling: An assessment of current methodology. In T. F. Liao (Ed.), *Sociological methodology 2010* (Vol. 40, pp. 285–327). Washington, DC: American Sociological Association.

Heckathorn, D. D. (1997). Respondent driven sampling: A new approach to the study of hidden populations. *Social Problems, 44,* 174–199.

Heckathorn, D. D. (2002). Respondent driven sampling II: Deriving valid population estimates from chain-referral samples of hidden populations. *Social Problems, 44,* 11–34.

Koerber, A., & McMichael, L. (2008). Qualitative sampling methods: A primer for technical communication. *Journal of Business and Technical Communication, 22,* 454–473.

Kuzel, A. (1999). Sampling in qualitative inquiry. In B. Crabtree & W. Miller (Eds.), *Doing qualitative research* (pp. 33–45). Thousand Oaks, CA: Sage.

Miles, M. B., & Huberman, A. M. (1994). *Qualitative data analysis: An expanded sourcebook* (2nd ed.). Thousand Oaks, CA: Sage.

Morrow, K. M., Vargas, S., Rosen, R. K., Christensen, A. L., Salomon, L., Shulman, L., Barroso, C., & Fava, J. L. (2007). The utility of non-proportional quota sampling for recruiting at-risk women for microbicide research. *AIDS Behavior, 11,* 586–595.

Penrod, J., Preston, D. B., Cain, R. E., & Starks, M. T. (2003). A discussion of chain referral as a method of sampling hard-to-reach populations. *Journal of Transcultural Nursing, 14,* 100–107.

Peterson, J. A., Penrod, J., Preston, D. B., Cain, R. E., & Starks, M. T. (2003). A discussion of chain referral as a method of sampling hard-to-reach populations. *Journal of Transcultural Nursing, 14,* 100–107.

Reisinger, H. S., Schwartz, R. P., Mitchell, S. G., Kelly, S. M., Brown, B. S., & Agar, M. H. (2008). Targeted sampling in drug abuse research: A review and case study. *Field Methods, 20,* 155–170.

Salganik, M. J. (2006). Variance estimation, design effects, and sample size calculations for respondent driven sampling. *Journal of Urban Health, 83,* 98–112.

Volz, E., & Heckathorn, D. D. (2008). Probability based estimation theory of respondent driven sampling. *Journal of Official Statistics, 24,* 79–97.

CHAPTER 5

CHOOSING THE TYPE OF PROBABILITY SAMPLING

What you will learn in this chapter:

- The types of probability sampling and how they differ from each other
- Steps in carrying out the major probability sample designs
- The strengths and weaknesses of the various types of probability sampling
- Differences between stratified sampling and quota sampling
- Differences between stratified sampling and cluster sampling
- Differences between multistage cluster sampling and multiphase sampling

INTRODUCTION

Once a choice is made to use a probability sample design, one must choose the type of probability sampling to use. This chapter includes descriptions of the major types of probability sampling. It covers steps involved in their administration, their subtypes, their weaknesses and strengths, and guidelines for choosing among them.

There are four major types of probability sample designs: simple random sampling, stratified sampling, systematic sampling, and cluster sampling (see Figure 5.1). Simple random sampling is the most recognized probability sampling procedure. Stratified sampling offers significant improvement to simple random sampling. Systematic sampling is probably the easiest one to use, and cluster sampling is most practical for large national surveys. These sampling procedures are described below.

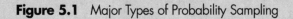

Figure 5.1 Major Types of Probability Sampling

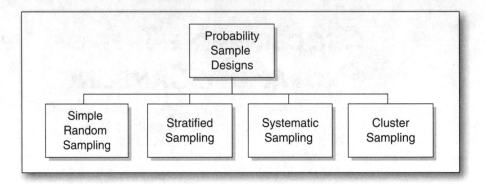

SIMPLE RANDOM SAMPLING

What Is Simple Random Sampling?

Simple random sampling is a probability sampling procedure that gives every element in the target population, and each possible sample of a given size, an equal chance of being selected. As such, it is an equal probability selection method (EPSEM).

What Are the Steps in Selecting a Simple Random Sample?

There are six major steps in selecting a simple random sample:

1. Define the target population.

2. Identify an existing sampling frame of the target population or develop a new one.

3. Evaluate the sampling frame for undercoverage, overcoverage, multiple coverage, and clustering, and make adjustments where necessary.

4. Assign a unique number to each element in the frame.

5. Determine the sample size.

6. Randomly select the targeted number of population elements.

Three techniques are typically used in carrying out Step 6: the lottery method, a table of random numbers, and randomly generated numbers using a computer program (i.e., random number generator). In using the lottery method (also referred to as the "blind draw method" and the "hat model"), the numbers representing each element in the target population are placed on chips (i.e., cards, paper, or some other objects). The chips are then placed in a container and thoroughly mixed. Next, blindly select chips from the container until the desired sample size has been obtained. Disadvantages of this method of selecting the sample are that it is time-consuming, and is limited to small populations.

A table of random numbers may also be used. The numbers in a table of random numbers are not arranged in any particular pattern. They may be read in any manner, i.e., horizontally, vertically, diagonally, forward, or backward. In using a table of random numbers, the researcher should blindly select a starting point and then systematically proceed down (or up) the columns of numbers in the table. The number of digits that are used should correspond to the total size of the target population. Every element whose assigned number matches a number the researcher comes across is selected for the sample. Numbers the researcher comes across that do not match the numbers assigned the elements in the target population are ignored. As in using the lottery method, using a table of random numbers is a tedious, time-consuming process, and is not recommended for large populations. Instead, statistical software should be used for large populations. Most statistical software and spreadsheet software have routines for generating random numbers. Elements of the populations whose assigned numbers match the numbers generated by the software are included in the sample. One may select a number from a table of random numbers for use as the starting number for the process.

What Are the Subtypes of Simple Random Sampling?

There are two types of simple random sampling: sampling with replacement and sampling without replacement. In sampling with replacement, after an element has been selected from the sampling frame, it is returned to the frame and is eligible to be selected again. In sampling without replacement, after an element is selected from the sampling frame, it is removed from the population and is not returned to the sampling frame. Sampling without replacement tends to be more efficient than sampling with replacement in producing representative samples. It does not allow the same population element to enter the sample more than once. Sampling without replacement is more common than sampling with replacement. It is the type that is the subject of this text.

What Are the Strengths and Weaknesses of Simple Random Sampling?

Simple random sampling has the major strengths and weaknesses of probability sampling procedures when compared to nonprobability sampling procedures. Notably, among its strengths, it tends to yield representative samples, and allows the use of inferential statistics in analyzing the data collected. Compared to other probability sampling procedures, simple random sampling has several strengths that should be considered in choosing the type of probability sample design to use (see Table 5.1). Some of these include:

- Advanced auxiliary information on the elements in the population is not required. Such information is required for other probability sampling procedures, such as stratified sampling.
- Each selection is independent of other selections, and every possible combination of sampling units has an equal and independent chance of being selected. In systematic sampling, the chances of being selected are not independent of each other.
- It is generally easier than other probability sampling procedures (such as multistage cluster sampling) to understand and communicate to others.
- Statistical procedures required to analyze data and compute errors are easier than those required of other probability sampling procedures.
- Statistical procedures for computing inferential statistics are incorporated in most statistical software and described in most elementary statistics textbooks.

On the other hand, simple random sampling has important weaknesses. Compared to other probability sampling procedures, simple random samplings have the following weaknesses:

- A sampling frame of elements in the target population is required. An appropriate sampling frame may not exist for the population that is targeted, and it may not be feasible or practical to construct one. Alternative sampling procedures, such as cluster sampling, do not require a sampling frame of the elements of the target population.
- Simple random sampling tends to have larger sampling errors and less precision than stratified samples of the same sample size.

- Respondents may be widely dispersed; hence, data collection costs might be higher than those for other probability sample designs such as cluster sampling.
- Simple random sampling may not yield sufficient numbers of elements in small subgroups. This would not make simple random sampling a good choice for studies requiring comparative analysis of small categories of a population with much larger categories of the population.

Research Note 5.1 below describes simple random sampling procedures used in a study of inmate-on-inmate sexual assaults in California's prisons.

Table 5.1 Strengths and Weaknesses of Simple Random Sampling Compared to Other Probability Sampling Procedures

Strengths	Weaknesses
Compared to other probability sampling procedures:	Compared to other probability sampling procedures:
Advanced auxiliary information on the elements in the population is not required.	A sampling frame of elements in the target population is required.
Every possible combination of sampling units has an equal and independent chance of being selected.	Does not take advantage of knowledge of the population that the researcher might have.
Easier to understand and communicate to others.	May have larger sampling errors and less precision, than other probability sampling designs with the same sample size.
Tends to yield representative samples.	If subgroups of the population are of particular interests, they may not be included in sufficient numbers in the sample.
Statistical procedures required to analyze data and compute errors are easier.	If the population is widely dispersed, data collection costs might be higher than those of other probability sample designs.
Statistical procedures for computing inferential are incorporated in most statistical software.	May be very costly, particularly where populations are geographically dispersed and/or individuals may be difficult to locate because of change of last name due to marriage or migration.

RESEARCH NOTE 5.1

Example of Simple Random Sampling: Study of Inmate-on-Inmate Sexual Assaults in California's Prisons

Jenness, Maxson, Sumner, and Matsuda (2010) conducted a survey of adult prisoners in California's prisons in a study of inmate-on-inmate sexual assaults. Six prisons were selected using purposive sampling, and then simple random sampling was used to select inmates from the selected prisons. The authors described their simple random sampling procedures as follows:

We relied on a similar process in each facility to randomly sample inmates. About a week prior to the first day of data collection at a particular prison, the CDCR [California Department of Corrections and Rehabilitation] Office of Research sent us a facility roster that identified every inmate housed in the prison. The roster indicated the inmate's name, CDC number, custody level, classification score, housing location in the facility, and mental health status. Inmates housed in reception centers were excluded. Once we received the roster, we removed inmates categorized as EOP [Enhanced Outpatient, mental patients indicating the highest level of mental incapacity]. Importantly, inmates with other mental health designations (e.g., Correctional Clinical Case Management System [CCCMS]) and inmates on restricted status (e.g., inmates housed in administrative segregation or security housing units [SHUs]) were retained on the final roster from which we randomly selected study participants.

From the final roster, we used statistical software to randomly select 100 inmates from each prison to be study participants. This approach ensured that CDCR officials could not interfere with the random selection on purpose or inadvertently. We randomly ordered the CDCR numbers of selected study participants to eliminate bias and sent the list of selected inmates to our liaison at the prison, typically the Public Information Officer or another Lieutenant, so that inmates were scheduled and notified by a ducat to meet with an interviewer on the research team. Maintaining consistency in our sampling procedures, including providing detailed written instructions to our liaisons, supported our goal of attaining a representative sample of inmates.

Source: Jenness, Maxson, Sumner, & Matsuda, 2010 pp. 11-12. Reprinted with permission.

STRATIFIED SAMPLING

What Is Stratified Sampling?

Stratified sampling is a probability sampling procedure in which the target population is first separated into mutually exclusive, homogeneous segments (strata), and then a simple random sample is selected from each segment (stratum). The samples selected from the various strata are then combined into a single sample. This sampling procedure is sometimes referred to as "quota random sampling."

What Are the Steps in Selecting a Stratified Sample?

There are eight major steps in selecting a stratified random sample:

1. Define the target population.

2. Identify stratification variable(s) and determine the number of strata to be used. The stratification variables should relate to the purposes of the study. If the purpose of the study is to make subgroup estimates, the stratification variables should be related to those subgroups. The availability of auxiliary information often determines the stratification variables that are used. More than one stratification variable may be used. However, in order to provide expected benefits, they should relate to the variables of interest in the study and be independent of each other. Considering that as the number of stratification variables increases, the likelihood increases that some of the variables will cancel the effects of other variables, not more than four to six stratification variables and not more than six strata for a particular variable should be used.

3. Identify an existing sampling frame or develop a sampling frame that includes information on the stratification variable(s) for each element in the target population. If the sampling frame does not include information on the stratification variables, stratification would not be possible.

4. Evaluate the sampling frame for undercoverage, overcoverage, multiple coverage, and clustering, and make adjustments where necessary.

5. Divide the sampling frame into strata, categories of the stratification variable(s), creating a sampling frame for each stratum. Within-stratum

differences should be minimized, and between-strata differences should be maximized. The strata should not be overlapping, and altogether, should constitute the entire population. The strata should be independent and mutually exclusive subsets of the population. Every element of the population must be in one and only one stratum.

6. Assign a unique number to each element.

7. Determine the sample size for each stratum. The numerical distribution of the sampled elements across the various strata determines the type of stratified sampling that is implemented. It may be a proportionate stratified sampling or one of the various types of disproportionate stratified sampling.

8. Randomly select the targeted number of elements from each stratum. At least one element must be selected from each stratum for representation in the sample; and at least two elements must be chosen from each stratum for the calculation of the margin of error of estimates computed from the data collected.

What Are the Subtypes of Stratified Sampling?

There are two major subtypes of stratified sampling: proportionate stratified sampling and disproportionate stratified sampling (see Figure 5.2). Disproportionate stratified sampling has various subcategories.

Proportionate Stratified Sampling

In proportionate stratified sampling, the number of elements allocated to the various strata is proportional to the representation of the strata in the target population. That is, the size of the sample drawn from each stratum is proportional to the relative size of that stratum in the target population. As such, it is a self-weighting and EPSEM sampling procedure. The same sampling fraction is applied to each stratum, giving every element in the population an equal chance to be selected. The resulting sample is a self-weighting sample. This sampling procedure is used when the purpose of the research is to estimate a population's parameters.

A hypothetical example of **proportionate allocation** is presented in Table 5.2. In this example, the elements sampled were allocated across the four districts of a marketing region so as the proportion of elements sampled for each district is identical to the proportion of elements in each district in the total

Figure 5.2 Subtypes of Stratified Sampling Based on Stratum Allocation

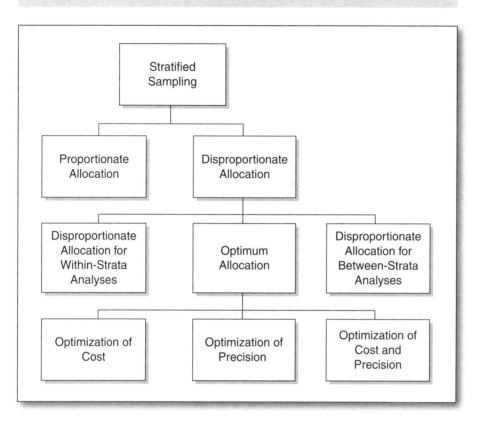

population. The sampling fraction in each district is the same 1 out of 22 elements. Each district is equally represented in the sample.

At times, a researcher may not only desire to estimate population parameters but also to make detailed analyses within a relatively small stratum and/or compare strata to each other. Proportionate stratified sampling may not yield sufficient numbers of cases in some of the strata for such analyses. Taking the example described in Table 5.2 as an example, it would not be possible to conduct a detailed analysis of elements in District 2 because only 12 elements are in the sample. Moreover, comparing District 2 elements to the elements in the other districts would be suspect. Proportionate stratified sampling is a poor sampling choice for carrying out such analyses. Disproportionate stratified sampling may be a better choice.

Table 5.2 Example of Proportionate Stratified Sampling

Marketing Region	Population		Proportionate Stratified Sample	
	Frequency	Percent	Frequency	Percent
District 1	18000	33%	396	33%
District 2	600	1%	12	1%
District 3	12000	22%	264	22%
District 4	24000	44%	528	44%
Total	54600	100%	1200	100%

Disproportionate Stratified Sampling

Disproportionate stratified sampling is a stratified sampling procedure in which the number of elements sampled from each stratum is not proportional to their representation in the total population. Population elements are not given an equal chance to be included in the sample. The same sampling fraction is not applied to each stratum. On the other hand, the strata have different sampling fractions, and as such, this sampling procedure is not an EPSEM sampling procedure. In order to estimate population parameters, the population composition must be used as weights to compensate for the disproportionality in the sample. However, for some research projects, disproportionate stratified sampling may be more appropriate than proportionate stratified sampling.

Disproportionate stratified sampling may be broken into three subtypes based on the purpose of allocation that is implemented. The purpose of the allocation could be to facilitate within-strata analyses, between-strata analyses, or optimum allocation. Optimum allocation may focus on the optimization of costs, the optimization of precision, or the optimization of both precision and costs.

Disproportionate allocation for within strata analyses. The purpose of a study may require a researcher to conduct detailed analyses within the strata of the sample. If using proportionate stratification, the sample size of a stratum is very small; it may be difficult to meet the objectives of the study. Proportionate allocation may not yield a sufficient number of cases for such detailed analyses. One option is to oversample the small or rare strata. Such oversampling would create a disproportional distribution of the strata in the sample when compared to the population. Yet, there may be a sufficient number of cases to carry out the within-strata analyses required by the study's objectives. Examples of research for which such a sample design would be appropriate include a study of Muslims in the military, a study of persons with a rare medical problem, or a study of persons who spent most of their youth in foster care. Using the hypothetical example described in Table 5.2, if it was desired to conduct a detailed analysis of District 2, one might oversample elements from that district; for example, instead of sampling only 12 elements, sample 130 elements. In order to conduct a meaningful, detailed analysis within District 2, the sample size for that district must be larger than 12 elements. The resulting distribution of elements in the sample by district may look like the distribution presented in Table 5.3.

Disproportionate allocation for between-strata analyses. The purpose of a study may require a researcher to compare strata to each other. If this is the case, sufficient numbers of elements must be selected for each category. A researcher may desire to maximize the sample size of each stratum. For such a study, equal allocation (also referred to as "balanced allocation" and "factorial sampling") may be appropriate. A researcher may seek to select an equal number of elements from each stratum.

An example of equal allocation disproportionate allocation is presented in Table 5.4. In this example, the elements sampled were allocated across the four districts of our hypothetical example so that the number of elements sampled for each district is equal. Compared to the proportionate sample distribution in Table 5.2, the sampling allocations presented in Table 5.4 provide a minimum number of elements for each district, making for a more

Table 5.3 Example of Disproportionate Allocation Stratified Sampling

Marketing Region	Population		Disproportionate Stratified Sample	
	Frequency	Percent	Frequency	Percent
District 1	18000	33%	357	30%
District 2	600	1%	130	11%
District 3	12000	22%	238	20%
District 4	24000	44%	475	39%
Total	54600	100%	1200	100%

Table 5.4 Example of Disproportionate Allocation Stratified Sampling to Facilitate Between-Strata Analyses

Marketing Region	Population		Disproportionate Stratified Sample Using Equal Allocation	
	Frequency	Percent	Frequency	Percent
District 1	18000	33%	300	25%
District 2	600	1%	300	25%
District 3	12000	22%	300	25%
District 4	24000	44%	300	25%
Total	54600	100%	1200	100%

balanced comparative analysis across the districts. Moreover, a relatively large number of elements are sampled from District 2, permitting detailed analysis within that stratum.

Optimum allocation. Although proportionate stratified sampling may yield smaller margins of error than simple random sampling in estimating population parameters, it may be possible to do better yet. **Optimum allocation** is designed to achieve even greater overall accuracy than that achieved using proportionate stratified sampling. It sets the sample size of the different strata, taking into account two important aspects of doing research: costs and precision. The sampling fraction varies according to the costs and variability within the various strata. Disproportionate stratified sampling, more specifically, optimum allocation, may be more appropriate for a study than proportionate stratified sampling when the strata differ in terms of data collection costs and the variability of the variables of interest. Optimum allocation may be applied focusing on cost only, precision only, or both cost and precision jointly.

Homogeneous strata with a smaller sample size can have the same level of precision as heterogeneous strata with a larger sample size. Applying this principle, it may be useful to make the number of elements selected from each stratum directly related to the standard deviation of the variable of interest in the stratum. The greater the variability of the variable in a stratum, the higher the sample size of the stratum should be. Moreover, taking into account data collection costs, the higher the data collection costs of a stratum, the lower the targeted sample size. Hypothetical data illustrating optimum allocation are presented in Table 5.5.

The hypothetical data presented in Table 5.5 indicate that the data collection costs within the four districts range from $10 to $39 per unit (see Column 4). Differences in the geographical distribution of the elements in the different strata may account for these differences. The distribution of sample sizes for the various strata in Column 7 takes into account these varying data collection costs.

Hypothetical standard deviations of the variable of interest for the four districts are presented in Column 5 of Table 5.5. The standard deviations range from 4.3 to 9.4. If data collection costs for the various districts are unavailable or essentially the same, one may yet optimize the sample sizes of the various strata by allocating the sample size of each stratum by taking into account the variability of the strata. This type of allocation was first proposed by Jerzy Neyman (1934), and is often referred to as the Neyman allocation. A distribution of the sample size of the different strata in the hypothetical example, taking into account the variability of the strata, is presented in Column 8. The use of this optimization procedure is dependent on data on the variability of the variable of interests for the different strata. Often such data are not available. Moreover, if the study has multiple purposes and more than one variable of interest, their optimization might conflict with each other.

Table 5.5 Examples of Optimum Allocation Disproportionate Stratified Sampling

Marketing Regions (1)	Population Frequency (2)	Population Percent Distribution (3)	Data Collection Cost Per Unit (j) (4)	Variability (s) (5)	$\frac{s}{\sqrt{j}}$ (6)	Sample Size Optimizing Costs (7)	Sample Size Optimizing Variability (8)	Sample Size Optimizing Costs and Variability (9)
District 1	18000	33%	$18	4.3	1.014	300	190	203
District 2	600	1%	$10	6.4	2.024	538	282	405
District 3	12000	22%	$39	9.4	1.505	138	415	302
District 4	24000	44%	$24	7.1	1.449	224	313	290
Total	54600	100%				1200	1200	1200

If data are available for both the data collection costs and the variability of the variable of interest, one may optimize for both costs and precision. A weighting factor taking into account both data collection costs and standard deviation may be computed as $s/\sqrt{j}$, where "s" represents the standard deviation within the stratum, and "j" represents the per-unit data collection costs within the strata. A distribution of this factor is presented in Column 6 of Table 5.5 for our hypothetical example. Taking this factor into account, the sample sizes for the various strata were optimized, taking into account both the data collection costs and the variability with the strata and presented in Column 9.

What Are the Strengths and Weaknesses of Stratified Sampling?

Stratified sampling has many of the strengths and weaknesses associated with most probability sampling procedures when they are compared to non-probability sampling procedures. In determining whether to choose stratified sampling, one may compare its strengths and weaknesses to those of simple random sampling (see Table 5.6). Compared to simple random sampling, the strengths of stratified sampling include:

- Ability to not only estimate population parameters, but also to make within-stratum inferences and comparisons across strata. Sufficient data on subgroups of interest may not be captured in simple random sampling. Stratified samples yield smaller random sampling errors than those obtained with a simple random sample of the same sample size, especially if optimum allocation is used. Stratification makes for a gain in precision, eliminating the variation of the variable that is used for stratifying. The amount of gain in precision is determined by the extent the within-stratum variances of the study variables are minimized and the between-stratum variances of the study variables are maximized. Stratification will yield a sample that is at least as precise as a simple random sample of the same sample size.
- Stratified samples yield smaller random sampling errors than those obtained with a simple random sample of the same sample size, especially if optimum allocation is used. Stratification makes for a gain in precision, eliminating the variation of the variable that is used for stratifying. The amount of gain in precision is determined by the extent the within-stratum variances of the study variables are minimized and the between-stratum variances of the study variables are maximized. Stratification will yield a sample that is at least as precise as a simple random sample of the same

size. If it is ineffective in increasing the level of precision, the results would not be worse than if simple random sampling were used.

- Stratified samples tend to be more representative of a population because they ensure that elements from each stratum in the population are represented in the sample. Sampling may be stratified to ensure that the sample is spread over geographic subareas and population subgroups.
- In using stratified sampling, advantage is taken of knowledge the researcher has about the population.
- If the stratification variable breaks up the population into homogeneous geographical areas, data collection costs may be lower than the data collection costs of sample random sampling.
- Utilizing stratified sampling permits the researcher to use different sampling procedures within the different strata.
- In using stratified sampling, a researcher may be created taking into account administrative convenience in carrying out the study. The researcher may take into account the clustering of the population in metropolitan areas, institutionalized segments of the population, and the distribution of data collection staff.

Compared to simple random sampling, weaknesses of stratified sampling include:

- Stratified sampling has a greater requirement for prior auxiliary information than is the case for simple random sampling. Information on stratification variables is required for each element in the population. Such information includes information on the proportion of the target population that belongs to each stratum; if optimum allocation is used, information on the variability of the variables of interest and information on the data collection costs are necessary for each stratum. Acquiring such information may be time-consuming and costly.
- Selection of stratification variables may be difficult if a study involves a large number of variables. These variables should be correlated with the variables of interests in the study.
- Stratified sampling requires more effort in terms of preparation for sampling, executing the sample design, and analyzing the data collected.
- In order to calculate sampling estimates, at least two elements must be selected from each stratum.
- The analysis of data collected is more complex than the analysis of data collected via simple random sampling.
- Misclassification of elements into strata may increase variability.

- If disproportionate allocation is used, the data collected must be adjusted (weighted) in estimating population parameters. The effect of the weighting is to lower precision of some population estimates.

Table 5.6 Strengths and Weaknesses of Stratified Sampling Compared to Simple Random Sampling

Strengths	Weaknesses
Unlike simple random sampling, stratified sampling:	Unlike simple random sampling, stratified sampling:
Has greater ability to make inferences within a stratum and comparisons across strata.	Requires information on the proportion of the total population that belongs to each stratum.
Has slightly smaller random sampling errors for samples of same sample size, thereby requiring smaller sample sizes for the same margin of error.	Information on stratification variables is required for each element in the population. If such information is not readily available, they may be costly to compile.
Obtains a more representative sample because it ensures that elements from each stratum are represented in the sample.	More expensive, time-consuming, and complicated than simple random sampling.
Takes greater advantage of knowledge the researcher has about the population.	Selection of stratification variables may be difficult if a study involves a large number of variables.
Data collection costs may be lower if the stratification variable breaks up the population into homogeneous geographical areas, or so as to facilitate data collection.	In order to calculate sampling estimates, at least two elements must be taken in each stratum.
Permits different research methods and procedures to be used in different strata.	The analysis of the data collected is more complex than the analysis of data collected via simple random sampling.
Permits analyses of within-stratum patterns and separate reporting of the results for each stratum.	If disproportionate allocation is used, weighting is required to make accurate estimates of population parameters.

What Is the Difference Between Stratified Sampling and Quota Sampling?

Stratified sampling and quota sampling are somewhat similar to each other. Both involve dividing the target population into categories and then selecting a certain number of elements from each category (see Table 5.7). Both procedures have as a primary purpose the selection of a representative sample and/or the facilitation of subgroup analyses. However, there are important differences. Stratified sampling utilizes a simple random sampling once the categories are created; quota sampling utilizes availability sampling. A sampling frame is required for stratified sampling, but not for quota sampling. More importantly, stratified sampling is a probability sampling procedure permitting the estimation of sampling error. This is not possible with quota samples.

Listed below are research notes presenting examples of stratified sampling. Research Note 5.2 describes a proportionate allocation stratified sample of students at a Southern university in a study of perception of racism. The next three research notes provide examples of disproportionate allocation stratified samples. Research Note 5.3 describes a disproportionate stratified sample design used in a study of police chiefs. The sample was stratified by size of the city. Large cities and cities with Latino chiefs were oversampled. Research Note 5.4 describes a study of HIV risk behavior among prison inmates. In order to have a sufficient number of women in their study, disproportionate allocation was used oversampling female inmates. The research described in Research Note 5.5 examines differences in the relationship between socioeconomic status and

Table 5.7   Comparison of Stratified Sampling and Quota Sampling

Stratified Sampling	Quota Sampling
Stratified sampling and quota sampling are similar in that:	
Population is divided into categories; elements are then selected from each category.	Population is divided into categories; elements are then selected from each category.
Purpose is to select a representative sample and/or facilitate subgroup analyses.	Purpose is to select a representative sample and/or facilitate subgroup analyses.
Stratified sampling and quota sampling are dissimilar in that:	
Elements within each category are selected using simple random sampling, and as a result:	Elements within each category are selected using availability sampling, and as a result:
A sampling frame is required.	A sampling frame is not required.
Random sampling error can be estimated.	Random sampling error cannot be estimated.
Selection bias is minimized.	Selection bias is not minimized.
Purpose is to reduce sampling error.	

health among African Americans and Whites. In order to have a sufficient number of African Americans, they were oversampling via a disproportionate stratified sampling design.

RESEARCH NOTE 5.2

Example of Proportionate Stratified Sampling: Study of Perception of Racism Among Students at a Southern University

Marcus et al. (2003) utilized proportionate stratified sampling in their study of students' perceptions of racial discrimination in classrooms, on campus, and in contacts with instructors at a Southern university. They described their sampling as follows:

The data for this study were collected from 398 students who were in 26 randomly selected classes during the spring quarter of 1998. The 26 classes were selected from the entire 555 class sections, excluding laboratory sections and internships, from all of the academic schools using a proportionate stratified sampling approach. Classes in all periods of the day, night, and the weekend were included.

The proportionate sampling plan called for 60% of the sample from day classes, 35% of the sample from evening classes, and 5% of the sample from weekend classes. (This accurately represents the proportion of these classes in these time periods.) This approach resulted in the 26 selected classes; 16 day classes (62%), 9 evening classes (35%) and one weekend class (4%). Of the original 26 classes selected seven instructors (27%) refused permission for their classes to participate. An additional seven classes were selected taking into account the time of day/week of the class. One (14%) of these seven classes was not allowed to participate. It, too, was replaced.

The class rolls of the 26 selected classes indicated a total of 496 enrolled students. The 398 returned instruments are 80% of the enrolled students in the selected classes. If we consider that on the day of administration as many as 10% of the students were either not in attendance or had dropped the course, then the rate of return was over 90%. On the day of administration, 100% of those in attendance responded.

Source: Marcus et al., 2003, p. 614. Reprinted with permission.

RESEARCH NOTE 5.3

Example of Disproportionate Stratified Sampling: Study of Police Chiefs

Hays, Regoli, and Hewitt (2007) used a two-stage stratified sample in their study of police chiefs. They described their sampling procedures as follows:

Data were derived from a national sample of 1,500 American police chiefs. . . . The sampling frame was constructed from each state's Chiefs of Police Association, which provided separate lists. A two-stage random stratified sampling procedure was used to select participants. First, departments were coded by city size, and eight categories were created to obtain a sample with representatives from all size cities. Second, 200 chiefs were chosen from the first six categories: less than 3,000 in population; 3,000 to 4,999; 5,000 to 9,999; 10,000 to 24,999; 25,000 to 49,999; and 50,000 to 99,999. Because there were only few cities with more than 100,000 populations, all the cases were chosen from the largest two categories, 100,000 to 499,999 and more than 500,000.

In addition to oversampling large cities, Latino chiefs were also oversampled to obtain a sufficient number of Latino chiefs. This was accomplished by carefully perusing the entire sampling frame (more than 10,000 names) and identifying the surnames that appeared to be Latino. Although this methodology is not without its shortcomings, it did result in 77 self-identified Latino chiefs.

Source: Hays, Regoli, & Hewitt, 2007, pp. 8–9. Reprinted with permission.

RESEARCH NOTE 5.4

Example of Disproportionate Stratified Sampling: Study of HIV Risk Behavior Among Prison Inmates

Swartz, Lurigio, and Weiner (2004) used disproportionate sampling in assessing Illinois prison inmates' sexual and drug-use practices, their knowledge about HIV risk-reduction techniques, and their beliefs regarding their own HIV-risk status

(Continued)

(Continued)

and their ability to avoid HIV infection. They described their sampling procedure as follows:

> Research staff recruited participants from the four reception and classification centers (RCCs) that process admittees to the Illinois Department of Corrections (IDOC) prisons in Joliet, Graham, Dwight, and Menard. All IDOC admittees, 18 years or older, were eligible for the study, with the exceptions of federal prisoners, inmates admitted to boot camps, those sentenced to death row, and those sent to RCCs for a transfer to other facilities. To select recruits for the study, we used a probability sampling strategy based on the proportionate number of admissions to each RCC. In addition, because women constituted a small proportion of IDOC admissions (about 7%), we oversampled them, relative to men, at an approximate ratio of 2 to 1. . . . Interviewers sampled participants on site during each day of interviewing. Because of the large variation in the numbers of inmates processed at each RCC, the sampling strategy varied across the four sites. Joliet Prison processed the largest number of admissions. Using a table of random numbers, interviewers selected a sample of inmates to be recruited for the study on that day only. At Graham Prison, interviewers randomly selected every second inmate for study recruitment. At Dwight and Menard Prisons, because of the small number of inmates processed there each week (e.g., on average, Dwight Prison processed approximately 30 to 40 inmates per week), interviewers selected all processed inmates for study recruitment.

Source: Swartz, Lurigio, & Weiner, 2004, pp. 491–492. Reprinted with permission.

RESEARCH NOTE 5.5

Example of Disproportionate Stratified Sampling: Study of the Relationship of Socioeconomic Status and Health Among African Americans and Whites

Ostrove, Feldman, and Adler (1999) analyzed the differences between African Americans and Whites in the relationship between socioeconomic status and health. They used data from two nationally representative surveys of adults in the United States: the Americans' Changing Lives (ACL) survey and the Health and

Retirement Survey (HRS). These samples were appropriate for their study as they were stratified samples with disproportionate allocation due to an oversampling of African Americans. They described the sample designs as follows:

> The ACL survey is a national longitudinal panel survey of African-American and white non-institutionalized adults that was designed to investigate adult activities and social relationships, and adaptation to life events and stress. The first wave of data collection in 1986 used a multistage stratified area probability sampling strategy, with oversampling of African-Americans and those over 60 years of age, and obtained responses from 3617 people. . . . The data were weighted to adjust for variations in probabilities of selection and in response rates, making the data representative of the US population. . . . The HRS is a national panel survey of non-institutionalized adults between the ages of 51 and 61 years (in 1992) and their spouses. The data for the current study are from the original wave of data collection from 1992, in which over 7600 households were sampled, yielding interviews with over 12,600 people. . . . The study used a multistage area probability sample design and oversampled for African-Americans, Latino/as, and residents of Florida. . . . The data were weighted to adjust for unequal selection probabilities, and for geographic and race group differences in response rates, creating a nationally representative sample.

Source: Ostrove, Feldman, & Adler, 1999, p. 454. Reprinted with permission.

SYSTEMATIC SAMPLING

What Is Systematic Sampling?

Systematic sampling (or interval random sampling) is a probability sampling procedure in which a random selection is made of the first element for the sample, and then subsequent elements are selected using a fixed or systematic interval until the desired sample size is reached. The random start distinguishes this sampling procedure from its nonprobability counterpart, nonprobability systematic sampling (discussed above). In some instances, a sampling frame is not used. The target population need not be numbered and a sampling frame compiled if there is physical presentation such as a continuous flow of population elements at specific locations. For example, after a random start, one may systematically select every *i*th patient visiting an emergency room in a hospital, store customers standing in line, or records in file drawers.

What Are the Steps in Selecting a Systematic Sample?

Generally, there are eight major steps in selecting a systematic sample:

1. Define the target population.

2. Determine the desired sample size (n).

3. Identify an existing sampling frame or develop a sampling frame of the target population.

4. Evaluate the sampling frame for undercoverage, overcoverage, multiple coverage, clustering, and periodicity, and make adjustments where necessary. Ideally, the list will be in a random order with respect to the study variable or, better yet, ordered in terms of the variable of interest or its correlate, thereby creating implicit stratification. If the sampling frame is randomized, systematic sampling is considered to be a good approximation of simple random sampling.

5. Determine the number of elements in the sampling frame (N).

6. Calculate the sampling interval (i) by dividing the number of elements in the sampling frame (N) by the targeted sample size (n). One should ignore a remainder and round down or truncate to the nearest whole number. Rounding down and truncating may cause the sample size to be larger than desired. If so, one may randomly delete the extra selections. If the exact size of the population is not known and impractical to determine, one may fix the sampling fraction.

7. Randomly select a number, r, from "1" through i.

8. Select for the sample, r, $r + i$, $r + 2i$, $r + 3i$, and so forth, until the frame is exhausted.

At a technical level, systematic sampling does not create a truly random sample. It is often referred to as "pseudo random sampling," "pseudo simple random sampling," or "quasi-random sampling." Only the selection of the first element in systematic sampling is a probability selection. Once the first element is selected, some of the elements will have a zero probability of selection. Moreover, certain combinations of elements, such as elements that are adjacent to each other in the sampling frame, are not likely to be selected. Repeated systematic sampling, described below, may be used to address this problem.

What Are the Subtypes of Systematic Sampling?

Systematic sampling may be classified into three major types: linear systematic sampling, circular systematic sampling, and repeated (or replicated) systematic sampling. Linear systematic sampling is the most frequently used form of systematic sampling. The steps in selecting a linear systematic sample are those listed above. Circular systematic sampling may be viewed as a subtype of linear systematic sampling. In using this procedure, in Step 7, instead of selecting a random number between "1" and "i," the size of the interval, a random number is selected between "1" and "N." When one gets to the end of the list in selecting the sample, one would continue from the beginning of the list. This creates a circular pattern in selecting the sample.

Linear systematic sampling and circular systematic create a single sample. Repeated systematic sampling involves the selection of multiple samples from the target population and then combining them into a single sample. Instead of only one random start, several smaller systematic samples are selected using multiple random starts. This makes the process more time-consuming than linear systematic sampling. However, repeated sampling minimizes the effect of bias due to periodicity, a regularly occurring pattern in the sampling frame (see below). Moreover, because linear systematic sampling generates only one "cluster" of elements (although the cluster may contain multiple elements), technically, an unbiased estimate of sampling error cannot be obtained without making certain assumptions. At least two independently chosen clusters must be made. Repeated sampling provides more than one cluster of elements and facilitates the calculation of variances and standard error of estimates from the sample.

What Are the Strengths and Weaknesses of Systematic Sampling?

Systematic sampling has the strengths and weaknesses associated with most probability sampling procedures when compared to nonprobability sampling procedures. In highlighting the strengths and weaknesses of systematic sampling, we may compare it to simple random sampling. Systematic sampling is often used when it is impractical or impossible to use simple random sampling. When compared to simple random sampling, in some instances it is a stronger sampling procedure, and in other instances it is a weaker sampling procedure (see Table 5.8). Compared to simple random sampling, the strengths of systematic sampling include:

- If the selection process is manual, systematic sampling is easier, simpler, less time-consuming, and more economical than simple random sampling. One needs to use a random process to select only the first element. On the other hand, if the selection process is computerized, the ease in the selection process of systematic sampling and simple random sampling may be comparable to each other.
- If the sampling frame has a monotonic ordering that is related to a study variable (e.g., ordering of stores by dollar value, listing of employees by number of years employed, and listings of schools by graduation rates), implicit stratification may result in the statistical efficiency equivalent to that of proportionate stratified sampling and is thereby more efficient than simple random sampling. If the ordering is randomized, systematic sampling may yield results similar to simple random sampling.
- Systematic sampling ensures that the sample is more spread across the population.

Table 5.8 Strengths and Weaknesses of Systematic Sampling Compared to Simple Random Sampling

Strengths	Weaknesses
Unlike simple random sampling:	Unlike simple random sampling:
If the selection process is manual, systematic sampling is easier, simpler, less time-consuming, and more economical.	If the sampling interval is related to periodic ordering of the elements in the sampling frame, increased variability may result.
The target population need not be numbered and a sampling frame compiled if there is physical representation.	Combinations of elements have different probabilities of being selected.
If the ordering of the elements in the sampling frame is randomized, systematic sampling may yield results similar to simple random sampling.	Technically, only the selection of the first element is a probability selection since for subsequent selections, there will be elements of the target population that will have a zero chance of being selected.
If the ordering of the elements in the sampling frame is related to a study variable creating implicit stratification, systematic sampling is more efficient than simple random sampling.	Principle of independence is violated, for the selection of the first element determines the selection of all others.
Systematic sampling eliminates the possibility of autocorrelation.	Estimating variances is more complex than that for simple random sampling.
Systematic sampling ensures that the sample is spread across the population.	

Similarity of adjacent elements in a list makes for autocorrelation, the correlation among elements in the population. Although rare, this may occur in simple random sampling. Spatial autocorrelation is likely to exist in a listing of addresses. Persons who live at addresses that are close to each other are likely to be more similar to each other, say in terms of socioeconomic status, than they are to persons living at addresses that are not as close. A positive autocorrelation creates lower precision, and a negative autocorrelation creates higher precision when compared to simple random sampling. However, systematic sampling eliminates the possibility of autocorrelation. For example, in using a voter's list for the selection of a sample for a study of voter preferences, it is possible that members of the same family are selected using simple random sampling, but this is not possible using systematic sampling.

Compared to simple random sampling, systematic sampling has a number of weaknesses. Some of them include:

- Although its occurrence is relatively rare, periodicity in the sampling frame is a constant concern in systematic sampling. A biased sample could result if a periodic or cyclical pattern in the sampling frame corresponds to the sampling fraction. This problem will exist if the sampling fraction is equal to or a multiple of a periodic interval in the list. For example, a systematic sample of students would be biased if students are listed by class and within each class ranked by performance on an achievement test. If the classes have approximately the same number of students, periodic bias will result.
- Moreover, whereas in simple random sampling every combination of n elements has an equal chance of selection, this is not the case for systematic sampling.
- Technically only the selection of the first element is a probability selection since for subsequent selections there will be members of the target population that will have a zero chance of being selected.
- Principle of independence is violated, for the selection of the first element determines the selection of all the others.
- Estimating variances is more complex than that for simple random sampling.

Research Note 5.6 provides an example of systematic sampling. It describes the sampling procedures used by Chandek and Porter (1998) in their study of victims of robbery and burglary. Another example of systematic sampling is presented in Research Note 5.7. In this study, systematic sampling was used in selecting cases in a study of child abuse cases filed in Dallas, Texas, between December 2001 and December 2003.

RESEARCH NOTE 5.6

Example of Systematic Sampling: Study of Victims of Robbery and Burglary

Chandek and Porter (1998) utilized systematic sampling in their study of victims of robbery and burglary. They described their sampling procedures as follows:

> The data for this study were obtained from telephone surveys and official complainant records from a medium-size Midwestern police department. The sample was obtained from the total population of burglary and robbery victims whose crimes were reported to the department between May 15th and August 14th of 1995—a total of 2,000 burglary and 999 robbery victims. Systematic sampling procedures were used to create a manageable sample size given the project's resource constraints.
>
> After using systematic sampling procedures and eliminating cases with missing information on the official complainant records, cases where the victim was under the age of 18 and cases where the victim was a business rather than an individual, the sample comprised 216 robbery victims and 200 burglary victims. A telephone survey was then conducted using a questionnaire specifically designed for the present study.

Source: Chandek & Porter, 1998, pp. 26–27. Reprinted with permission.

RESEARCH NOTE 5.7

Example of Systematic Sampling: Study of Evidence and Filing of Charges in Child Abuse Cases

Walsh, Jones, Cross, and Lippert (2010) used systematic sampling in their study of the type of evidence and whether charges were filed in child abuse cases in Dallas, Texas. They described their sampling procedures as follows:

> Systematic sampling (e.g., taking every third case) was used to enroll research cases from the Children's Advocacy Center and from comparison community agencies (e.g., Child Protective Services, police). If there were multiple victims in the same family or multiple perpetrators per case, data collection focused

on one randomly selected victim or perpetrator. The initial sample for this analysis included only child sexual abuse cases with adult offenders (N = 360). Five cases were missing information on whether charges were filed; thus, they were not included. In 26 cases, an offender could not be identified; the offender or family fled during the investigation; or the family was unwilling to press charges. . . . The final sample included 329 cases.

Source: Walsh, Jones, Cross, & Lippert, 2010, pp. 440–441. Reprinted with permission.

CLUSTER SAMPLING

What Is Cluster Sampling?

Often it is impossible or impractical to create a sampling frame of a target population, and/or the target population is widely dispersed geographically, making data collection costs relatively high. Such situations are ideal for cluster sampling. **Cluster sampling** is a probability sampling procedure in which elements of the population are randomly selected in naturally occurring groupings (clusters). In the context of cluster sampling, a "cluster" is an aggregate or intact grouping of population elements. Element sampling is the selection of population elements individually, one at a time. On the other hand, cluster sampling involves the selection of population elements not individually, but in aggregates. The sampling units or clusters may be space-based, such as naturally occurring geographical or physical units (e.g., states, counties, census tracts, blocks, or buildings); organization-based, such as such units as school districts, schools, grade levels, or classes; or telephone-based, such as area codes or exchanges of telephone numbers. For the most part, the cluster sample designs described in this chapter are space-based or area-based sampling procedures. Telephone-based sampling procedures are described in Chapter 6.

The heterogeneity of the cluster is central to a good cluster sample design. Ideally, the within-cluster differences would be high, and the between-cluster differences would be low. The clusters should be like each other. On the other hand, the elements within each cluster should be as heterogeneous as the target population. Ideally, the clusters would be small but not so small as to be homogeneous.

What Are the Steps in Selecting a Cluster Sample?

There are six major steps in selecting a cluster sample:

1. Define the target population.

2. Determine the desired sample size.

3. Identify an existing sampling frame or develop a new sampling frame of clusters of the target population.

4. Evaluate the sampling frame for undercoverage, overcoverage, multiple coverage, and clustering, and make adjustments where necessary. Ideally, the clusters would be as heterogeneous as the population, mutually exclusive, and collectively exhaustive. Duplication of elements in the sample may result if population elements belonged to more than one cluster. Omissions will result in coverage bias.

5. Determine the number of clusters to be selected. This may be done by dividing the sample size by estimated average number of population elements in each cluster. To the extent the homogeneity and heterogeneity of the clusters are different from that of the population, as cluster number increases, precision increases. On the other hand, as differences between clusters increases, precision decreases.

6. Randomly select the targeted number of clusters.

What Are the Subtypes of Cluster Sampling?

Two major dimensions are used to classify different types of cluster sampling. One is based on the number of stages in the sample design, and the other is based on the proportional representation of the clusters in the total sample.

Subtypes Based on Number of Stages

Often cluster sampling is carried out in more than one "stage." A stage is a step in the sampling process in which a sample is taken. Considering the number of stages in the design, there are three major subtypes of cluster sampling: single-stage cluster sampling, two-stage cluster sampling, and multistage cluster sampling.

Single-stage cluster sampling. In a single-stage cluster sample design, sampling is done only once. As an example of single-stage cluster sampling, let us say one is interested in studying homeless persons who live in shelters. If there are five shelters in a city, a researcher will randomly select one of the shelters and then include in the study all the homeless persons who reside at the selected shelter. A market researcher might choose to use a single-stage cluster sample design. Say a researcher was interested in test marketing a product. The researcher may randomly select zip codes; send samples of the product together with a mail-back evaluation questionnaire to each address within the selected clusters.

Two-stage cluster sampling. A **two-stage cluster sample design** includes all the steps in single-stage cluster sample design with one exception, the last step. Instead of including all the elements in the selected clusters in the sample, a random sample (either a simple random sample, stratified sample, or systematic sample) is taken from the elements in each selected cluster. Sampling beyond the first stage is sometimes referred to as subsampling. Generally, unless the clusters are homogeneous, a two-stage cluster sample design is better than a one-stage cluster sample design. A self-weighting sample will result if at the first stage sampling is conducted with probability proportional to size (see below). Using the example of the study of homeless persons described above, instead of selecting all the persons who reside at the selected shelter for inclusion in the study, the researcher would randomly select a subset of the residents of the shelter.

Multistage cluster sampling. Surveys of large geographical areas require a somewhat more complicated sample design than those described up to this point. Typically, a multistage cluster sample design must be used. **Multistage cluster sampling** involves the repetition of two basic steps: listing and sampling. Typically, at each stage, the clusters get progressively smaller in size; and at the last stage element sampling is used. Sampling procedures (simple random sampling, stratified sampling, or systematic sampling) at each stage may differ. It is not necessary that the sampling procedures at each stage be the same. The number of stages that are used is often determined by the availability of sampling frames at different stages.

Special terminology is used to refer to the different sampling units. The sampling unit that is used in the first stage is referred to as the **primary sampling unit** (PSU). The units of subsequent sampling are referred to as the **secondary sampling unit** (SSU), tertiary sampling units (TSU), etc., until one gets to the "final" or "ultimate" sampling unit.

Typically, as the sampling process moves from the selection of PSUs to the other sampling stages, the sampling units become more homogeneous. The large clusters tend to be more heterogeneous than small clusters. Because of the greater heterogeneity of the PSUs, sampling error is minimized if one sample has more PSUs than SSUs, more SSUs than TSUs, and so forth.

Subtypes Based on the Proportional Representation of Clusters in Sample

Clusters may be selected in such a way that it is an EPSEM sampling procedure; that is, every element in the population would have an equal chance to be included in the sample. If the clusters sampled are roughly the same size, the sample design may be considered to be an EPSEM sample design. If the clusters have unequal sizes, an EPSEM sample design may be achieved by using a probability proportionate to size (PPS) selection procedure. The probability of selecting a cluster is dependent on the proportional distribution of its elements in the target population. Using PPS, a self-weighting sample is obtained. Probability disproportional to size (PDS) sampling involves selecting clusters without considering the proportional distribution of the elements in the target population.

Respondent Selection Procedures

Typically, in household surveys employing a two-stage cluster sample design or a multistage cluster sample design, individual elements are selected at the last stage of the sample design. If the household contains more than one member of the target population, one element must be selected. Both nonprobability and probability procedures are used to select the element from whom to collect data.

Two principal nonprobability household respondent selection procedures are used: head of household selection and first-adult selection. In using the head of household selection the researcher simply asks to speak to the head of household. One may alternatively ask for the male and female heads of household. The first-adult approach involves the selection of the first adult contacted, providing he/she is a member of the target population. These procedures are easy to administer, do not take much time, and are not intrusive. However, they incur selection bias, and are likely to oversample females as they are more likely than males to be available to be interviewed. The head of household method tends to oversample women, especially in urban areas, due to the greater number of single-parent female-headed households than single-parent male-headed households. The first-adult selection method tends to oversample women because women are more likely to be at home.

These respondent selection procedures do not give every member of the target population a chance to be included in the sample. Combining the probability selection of clusters with the nonprobability selection of household members makes the sampling procedure a mixed-methods procedure. Mixed-methods sampling procedures are described in more detail in the next chapter.

There are several probability household respondent selection procedures. The most frequently used probability approaches are the Kish tables, the Troldahl-Carter-Bryant tables, the Hagan and Carter selection method, and the last/next birthday method (Binson, Canchola, & Catania, 2000). These procedures reflect a struggle among researchers to minimize systematic error. Typically, the introduction to the interview is lengthened as they involve two consents: the initial consent from the first contact in the household and second from the person selected to be interviewed. This has the effect of decreasing undercoverage bias but increasing refusal rates. Moreover, if the selected person is not at home, the interviewer is restricted from selecting someone else in the household. Callbacks must be made. The success of the callbacks affects the study's unit nonresponse bias.

Kish Tables

In 1949, Kish created tables to facilitate the random selection of household members from among those eligible to participate in a study. The tables included a listing of household sizes one through five, and six or more; and for each household size a random number indicating the household member to be included in the study (see Table 5.9). Tables are prepared so that each household member (except those in households with six or more members of the target population) will have an equal chance to be selected and randomly applied to interview being conducted. Once making contact with a household, as part of the screening process, an interviewer would:

- Create a listing (sampling frame) of members of the household that are in the target population including their gender, relationship to household head, and age.
- Assign a unique number to each element listed in the frame.
- Using the randomized response table assigned to interview, determine the household member indicated in the table that should be interviewed.

Using the Kish tables produces a random sample to household members and decreases undercoverage bias; however, it does so at a cost. The process increases the amount of training of interviewers, the amount of time required

Table 5.9 Summary of Kish Tables Used for Selecting One Adult in Each Dwelling

Proportions of Assigned Tables	Table Number	If the number of adults in the household is:					
		1	2	3	4	5	6 or more
		Select adult numbered:					
1/6	A	1	1	1	1	1	1
1/12	B1	1	1	1	1	2	2
1/12	B2	1	1	1	2	2	2
1/6	C	1	1	2	2	3	3
1/6	D	1	2	2	3	4	4
1/12	E1	1	2	3	3	3	5
1/12	E2	1	2	3	4	5	5
1/6	F	1	2	3	4	5	6

Source: Kish, 1965, p. 399. Reprinted with permission.

for the screening process, the difficulty interviewers experience in establishing rapport, and the resistance of respondents to be interviewed. Due to the complexity of the method, some interviewers may improvise and use inappropriate shortcuts in selecting the person to be interviewed. The Kish tables were developed at a time when surveys were conducted primarily via personal interviews. As telephone surveys became more and more popular, the need for a less time-consuming respondent-selection procedure became more apparent. Other procedures were developed to satisfy such needs.

Troldahl-Carter-Bryant Tables

Troldahl-Carter-Bryant (TCB) tables are representative of a number of approaches designed to simplify the Kish tables (Bryant, 1975; Czaja, Blair, & Sebestik, 1982; Groves & Kahn, 1979; Paisley & Parker, 1965; Troldahl & Carter, 1964). Using TCB tables, a researcher asks only two questions: How many persons live in the household who are in the target population (say, 18 years of age or older), and how many of them are women? The TCB randomized response tables are then used by the interviewer in selecting to interview either the man, the woman, oldest man or woman, youngest man or woman, or the middle man or woman (for an example, see Table 5.10). As

Table 5.10 Example of Troldahl-Carter-Bryant Randomized Response Table

Number of Women in Household	Number of Adults in Household			
	1	2	3	4 or more
0	Man	Youngest man	Youngest man	Oldest man
1	Woman	Woman	Oldest man	Woman
2		Oldest woman	Man	Oldest man
3			Youngest woman	Man or oldest man
4 or more				Oldest woman

done for the Kish tables, these tables are randomly assigned to the interviews conducted. The Kish tables and the TCB tables provide a means of randomly selecting the person to be interviewed; however, each member of the target population does not have an equal chance to be selected. Although believed to be a minor violation of randomness, the TCB method does not allow the selection of persons who fall between the youngest and oldest persons.

Hagan and Carter Selection Method

Hagan and Collier (1983) used an even simpler method. Their approach involves the random assignment of four forms to the interviews that are conducted. One form instructs the interviewer to ask to speak with the youngest adult male, another instructs the interviewer to ask to speak to the youngest adult female, another instructs the interviewer to speak to the oldest adult male, and the fourth instructs the interviewer to speak to the oldest adult female. If no such person is present, the interviewer asks to speak to the opposite sex of the same age group. In order to compensate for the greater difficulty in contacting men and younger females, these subpopulations are often given higher probabilities to be selected. This procedure is easier than using the Kish tables and the TCB tables. However, it assumes that only two members of the target population are in the household and, as for TCB tables, does not allow the selection of persons who are inbetween the oldest and youngest persons in the household.

Last/Next Birthday Method

The approach developed by Salmon and Nichols (1983) does not involve enumeration of household members nor randomized selection tables. A researcher merely asks to speak to the member of the target population who had the last birthday or will have the next birthday. One may randomly alternate either the last or next birthday. Compared to the procedures described above, this method is the easiest and the least time-consuming in terms of the training required and its administration. However, the validity of the procedure is dependent on whether the person answering the screening questions actually knows the birthday of all the members of the household. The larger the household, the more likely this the person does not know the birthday of all eligible persons for the study. Moreover, the procedure is considered a quasi-probability procedure because the respondent is determined when the date to conduct the interview is determined.

Alphabetic Ordering of Names

Another approach is the alphabetic ordering of the first names of those in the target population. As the last, or next, birthday method, this method is relatively easy to administer but is dependent on the knowledge of the contact person. Moreover, it requires time to obtain the names, put them in alphabetical order, and then to make a selection.

What Are the Strengths and Weaknesses of Cluster Sampling?

Cluster sampling has the strengths and weaknesses associated with most probability sampling procedures when compared to nonprobability sampling procedures. However, it has several special strengths and weaknesses when compared to other probability sampling procedures, such as simple random sampling (see Table 5.11). Some of the strengths of cluster sampling when compared to simple random sampling are:

- If the clusters are geographically defined, cluster sampling requires less time, money, and labor than simple random sampling. It is the most cost-effective probability sampling procedure.
- For the same level of costs, cluster sampling with a higher sample size may yield less sampling error than that resulting from simple random sampling with a smaller sample size.

Table 5.11   Strengths and Weaknesses of Cluster Sampling Compared to Simple Random Sampling

Strengths	Weaknesses
Compared to simple random sampling:	Compared to simple random sampling:
If the clusters are geographically defined, cluster sampling requires less time, money, and labor.	A cluster sample may not be as representative of the population as a simple random sample of the same sample size.
Cluster sampling permits subsequent sampling because the sampled clusters are aggregates of elements.	Variances of cluster samples tend to be much higher than variances of simple random samples.
One can estimate characteristics of the clusters as well as the population.	Cluster sampling introduces more complexity in analyzing data and interpreting results of the analyses.
Cluster sampling does not require a sampling frame of all of the elements in the target population.	Cluster sampling yields larger sampling errors for samples of comparable size than other probability samples.

- Cluster sampling permits subsequent sampling because the sampled clusters are aggregates of elements.
- Unlike simple random sampling, cluster sampling permits the estimation characteristics of subsets (clusters) as well as the target population.
- Single-stage cluster sampling requires a sampling frame of the clusters only, and two-stage cluster sampling and multistage cluster sampling require a sampling frame of the elements of the population only for the clusters sampled at the last stage of the process.
- Cluster sampling is much easier to implement than simple random sampling.

Some of the weaknesses of cluster sampling when compared to simple random sampling include:

- The sampled clusters may not be as representative of the population as a simple random sample of the same sample size.
- Combining the variance from two separately homogeneous clusters may cause the variance of the entire sample to be higher than that of simple random sampling.
- Cluster sampling introduces more complexity in analyzing data. Inferential statistical analysis of data collected via cluster sampling is more difficult to

compute and interpret results than inferential statistical analysis of data collected via simple random sampling. The statistical software used to analyze the data collected must use formulas that take into account the use of a cluster sample design. Many statistical software programs utilize formulas for simple random sampling and, as a result, overestimate levels of significance.

- The more stages there are in a cluster sample design, the greater overall sampling error.
- If clusters are not similar to each other, the fewer the number of clusters, the greater the sampling error.
- Cluster sampling yields larger sampling errors for samples of comparable size than other probability samples. If the clusters are similar to each other, this error is minimized. Moreover, these errors can be reduced by increasing the number of clusters. Note, this has the effect of increasing data collection costs.
- The more clusters one selects, the less the difference in data collection costs between cluster sampling and simple random sampling.
- Since elements within a cluster tend to be alike, we receive less new information about the population when we select another element from that cluster rather than from another cluster. This lack of new information makes a cluster sample less precise than a simple random sample.

What Is the Difference Between Cluster Sampling and Stratified Sampling?

Cluster sampling is similar to stratified sampling in that both involve separating the population into categories and then sampling within the categories (see Table 5.12). Both sampling procedures permit analysis of individual categories (strata or clusters) in addition to analysis of the total sample. However, there are important differences. Some of these differences include:

- In stratified sampling, once the categories (strata) are created, a random sample is drawn from each category (stratum). On the other hand, in cluster sampling, elements are not selected from each cluster. In single-stage cluster sampling, once the categories (clusters) are created, a random sample of cluster is drawn. All elements in the selected cluster are included in the sample. In two-stage cluster sampling and multi-stage cluster sampling, a random sample of cluster is drawn and then elements are randomly selected from the selected clusters.

Table 5.12 Comparison of Stratified Sampling and Cluster Sampling

Stratified Sampling	Cluster Sampling
The population is separated into strata, and then sampling is conducted within each stratum.	The population is separated into clusters, and then clusters are sampled.
Analysis of individual strata is permitted in addition to analysis of the total sample.	Analysis of individual categories (clusters) are permitted in addition to analysis of the total sample.
In order to minimize sampling error, within-group differences among strata should be minimized, and between/group differences among strata should be maximized.	In order to minimize sampling error, within-group differences should be consistent with those in the population, and between-group differences among the clusters should be minimized.
A sampling frame is needed for the entire target population.	In single-state cluster sampling, a sampling frame is needed only for the clusters. In two-stage and multistage cluster sampling, a sampling frame of individual elements is needed only for the elements in the clusters selected at the final stage.
Main purpose: increase precision and representation.	Main purpose: decrease costs and increase operational efficiency.
Categories are imposed by the researcher.	Categories are naturally occurring pre-existing groups.
More precision compared to simple random sampling.	Lower precision compared to simple random sampling.
The variables used for stratification should be related to the research problem.	The variables used for clustering should not be related to the research problem.
Common stratification variables: age, gender, income, race.	Common classification variables: geographical area, school, grade level.
Requires more prior information than cluster sampling.	Requires less prior information than stratified sampling.

- In stratified sampling, in order to minimize sampling error, within-group differences among strata should be minimized, and the strata should be as homogeneous as possible. In cluster sampling, in order to minimize sampling error, within-group differences should be consistent with those in the population, and the clusters should be as heterogeneous as the population. The ideal situation for stratified sampling is to have the homogeneity within each stratum and the strata means to differ from each other. The ideal situation for cluster sampling is to have heterogeneity within the clusters and the cluster means not to differ from each other.

- In stratified sampling, in order to minimize sampling error, between-group differences among strata should be maximized. In cluster sampling, in order to minimize sampling error, between-group differences among the clusters should be minimized.

- In stratified sampling, categories are conceptualized by the researcher. In cluster sampling, the categories are naturally occurring groups.

- In stratified sampling, a sampling frame is needed for the entire target population. In single-stage cluster sampling, a sampling frame is needed only for the clusters. In two-stage cluster sampling and multistage cluster sampling, in addition to a sampling frame of the clusters in the first stage of the process, a sampling frame is needed only for elements of each one of the selected clusters.

- The main purpose of stratified sampling is to increase precision and representativeness. The main purpose of cluster sampling is to decrease costs and increase operational efficiency.

- Compared to simple random sampling, stratified sampling has higher precision and cluster sampling has lower precision. The increase in precision by stratification is not that much. However, clustering can cause a significant decrease in precision.

- The variables used for stratification should be related to the variables under study. The variable used for clustering should not be related to the variables under study.

- Commonly used stratification variables are age, gender, and income. Commonly used classification variables in cluster sampling are geographical area, school, and grade level.

- Stratified sampling requires more prior information than cluster sampling; likewise, cluster sampling requires less prior information than stratified sampling.

- In stratified sampling, the researcher strives to divide the target population into a few subgroups, each with many elements in it. In cluster sampling, the researcher strives to divide the target population into many subgroups, each with few elements in it.

What Is the Difference Between Multistage Sampling and Multiphase Sampling?

Multistage sampling (two-stage cluster sampling and multistage cluster sampling) is often confused with multiphase sampling (also referred to as two-phase sampling, double sampling, and post-stratification sampling). Both sampling procedures involve the multiple sampling at different stages or phases, and in some circumstances may be viewed as mixed-methods sampling. In multistage sampling the sampling units for the different stages are different. On the other hand, in multiphase sampling the same sampling unit is sampled multiple times.

Typically, multiphase sampling is used when one does not have a sampling frame with sufficient auxiliary information to allow for stratification. The first phase is used for screening purposes. Using the available sampling frame, one may proceed as follows:

1. Select an initial sample of elements from the available sampling frame.

2. Conduct a short screening interview to collect the necessary auxiliary information for further sampling and stratification.

3. Poststratify the initial sample into strata using the auxiliary information collected.

4. Using the strata for which one desires to collect additional information, select either all the elements in the strata or a probability sample of the elements in the strata for additional data collection.

Multiphase sampling typically is carried out to increase precision, reduce costs, and reduce nonresponse. As noted earlier, stratified samples have higher levels of precision than simple random samples of the same sample size. However, a sampling frame must include information on the stratification variable(s) for all population elements to employ stratification. Multiphase sampling is an option when a sampling frame does not include such information.

Multiphase sampling may also be employed to reduce data collection costs if it took more time and effort to collect data on some variables than to collect data on other variables. In Phase 1, the easily accessible data may be collected from the entire sample. In Phase 2 and other subsequent phases, if desired or necessary, the data that take greater effort or expense to be collected are collected from a smaller subsample. Data collection costs are minimized.

Multiphase sampling may also be used to obtain information on nonrespondents.

Typically, it costs more to collect data on persons who initially refused to participate in a study and other nonrespondents than to collect data from the initial respondents. Such costs might be minimized by employing a multiphase sampling of nonrespondents.

Below are descriptions of several popular national surveys that are representative of multistage cluster sampling: the National Home and Hospice Care Survey (Research Note 5.8), the National Ambulatory Medical Care Survey (Research Note 5.9), the National Health and Nutrition Examination Survey (Research Note 5.10), the National Survey of Family Growth (Research Note 5.11), and the National Health Interview Survey (Research Note 5.12).

RESEARCH NOTE 5.8

Example of Two-Stage Cluster Sampling With Probability Proportional to Size: The National Home and Hospice Care Survey

The National Home and Hospice Care Survey (NHHCS) is a continuing series of surveys of home and hospice care agencies in the United States. Data have been collected about agencies that provide home and hospice care and about their current patients and discharges. Beginning in 1992, the survey was repeated in 1993, 1994, 1996, 1998, and 2000, and most recently in 2007. The 2007 NHHCS used a stratified two-stage probability sample design with probability proportional to size. The sample design included these two stages:

The first stage, carried out by the Centers for Disease Control and Prevention's National Center for Health Statistics (NCHS), was the selection of home health and hospice agencies from the sample frame of over 15,000 agencies, representing the universe of agencies providing home health care and hospice services in the United States. The primary sampling strata of agencies were defined by agency type and metropolitan statistical area (MSA) status. Within these sampling strata, agencies were sorted by census region, ownership, certification status, state, county, ZIP code, and size (number of employees). For the 2007 NHHCS, 1,545 agencies were systematically and randomly sampled with probability proportional to size. . . . The second stage of sample selection was completed by the interviewers during the agency interviews. The current home health patients and hospice discharges were randomly selected by a computer algorithm, based on a census list provided by each agency director or his/her designee. Up to 10 current home health patients were randomly selected per home health agency, up to 10 hospice discharges were randomly selected per hospice agency, and a combination of up to 10 current home health patients and hospice discharges were randomly selected per mixed agency.

Source: Centers for Disease Control and Prevention, 2007.

RESEARCH NOTE 5.9

Example of Multistage Cluster Sampling: The National Ambulatory Medical Care Survey

The National Ambulatory Medical Care Survey (NAMCS) is a national survey designed to collect data on the provision and use of ambulatory medical care services in the United States. The survey involves the sampling of visits to non-federally employed office-based physicians who are primarily engaged in direct patient care. The survey was conducted annually from 1973 to 1981, in 1985, and annually since 1989. It utilizes the following multistage sample design:

> The NAMCS utilizes a multistage probability design that involves probability samples of **primary sampling units** (PSUs), physician practices within PSUs, and patient visits within practices. The first-stage sample includes 112 PSUs. PSUs are geographic segments composed of counties, groups of counties, county equivalents (such as parishes or independent cities) or towns and townships (for some PSUs in New England) within the 50 States and the District of Columbia.
>
> The second stage consists of a probability sample of practicing physicians selected from the master files maintained by the American Medical Association and the American Osteopathic Association. Within each PSU, all eligible physicians were stratified by 15 groups: general and family practice, osteopathy, internal medicine, pediatrics, general surgery, obstetrics and gynecology, orthopedic surgery, cardiovascular diseases, dermatology, urology, psychiatry, neurology, ophthalmology, otolaryngology, and a residual category of all other specialties.

(Continued)

(Continued)

The final stage is the selection of patient visits within the annual practices of sample physicians. This involves two steps. First, the total physician sample is divided into 52 random subsamples of approximately equal size, and each subsample is randomly assigned to 1 of the 52 weeks in the survey year. Second, a systematic random sample of visits is selected by the physician during the reporting week. The sampling rate varies for this final step from a 100 percent sample for very small practices, to a 20 percent sample for very large practices as determined in a presurvey interview.

Source: Centers for Disease Control and Prevention, 2010.

RESEARCH NOTE 5.10

Example of Multistage Cluster Sampling: The National Health and Nutrition Examination Survey (NHANES)

The National Health and Nutrition Examination Survey (NHANES) is a series of studies designed to assess the health and nutritional status of adults and children in the United States. The series began in the early 1960s. Its sample design consists of the following stages:

Stage 1: Primary sampling units (PSUs) are selected. These are mostly single counties or, in a few cases, groups of contiguous counties with probability proportional to a measure of size (PPS).

Stage 2: The PSUs are divided up into segments (generally city blocks or their equivalent). As with each PSU, sample segments are selected with PPS.

Stage 3: Households within each segment are listed, and a sample is randomly drawn. In geographic areas where the proportion of age, ethnic, or income groups selected for oversampling is high, the probability of selection for those groups is greater than in other areas.

Stage 4: Individuals are chosen to participate in NHANES from a list of all persons residing in selected households. Individuals are drawn at random within designated age-sex-race/ethnicity screening subdomains. On average, 1.6 persons are selected per household.

Source: Centers for Disease Control and Prevention, 2010.

RESEARCH NOTE 5.11

Example of Multistage Cluster Sampling: The National Survey of Family Growth

Beginning in 1971, the National Survey of Family Growth (NSFG) obtains detailed information on factors affecting childbearing, marriage, and parenthood from a national probability sample of women and men 15 to 44 years of age. Its 2006 to 2010 sample design consists of the following steps:

The NSFG sample design consisted of *five stages* of selection to choose eligible sample persons. Women, teens 15–19 years of age, and black and Hispanic persons are selected at higher rates, yielding an oversample of such persons.

The 2006–2010 NSFG sample design started with the same national sample of PSUs used in the 2002 ("Cycle 6") NSFG national sample design. . . . Following the creation of the PSUs, a process called stratification was used to partition the PSUs into three major groups or strata: 28 large metropolitan areas, 290 other metropolitan areas, and 2,084 nonmetropolitan areas. The 28 large metropolitan areas are referred to as self-representing (SR) areas. SR areas are those that have such large populations that a national sample of the size used for continuous NSFG virtually required that they be represented. As such "certainty" selections, the sample from each of these areas represents only those areas. That is, the sample from these 28 PSUs represents only the population of that area. Hence, in the sampling literature, these types of units are referred to as representing only themselves, or "self-representing."

The remaining 2,374 PSUs are called non-self-representing (NSR) areas. A sample of the NSR PSUs was selected so that each sample PSU represented itself and other NSR PSUs of a similar nature. In order to make the representation more complete, the NSR PSUs were further grouped by geography and population size into 82 sets or strata. Each NSR stratum had two or more PSUs, and some strata had more than 100 PSUs. The number of PSUs in a stratum varied because the strata were created to have approximately equal 2000 Census population across the PSUs. . . In the second stage of selection, census blocks were stratified into four domains within each PSU, and the housing units on those blocks were listed. . . . The third stage of selection chooses housing units from the list of addresses available

(Continued)

(Continued)

in each sample segment. . . . The fourth stage of sampling is the selection of eligible persons within sample households. Interviewers visit housing units selected in the third stage, and when the housing unit is found to be occupied, attempt to list all persons living there. One eligible person is chosen randomly in every household containing one or more eligible persons. . . . The fifth stage in sample selection occurs in each 12-week "quarter" of interviewing: the selection of the "double sample" (because it is a sample of a sample). After 10 of the 12 weeks of data collection in each 12-week quarter, a set of selected housing units has not been successfully screened or, if successfully screened, the sampled person has not been interviewed yet.

Source: Lepkowski, Mosher, Davis, Groves, & Van Hoewyk, 2010, pp. 5–6. Reprinted with permission.

RESEARCH NOTE 5.12

Example of Multistage Cluster Sampling: Sample Design of the National Health Interview Survey

Since 1957, the National Health Interview Survey has been the principal source of health information on the U.S. population. In 2006, it utilizes a multistage area probability design:

The National Health Interview Survey is a cross-sectional household interview survey. Sampling and interviewing are continuous throughout each year. The sampling plan follows a multistage area probability design that permits the representative sampling of households and noninstitutional group quarters (e.g., college dormitories) . . . The first stage of the current sampling plan consists of a sample of 428 primary sampling units (PSUs) drawn from approximately 1,900 geographically defined PSUs that cover the 50 States and the District of Columbia. A PSU consists of a county, a small group of contiguous counties, or a metropolitan statistical area.

Within a PSU, two types of second-stage units are used: area segments and permit segments. Area segments are defined geographically and contain an expected eight, twelve, or sixteen addresses. Permit segments cover housing units built after the 2000 census. The permit segments are defined using updated lists of building permits issued in the PSU since 2000 and contain an expected four addresses. . . . As with the previous sample design, the NHIS sample is drawn from each State and the District of Columbia. Although the NHIS sample is too small to provide State level data with acceptable precision for each State, selected estimates for most states may be obtained by combining data years.

The total NHIS sample is subdivided into four separate panels, or subdesigns, such that each panel is a representative sample of the U.S. population. This design feature has a number of advantages, including flexibility for the total sample size. For example, the 2006 and 2007 NHIS samples both were reduced because of budget shortfalls; two panels were cut from the sample in the third calendar quarter of each year.

The households and noninstitutional group quarters selected for interview each week in the NHIS are a probability sample representative of the target population. With four sample panels and no sample cuts, the expected NHIS sample size (completed interviews) is approximately 35,000 households containing about 87,500 persons.

Source: Centers for Disease Control and Prevention, 2009.

GUIDELINES FOR CHOOSING TYPE OF PROBABILITY SAMPLE DESIGN

Considering the features of the sample designs described above, and their strengths and weaknesses, the following guidelines may be offered for using the following types of sample designs:

- Simple random sampling
- Stratified sampling
- Systematic sampling
- Cluster sampling
- Mixed sample designs

Guideline 5.1. *Simple random sampling.* Consider choosing simple random sampling if one has access to a complete and accurate sampling frame of the target population that is complete and accurate but does not contain auxiliary information that may be used for stratification purposes.

Guideline 5.2. *Stratified sampling*. Consider choosing stratified sampling if:

- It is possible to divide a population into two or more homogeneous strata and construct a sampling frame for each stratum.
- One has access to a sampling frame of the target population that is complete and accurate and contains auxiliary information that may be used for stratification purposes.
- Some subgroups of the population are vastly different from other subgroups.
- It is very important to minimize sampling error.
- There is a concern about underrepresenting smaller subgroups.
- The population is heterogeneous.
- There is a desire to use different selection methods for different strata.
- It is likely that answers to the research questions of a study are likely to be different for different subgroups.
- It is useful when each stratum needs to be reported separately.
- Comparative analysis of strata is desired.

Guideline 5.3. *Proportionate stratified sampling*. Consider choosing proportionate stratified sampling if subgoups of approximately the same size are to be investigated or compared.

Guideline 5.4. *Disproportionate stratified sampling*. Consider choosing disproportionate stratified sampling if:

- Subgoups of vastly different sizes are to be investigated or compared.
- It is important to include a large number of elements from a small segment of the population.
- One is primarily interested in key similarities and differences among strata.
- Some observations are limited or hard to obtain.
- It is important to make statistically valid statements about subgroups.
- Subgroups of the population have different variances for the variables of interest.
- Costs of data collection are different across population subgroups.

Guideline 5.5. *Systematic sampling*. Consider choosing systematic sampling if:

- It is difficult to identify items using a simple random sampling method.
- It is important to use a probability sampling procedure that can be easily implemented.
- A sampling frame is not available or impractical to prepare, but a stream of representative elements of the population is available.
- The listing of the population is essentially random or can be randomized.

Guideline 5.6. *Cluster sampling.* Consider choosing cluster sampling if:

- It is important to minimize data collection costs and there are substantial fixed costs associated with each data collection location.
- A sampling frame of individual population elements is not available but a sampling frame of clusters of elements is available.
- Travel costs can be substantially reduced.

Guideline 5.7. *Double sampling and multiphase sampling.* Consider double sampling and multiphase sampling if there is a need to identify and collect information from a subgroup of the population that is difficult to collect prior information on.

SUMMARY

There are four major choices of probability sample designs: simple random sampling, stratified sampling, systematic sampling, and cluster sampling. The strengths and weaknesses of the above sample designs are compared, and guidelines are presented for their selection.

Simple random sampling is a probability sampling procedure that gives every element in the target population and each possible sample of a given size, an equal chance of being selected. As with other probability sampling procedures, it tends to yield representative samples, and allows the use of inferential statistics to compute margin of errors. However, it tends to have larger sampling errors and less precision than stratified samples of the same sample size. If the target population is widely dispersed, data collection costs might be higher for simple random sampling than those for other probability sample designs, such as cluster sampling.

Stratified sampling is a probability sampling procedure in which the target population is first separated into mutually exclusive, homogeneous segments (strata), and then a simple random sample is selected from each segment (stratum). There are two major subtypes of stratified sampling: proportionate stratified sampling and disproportionate stratified sampling. In proportionate stratified sampling, the number of elements allocated to the various strata is proportional to the representation of the strata in the target population. This condition is not satisfied in disproportionate stratified sampling. In this type of stratification, unequal disproportionate allocation, equal disproportionate allocation, or optimum allocation may be applied.

Compared to unstratified sampling, stratified sampling (1) permits the estimation of population parameters and within-strata inferences and comparisons across strata; (2) tends to be more representative of a population; (3) takes advantage of knowledge the researcher has about the population; (4) possibly makes for lower data collection costs; and (5) permits the researcher to use different sampling procedures within the different strata. On the other hand, unlike unstratified sampling, stratified sampling requires prior information on the stratification variables and more complex analysis procedures.

Systematic sampling is a probability sampling procedure in which a random selection is made of the first element for the sample, and then subsequent elements are selected using a fixed or systematic interval until the desired sample size is reached. Generally, systematic sampling is easier, simpler, less time-consuming, and more economical than simple random sampling. If the ordering is unrelated to the study variables, but randomized, systematic sampling will yield results similar to simple random sampling. On the other hand, periodicity in the sampling frame is a constant concern in systematic sampling.

Cluster sampling is a probability sampling procedure in which elements of the population are randomly selected in naturally occurring aggregates or clusters. Subtypes of cluster sampling may be classified on the basis of the number of sampling events (single-stage cluster sampling, two-stage cluster sampling, and multistage cluster sampling) and on the basis of the proportional representation of the clusters in the sample (probability proportional to size and probability disproportional to size). Some of the strengths of cluster sampling when compared to simple random sampling include requiring less time, money, and labor; and permitting subsequent sampling and the estimation characteristics of clusters as well as the target population. However, cluster sampling when compared to simple random sampling may not be as representative of the population as a simple random sample of the same sample size, and variances of cluster sampling are likely to be higher than those for simple random sampling.

REVIEW QUESTIONS

1. What are the principal differences and similarities between the major categories of probability sampling: simple random sampling, systematic sampling, stratified sampling, and cluster sampling?

2. What are the principal differences and similarities among the subcategories of these major categories of probability sampling?

3. Provide examples of research questions for which the different types of stratified sampling would be a good fit.

4. Which strengths and weaknesses of the major types of probability sampling are the most critical?

5. What are the similarities and differences between stratified sampling and quota sampling?

6. What guidelines should be followed in establishing the strata for a stratified sample?

7. Compare and contrast procedures that have been used to select a respondent to be interviewed from those in a household who are eligible to participate in a study.

8. What is a sampling frame? Is it necessary to use a sampling frame in selecting a probability sample? Justify your answer.

9. What are the similarities and differences between cluster sampling and stratified sampling?

10. What are the similarities and differences between multistage sampling and multiphase sampling?

11. What do you consider to be the most critical guidelines for choosing among the various type of probability sampling? Why?

12. What guidelines should be considered in deciding between:

    a. Simple random sampling versus stratified sampling
    b. Element sampling versus cluster sampling
    c. Simple random sampling versus systematic sampling

13. A stratified sample of size $n = 60$ is to be taken from a population of size $N = 4000$, which consists of three strata of size $N_1 = 2000$, $N_2 = 1200$ and $N_3 = 800$. If the allocation is to be proportional, how large a sample must be taken from each stratum?

14. What alternative sample designs would you propose for the sample designs described in the research notes in this chapter?

15. Consider the sample designs described in the research notes in Chapter 4: Choosing the Type of Nonprobability Sample Design. What alternative probability sample designs may be used to achieve the purposes of the study? Compare and contrast the advantages and limitations of the probability sample designs you propose with the nonprobability sample designs described in the research notes in Chapter 4.

16. What procedures would you use to select a probability sample of homeless people and why? Once you have answered these questions, consider Burnam and Koegel's "Methodology for Obtaining a Representative Sample of Homeless Persons: The Los Angeles Skid Row Study" (1988).

KEY TERMS

Define and give examples of the following concepts:

cluster sampling	equal probability selection method
disproportionate allocation	multistage cluster sampling

optimum allocation

primary sampling unit

proportionate allocation

secondary sampling unit

simple random sampling

single-stage cluster sampling

systematic sampling

two-stage cluster sampling

REFERENCES FOR FURTHER STUDY

Binson, D., Canchola, J. A., & Catania, J. A. (2000). Random selection in a national telephone survey: A comparison of the Kish, next birthday, and last-birthday methods. *Journal of Official Statistics, 16,* 53–59.

Burnam, M. A., & Koegel, P. (1988). Methodology for obtaining a representative sample of homeless persons: The Los Angeles Skid Row Study. *Evaluation Review, 12,* 117–152.

Bryant, B. E. (1975). Respondent selection in a time of changing household composition. *Journal of Marketing Research, 12,* 129–135.

Czaja, R., Blair, J., & Sebestik, J. P. (1982). Respondent selection in a telephone survey: A comparison of three techniques. *Journal of Marketing Research, 19,* 381–385.

Hagan, D. E., & Collier, C. M. (1983). Must respondent selection procedures for telephone surveys be invasive? *Public Opinion Quarterly, 47,* 547–556.

Kish, L. (1949). A procedure for objective respondent selection within the household. *Journal of the American Statistical Association, 44,* 380–387.

Kish, L. (1965). *Survey sampling.* New York: Wiley & Sons.

Lavrakas, P. J., Bauman, S. L., & Merkle, D. M. (1993). The last-birthday method and within-unit coverage problems. *Proceedings of the section on survey research methods, American Statistical Association,* 1107–1112.

Levy, P. S., & Lemeshow, S. (2008). *Sampling of populations: Methods and applications.* New York: Wiley & Sons.

Salmon, C. T., & Nichols, J. S. (1983). The next-birthday method of respondent selection. *Public Opinion Quarterly, 47,* 270–276.

Scheaffer, R. L., Mendenhall, W., & Ott, L. (2006). *Elementary survey sampling.* Belmont, CA: Duxbury Press.

Sudman, S. (1976). *Applied sampling.* New York: Academic Press.

Thompson, S. K. (2002). *Sampling.* New York: Wiley & Sons.

Troldahl, V. C., & Carter, R. E. (1964). Random selection of respondents within households in phone surveys. *Journal of Marketing Surveys, 1,* 71–76.

CHAPTER 6

SAMPLING CHARACTERIZED BY THE NATURE OF THE SAMPLING UNIT AND MIXED-METHODS SAMPLE DESIGNS

What you will learn in this chapter:

- Sampling procedures distinguished by the nature of their sampling unit:
  - Telephone-based sampling
  - Web-based sampling
  - Address-based sampling
  - Time-based sampling
  - Space-based sampling
- Subtypes, strengths and weaknesses, and factors associated with trends in the use of the above sampling procedures
- Typology of types of mixed-methods sample designs
- The strengths and weaknesses of mixed-methods sampling

INTRODUCTION

Sampling procedures may be classified not only according to their operational procedures, as what has been done up to this point, but also according to the nature of the unit that is sampled. Although the unit of analysis of a study is population-based, units of the population may not be available or practical to be used as sampling units. As a result, alternative sampling units must be used. A number of sampling procedures characterized by the nature of the sampling unit have been developed. These include telephone-based sampling, web-based sampling, address-based sampling, time-based sampling, and space-based sampling.

These sampling procedures are distinguished by the nature of the sampling unit that is used. Telephone-based sampling utilizes telephone numbers as sampling units. Web-based sampling utilizes elements of electronic communications as sampling units. Address-based sampling utilizes addresses as sampling units. Time-based sampling utilizes units of time as the sampling unit. Space-based sampling utilizes space as sampling units. Venue-based sampling utilizes combinations of time and space as sampling units. The use of some of these sampling procedures has been greatly influenced by changes in technology, lifestyles, the legal environment, and nonresponse rates.

In addition to presenting descriptions of sample designs distinguished by the nature of the sample unit that is used, description of mixed-methods sample designs are presented in this chapter. Instead of implementing a single-method sample design, a researcher may combine multiple types of sample designs creating mixed-methods sample designs. Mixed-methods research designs are typically characterized by the mixing of qualitative and quantitative research designs. In this text, focusing on sampling, mixed-methods sample designs are based on the mixing of nonprobability sample designs and probability sample designs. Within-methods designs combine either multiple nonprobability sample designs or multiple probability sample designs. Cross-methods designs combine nonprobability sample designs and probability sample designs. These designs and their subtypes are also described in this chapter.

SAMPLING CHARACTERIZED BY THE NATURE OF THE SAMPLING UNIT

In efforts to minimize costs and total error in sampling, throughout the years researchers have made adjustments in their sampling procedures responding to changes in technology, lifestyles, the legal environment, and nonresponse rates. This may be illustrated as follows:

Changes in Technology + Changes in Lifestyles + Changes in Legal Environments + Increasing Nonresponse Rates + Need to Minimize Total Costs and Total Error = Changes in Research Operations

To a certain extent, all aspects of research operations have been impacted, including sampling, data collection, and data analysis. Over the last 50 years, the changes in technology and software that have impacted sampling choices include:

- Changes in communication technology including modems, answering machines, fax machines, PDAs, cell phones, etc.

- Changes in computer technology including the storage capacity, speed, and size of computers
- Development in geographic information systems (GIS) enhancing mapping capabilities

Over the last 50 years, major segments of the population have experienced lifestyle changes. The technological changes cited above have influenced life style changes, which in turn have impacted sampling. Some of these lifestyle changes include:

- Movements from no phone, to landline phone, to cell phone and landline phone, and to cell phone and no landline phone. For younger persons, this pattern is much stronger than that for older persons, and there is now a pattern of change from using cell phones to emailing, texting, and web-based social networking.
- Surfing the Internet for enjoyment, work, and personal needs

Critical changes in the legal environment that have impacted sampling procedures include:

- The Telephone Consumer Protection Act of 1991. Although surveys are not included in the restrictions imposed by the Do Not Call Registry, researchers are prevented from using autodialers in making calls to cell phones. In the event of a violation, individuals are entitled to collect damages directly for $500 to $1,500 for each violation.
- The Paper Reduction Act of 1995. This act requires approval from the Office of Management and Budget of data collection instruments used in federally sponsored data collection efforts that involve the collection of data from more than nine individuals. This increased the time for executing surveys, and impacted the sample size in some projects.

Since the last few decades unit nonresponse rates in survey research have been increasing (Groves et al. 2009). Decreasing nonresponse rates combined with the above factors have motivated researchers to explore different research modes to effectively achieve their research objectives. Over the last 50 years, the emphasis in the use of various research modes changed from population-based sampling, to telephone-based sampling, and then to web-based sampling and address-based sampling. This pattern is illustrated in Figure 6.1.

Figure 6.1 Changing Emphasis in Sampling Modes Over Past 50 Years

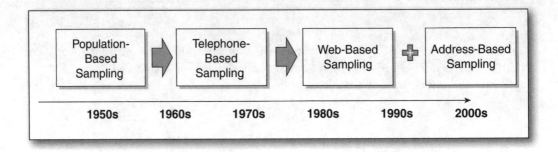

TELEPHONE-BASED SAMPLING

What Is Telephone-Based Sampling?

Telephone-based sampling consists of sampling procedures that utilize telephone numbers as sampling units. As the costs of personal interview surveys increased, and the percentage of households with telephones increased, telephone surveys supplanted personal interview surveys as the survey mode of choice. At the time of the failure of the *Literary Digest* in 1936, only 36% of the households in the United States had a telephone. Twenty-four years later, this percentage was around 80%, and by the 1970s the percentage was over 90%. Since then telephone usage has leveled off around 95%. By the 1980s telephone surveys were the dominant survey methodology.

Some of the factors making for this dominance include:

- Increase in telephone coverage minimizing the effect of noncoverage of persons without a telephone
- Decline in response rates in personal interview surveys
- Cost and effort required to conduct personal interview surveys
- Higher response rates and lower costs than personal interview surveys
- Technological advances in telecommunications such as automatic dialing and universal direct long distance dialing
- Separation of the listings of the telephone numbers of residential and nonresidential telephone numbers
- Availability of telephone directories in an electronic format
- Cleaning, updating, and availability of sampling frames of telephone numbers by commercial companies

- Development of computer-assisted telephone interviewing, which made for a reduction in interviewer effort, coding and data entry costs, and the time between data collection and report writing; and an increase in capacity for quality control and error checking, the use of complex questions utilizing branching, and automatic data entry

Yet, telephone-based sampling has major problems. At the top of the list is coverage bias. Although the percentage of households with a telephone is extremely high, there are yet differences between households that have telephones and households that do not have telephones. Nontelephone households tend to be more likely to:

- Live in the South
- Live in rural areas
- Have members who are African American
- Have low incomes
- Have members who have low levels of education
- Have either one household member or six or more persons
- Have children under 14
- Have unemployed members

What Are the Subtypes of Telephone-Based Sampling?

There are two major types of telephone-based sampling: list-based sampling and random digit dialing (RDD). These sampling procedures are described below.

List-Based Sampling

What is list-based sampling? List-based sampling is a set of sampling procedures that involves the sampling from a listing of telephone numbers of the target population. Examples include the selection of telephone numbers from telephone directories, city directories, lists of employees, lists of customers, lists generated by commercial firms, etc.

What are the subtypes of list-based sampling? There are three major subtypes of list-based sampling of telephone numbers: simple random sampling of the listings, systematic sample of the listings, and add-a-digit procedures. In selecting a simple random sampling of the listings, pages are randomly selected, and then telephone numbers are chosen randomly from the pages that are selected. Alternatively, one may proceed as follows:

1. Define the target population.

2. Identify a listing of telephone numbers of the target population or develop a new one.

3. Evaluate the listing for coverage bias (undercoverage bias, overcoverage bias, multiple coverage bias, and clustering bias), and make adjustments where necessary.

4. Assign a unique number to each element in the frame.

5. Determine the sample size.

6. Randomly select the targeted number of population elements.

The key strength of this procedure is that it is relatively easy to use. However, it has serious weaknesses. Most important is the problem of coverage bias. Moreover, the procedure is tedious and impractical for large target populations. In some areas up to 50% of the working telephone numbers are unlisted. Having an unlisted telephone number is directly related to having recently moved, being unmarried, renting instead of owning one's home, being Black, and living in urban areas, and inversely related to age and income (Blankenship, 1977a; Brunner & Brunner, 1971; Glasser & Metzger, 1975; Leuthold & Scheele, 1971; Rich, 1977; Roslow & Roslow, 1972). Persons with these characteristics are likely to be underrepresented in studies utilizing this sampling procedure.

A *systematic sampling* may be drawn from the directory listings. This sampling procedure may proceed as follows:

1. Define the target population.

2. Determine the desired sample size (n).

3. Identify a listing of telephone numbers of the target population.

4. Evaluate the listing of telephone numbers for undercoverage, overcoverage, multiple coverage, clustering, and periodicity, and make adjustments where necessary and possible.

5. Determine the number of elements in the listing (N). Often this number is estimated for large telephone directories.

6. Calculate the sampling interval, (i), by dividing the number of elements in the listing (N) by the targeted sample size (n).

7. Randomly select a number, r, from "1" through i.

8. Select for the sample, r, $r + i$, $r + 2i$, $r + 3i$, and so forth, until the frame is exhausted.

Similar to simple random sampling, a strength of systematic sampling is that it is relatively easy to use; however, unlike simple random sampling, it ensures that the entire range of the list will be covered. It has the same coverage bias issues as simple random sampling and, although not likely, it also has the possibility of having a problem of periodicity.

A number of add-a-digit procedures have been advanced since the 1970s to minimize the coverage bias in using telephone directories. These procedures add an additional step to the basic simple random procedure: Instead of dialing the number selected from the directory, a fixed or random number (i.e., one or two digits) is added to the number. The resulting number is then dialed. If a residence is not reached, another digit is added. This process continues until a residence is reached, or a stopping rule is satisfied (e.g., 10 consecutive unsuccessfully attempts in reaching a residence). This procedure is often referred to as the "plus-one" method and the "plus digit" method. If the digits that are added are randomly determined, this procedure becomes a form of list-assisted random digit dialing. A number of applications of this procedure have been proposed (e.g., Forsman & Danielsson, 1997; Ghosh, 1984; Potter, McNeill, Williams, & Waitman, 1991).

Add-a-digit procedures correct the coverage bias due to unlisted telephone numbers and newly acquired telephone numbers; however, they do not correct for households with no telephone and cell phone–only households.

Random Digit Dialing

What is random digit dialing? Random digit dialing is a set of procedures used to randomly generate telephone numbers. Random digit dialing was introduced by Cooper (1964) in the 1960s. The ideas of Cooper were further developed by Eastlack and Assael (1966), Glasser and Metzger (1972), and Mitofsky and Waksberg, as described by Waksberg (1978).

RDD procedures are based on the structure of telephone numbers. In the United States, telephone numbers have three basic components: a three-digit area code, a three-digit prefix or exchange, and a four-digit suffix. Area codes are assigned on a state basis. However, recently telephone numbers are portable, and a person may be able to keep a current telephone number after moving to another state. Not all theoretically possible exchanges are used as prefixes. The geographical area covered by an exchange is set by public service commissions, and generally do not correspond to political districts. The four-digit suffix may be seen as composed of 10 sets of 1,000 blocks of telephone numbers, ranging from 0000 through 9999. Each 1,000 block of numbers are composed of 100 banks of numbers ranging from the 00*xx* bank through the 99*xx* bank. Within the exchanges, telephone numbers tend to be assigned in clusters rather than randomly determined. The locations of the clusters are not known. The 100-banks vary in their percentage of residential numbers.

What are the subtypes of RDD? There are three main RDD approaches: a basic approach involving the random generation of telephone numbers, the Mitofsky-Waksberg RDD approach, and list-assisted RDD approaches. Basic RDD sampling procedures involve the random generation of suffixes for working six-digit area code and exchange combinations that serve the geographical area of the target population. Steps that may be used in carrying out basic RDD sampling are:

1. Utilizing information from the telephone company, identify telephone exchanges that are dedicated to nonresidential use. These should be excluded from the following steps.

2. Randomly generate suffixes for each six-digit area code/prefix combination utilized in the geographical area of the target population.

3. Dial the numbers generated.

4. Repeat the above steps until the targeted sample size is obtained.

As for the add-a-digit approaches, this procedure corrects the bias due to unlisted telephone numbers and newly acquired telephone numbers that are associated with list-based sampling. However, it does not correct for households with no telephone and cell phone–only households. A major weakness is that it creates many nonworking numbers. Only about 20% of all possible numbers are assigned. Much time and effort are involved in dialing these numbers. As interviewers dial and dial telephone numbers without contacting residential households, they get discouraged and have low morale. This problem is more severe in rural areas than in urban areas. In urban areas when a nonworking number is dialed, a message alerts the caller that a nonworking number was dialed. Such a message does not alert callers in rural areas. As a result, screening calls is much more expensive in rural areas.

In 1970, Mitofsky proposed a two-stage RDD sampling method to compensate for the inefficiency of basic RDD methods. Mitofsky was later joined by Waksberg in enhancing the procedures and placing them within a theoretical framework (Waksberg, 1978). The procedures that they worked out became the dominant sampling method for telephone surveys in the 1980s. Steps in the Mitofsky-Waksberg RDD approach include:

Stage 1

1. Randomly select the first two digits of the suffix of a six-digit area code/prefix combination used in the geographical area of the target population.

2. Add two random digits to the eight digits created in the first step.

3. Dial the number generated to determine whether it is a residential telephone number.

4. If the number generated is nonresidential, the bank is dropped and is not used in Stage 2. If the number generated is residential, the bank is used in Stage 2.

5. The above steps are continued until a set number of banks have been selected for Stage 2.

Stage 2

1. For the banks selected in Stage 1, repeat Step 2 of Stage 1, randomly generating additional numbers from the banks.

2. Dial the numbers generated in Step 1, and repeat the process until the targeted sample size is obtained.

As do other RDD approaches, the Mitofsky-Waksberg approach corrects the bias due to unlisted telephone numbers and newly acquired telephone numbers that are associated with list-based sampling. Moreover, by taking advantage of the clustering together of residential telephone numbers within 100-banks, the number of nonresidential calls that are made is reduced saving costs and interviewer efforts. However, the effect of the clustering is an increase in variance when compared to simple random sampling. It is possible that some banks comprised of residential numbers would be excluded, and other banks with only a few residential numbers included in Stage 2. Moreover, this process is tedious to carry out manually. A number of modifications have been proposed for the procedure (e.g., Alexander, 1988; Brick & Waksberg, 1991; Burke, Morganstein & Schwartz, 1981; Casady & Lepkowski, 1991; Casady & Lepkowski, 1993; Cummings, 1979; Hogue & Chapman, 1984; Lepkowski & Groves, 1986; Mason & Immerman, 1998; Palit, 1983; Palit & Blair, 1986; Tucker, Casady, & Lepkowski, 1993).

List-assisted RDD sampling represents a set of sampling procedures that involve a combination of list-based sampling and RDD sampling. Using electronic files of working area code/exchange combinations and electronic files of residential telephone directories listings, 100-banks of telephone numbers are classified according to the presence (e.g., zero-listed banks and 1+ listed banks) or a specific percentage of residential listings or a particular percentage of residential listing (e.g., 5%,10%, or 20%). Sampling procedures that are used may be limited to low-density banks that have no listed numbers, high-density banks that contain at least one listing, and a combination of low-density and high-density banks. Using a high-density bank increases selection bias and calling efficiency. By the 1990s, list-assisted sampling procedures were widely used.

Commercial companies using data from telephone directories, automobile registration files, zip code databases, and block statistics from the U.S. Bureau of the Census have created databases associated with different banks of telephone numbers. Sorting by telephone number, commercial companies are able to screen out zero-listed 100-banks of telephone numbers. This improves the likelihood that selected banks will have working residential telephone numbers, thereby reducing survey costs and effort.

List-assisted RDD is more efficient in sampling households than traditional RDD methods. The likelihood of selecting banks of telephone numbers with no residential numbers is minimized. Yet, this procedure does not resolve the problems of coverage bias due to nontelephone households and cellphone–only households. Earlier research indicated that the nonuse of zero-banks excludes only a small percentage of households (Brick, Waksberg, Kulp, & Starer, 1995). However, more recently changes in the structure of the U.S. telecommunications industry and an increasing number of residential exchanges have had a large impact on the clustering of residential telephone numbers. Recent research indicates that the selection of zero-banks excludes up to 20% of the households within a target population (Fahimi, Kulp, & Brick, 2009). Zero-banks tend to comprise a higher proportion of rural residents and persons who have recently moved. Several modifications and applications have been proposed for this sampling procedure (Brick et al., 1995; Casady & Lepkowski, 1993; Norris & Paton, 1991).

What Are the Strengths and
Weaknesses of Telephone-Based Sampling?

Researchers utilizing telephone-based sampling continue to deal with the trade-off of coverage bias versus costs and effort. Its principal strengths continue to be the widespread use of telephones and the various RDD approaches that have been developed to reduce sampling time and effort in sampling without affecting probability nature of the sampling.

There are yet significant weaknesses in telephone-based sampling. Decreasing response rates and increasing numbers of cell phone–only households aggravate these problems. Moreover, changes relating to telephone numbers themselves have had a ripple effect of increasing the costs and effort in conducting telephone surveys. Such changes include:

- Increase in the number of area codes
- Reduction in the "clustering" of residential numbers
- Increase in the number of unlisted telephone numbers
- Increase in the number of households with multiple telephones
- Decrease in the coverage rates and response rates of telephone surveys, which has led to an increased use of dual frames and multiple frames, increasing costs and effort involved; and mixed-methods designs combining telephone surveys with other modes, including electronic surveys utilizing web-based sampling procedures. Web-based sampling procedures are described below.

Moreover, telephone survey researchers face a number of challenges, including:

- One individual may have more than one phone, and one phone may be used by more than one individual.
- Caller ID, answering machines, modems, and fax machines add to nonresponse and data collection costs. An increasing use of call screening by respondents makes it more difficult to make contact.
- The Do Not Call registry has made the public more resistant to telephone surveys, although research telephone surveys are exempt from the regulation.
- The portability of telephone numbers has led to greater difficulty in linking the telephone number to a geographical area.
- The required costs, time, and effort to reach hidden and rare populations may be high.
- Limited calling and contact period for reaching respondents, 6:00 p.m. to 9:00 p.m., may restrict researchers.

- The growing usage of cell phones creates special challenges, such as the following:

  o The Telephone Consumer Protection Act of 1991 prohibits the calling of cell phones with automatic dialing systems. Numbers must be hand-dialed, adding to the cost of a study. As a result, cell phones are not included in telephone survey sampling frames. In order to avoid calls to cell phones, sampling frames of phone numbers must be cleaned to remove cell phone numbers, and calls made from the list must be screened to determine if a cell phone was reached. Cell phone–only and "cell-mostly" individuals tend to be younger and more mobile than the general public, renters, and living with unrelated individuals.

  o Landline phone numbers that have been ported to cell phones create special problems for call centers since automated dialing is employed. It is not possible to distinguish these ported numbers, and legally, automated dialing cannot be used in calling cell phones.

  o Safety issues such as the person called may be driving or in some other situation in which it would be unsafe to talk on the phone.

  o There may be a cost to the cell phone respondent that should be compensated.

  o The cost of completing a cell phone interview is twice the cost of completing a landline interview.

  o Although some listings of landline telephones may include auxiliary information on the elements in the frame, auxiliary information is rarely included in cell phone sampling frame. This limits the ability to utilize stratified sampling and to determine the nonresponse bias by comparing respondents to nonrespondents.

  o Cell phone calls are likely to encounter a higher percentage of young persons and persons with language barriers.

  o Cell phone numbers are not assigned on a geographical basis, which also limits the ability to utilize stratified sampling and mapping geographical data to the calls that are made.

  o Extensive screening is necessary as one cannot identify business numbers, prepaid phone cards or disposable phones, or the geographical area of the phone being called.

  o Whereas landline phones tend to be used by all household members, cell phones tend to be used by only one person in the household.

  o The use of dual sampling frames, a landline frame and a cell phone frame, may minimize some of the above issues. The frames must be screened for duplicates, and duplicates dropped.

The following research notes provide examples of telephone-based sampling. Research Note 6.1 describes the sampling procedures used in in the National Black Election Study, a series of telephone surveys of the U.S. Black population that began in 1984. Research Note 6.2 describes the sampling procedures used in the Behavioral Risk Factor Surveillance System, the largest health survey in the world initiated by the Centers for Disease Control and Prevention in 1984. Research Note 6.3 describes a dual frame telephone-based sample design used in a study of the political participation of Asian Americans.

RESEARCH NOTE 6.1

Example of RDD Sampling: Sample Design of the 1984 National Black Election Study

As part of his analysis of problems and progress in the measurement of Black public opinion, Smith (1987) described the RDD sample design of the 1984 National Black Election Study (NBES) conducted by the Institute for Social Research (ISR) at the University of Michigan. He described this sample design as follows:

In the NBES, the sample for the preelection wave was obtained by using a disproportionate random-digit dialing (RDD) design. ISR learned from a pilot study that, given an equal probability design (where every phone in the United States has the same chance of being selected), the eligibility of working numbers for black households would be too low and thus too costly (Inglis et al., 1985). Instead, the NBES assigned all telephone exchanges in the United States to one of three "black-household density" strata. These strata were defined as follows:

1. High black density—exchanges in all large SMSAs with a black population of 15 % or more.

2. Medium black density—exchanges in smaller SMSAs, and in all of Alabama, Florida, Georgia, Louisiana, Mississippi, North Carolina, South Carolina, and Virginia.

3. Low black density—all remaining exchanges.

The selection rate for the high density stratum was three times that for the low-density stratum, while the rate for the medium-density stratum was twice that of the low-density stratum.

Source: Smith, 1987, p. 452. Reprinted with permission.

RESEARCH NOTE 6.2

Example of List-Assisted RDD Sampling: Sample Design of the Behavioral Risk Factor Surveillance System

The Behavioral Risk Factor Surveillance System (BRFSS) was initiated in 1984 by the Centers for Disease Control and Prevention (CDC) as a state-based system for collecting prevalence data on risk behaviors and preventive health practices that affect health status in the United States (Centers for Disease Control and Prevention, 2006). More than 350,000 adults are interviewed each year, making the BRFSS the largest telephone health survey in the world. The BRFSS utilizes the following list-assisted RDD sample design procedures:

> With DSS [disproportionate stratified random sampling], as implemented in the BRFSS beginning in 2003, telephone numbers are drawn from two strata (lists) that are based on the presumed density of known telephone household numbers. In this design, telephone numbers are classified into strata that are either high density (listed 1+ block telephone numbers) or medium density (not listed 1+ block telephone numbers) to yield residential telephone numbers. Telephone numbers in the high density stratum are sampled at the highest rate.

Source: Centers for Disease Control & Prevention, 2006.

RESEARCH NOTE 6.3

Example of a Dual Frame Telephone-Based Sampling Design: Study of Political Participation of Asian Americans

Rim (2009) used a dual frame approach consisting of random digit dialing and listed surname frames in their study of political participation of Asian Americans. This study targeted Asian Americans living in Chicago, Los Angeles, New York, Honolulu, and San Francisco where 40% of the Asian Americans in the United States reside. They described their sampling procedures as follows:

> This study interviewed a total of 1,218 respondents by phone between November 16, 2000, and January 28, 2001. Within the sample, 308 Chinese (25%), 266 Filipino (22%), 198 Japanese (16%), 168 Korean (14%), 141 South Asians (12%; Indian/Pakistani), and 137 Vietnamese (11%) were interviewed, and 824 respondents (68%) were U.S. citizens.

The representativeness of the sample may be reduced because of the hybrid nature of the sampling design. With the exception of New York and Chicago, where only the listed surname approach was used, a dual-frame approach consisting of both random-digit dialing (RDD) at targeted Asian zip-code densities and listed surname frames was used to draw samples from Los Angeles, Honolulu, and San Francisco. Households with unlisted telephone numbers or respondents who do not bear Asian surnames in the targeted areas were excluded from the sample. Only adults who self-identified as Chinese, Filipino, Japanese, Korean, South Asian (Indian/Pakistani), or Vietnamese were included in the sample. Multilingual surveys were not available to Filipino, South Asian, and Japanese respondents. Finally, within each MSA, selection probability for each ethnic group in the sample was selected to approximate the size of the ethnic population of Asian Americans in the 1990 Census.

Source: Rim, 2009, p. 575. Reprinted with permission.

WEB-BASED SAMPLING

What Is Web-Based Sampling?

Web-based sampling is a set of sampling procedures that utilize email addresses, web site visits, and recruited users of the Internet as sampling units. As telephone surveys, web surveys provided an alternative to the high costs of personal interview surveys. Since its introduction in the mid-1980s, web-based surveys have increased dramatically. Today, probably more than 40% of all surveys are web-based.

What Are the Subtypes of Web-Based Sampling?

A number of typologies of web-based sampling have been proposed (see, e.g., see Couper, 2000; Fricker, 2008; Srivenkartaramana & Saisree, 2009). Building on these typologies, web-based sampling may be classified into three categories: list-based sampling, sampling of website visits, and sampling from recruited panels (see Figure 6.2). Each of these categories includes nonprobability sampling procedures and probability sampling procedures. They are described below.

Figure 6.2 Major Types of Web-Based Sampling

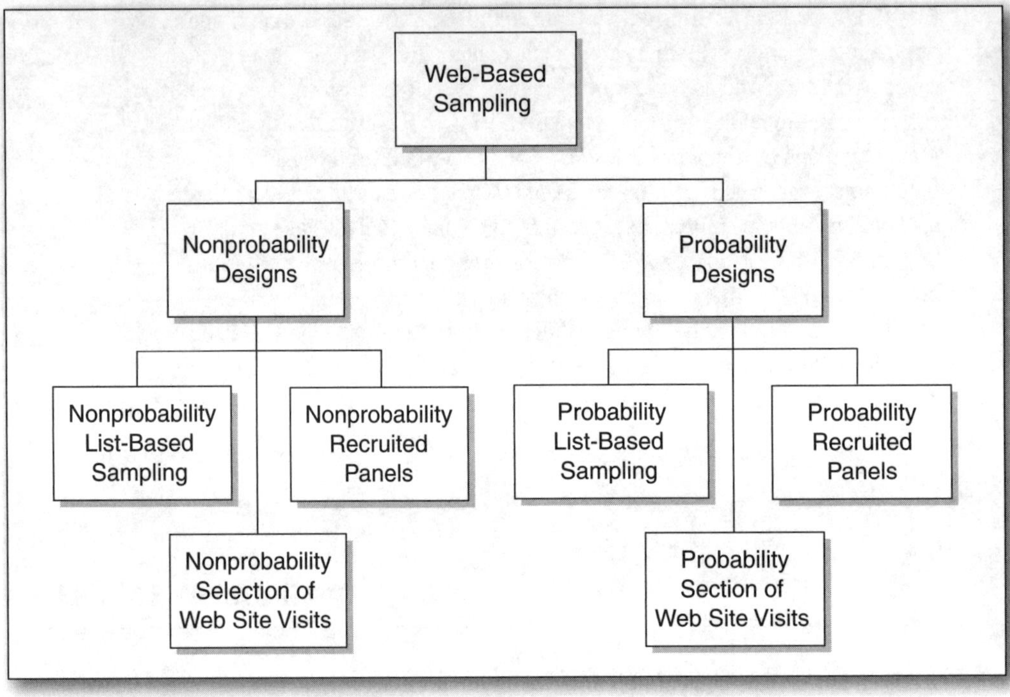

```
                        Web-Based
                        Sampling
              ┌──────────────┴──────────────┐
       Nonprobability                  Probability
         Designs                        Designs
      ┌──────┴──────┐              ┌───────┴───────┐
Nonprobability  Nonprobability  Probability   Probability
 List-Based      Recruited      List-Based     Recruited
 Sampling         Panels        Sampling        Panels

 Nonprobability                 Probability
  Selection of                   Section of
 Web Site Visits                Web Site Visits
```

List-Based Sampling

Much of web-based sampling involves list-based sampling. A sampling frame of postal addresses or email addresses is generated, and addresses are selected from the frame using either nonprobability or probability procedures. Elements selected are sent an invitation to go online and participate in the survey. Typically, the list is a listing of email addresses. The listing may be a basic listing of email addresses, with little additional information, or a listing that includes a great deal of auxiliary information that may be used for targeting specifically subsets of the target population and stratification. Lists may be created from administrative records; registration forms completed by visitors to web sites; employees' records; databases of customers; lists of suppliers; membership lists of discussion groups, newsgroups, and interest groups; and requests for email addresses via other survey modes. This type of sampling is used in surveys in which an email is sent with an embedded questionnaire, an attached questionnaire, or an invitation and link to a questionnaire on a web site. A probability sample will be generated if the listings do not have significant coverage bias, and a probability selection procedure is used to select elements from the lists. For a probability selection, every element in the target population must be given a chance to be selected. A nonprobability sample would be generated if the list has significant coverage bias, and elements are selected in such a way that every element in the target population would not have a chance to be selected. Email addresses may be haphazardly "harvested" and invitations sent to those at the top of the list.

Sampling of Web Site Visits

A listing of up-to-date email addresses is not always available or practical to be constructed for use in conducting web-based surveys. An alternative sampling procedure to list-based sampling is the sampling of web site visits. A web site may have a banner inviting visitors to complete a questionnaire, or a pop-up invitation may appear providing the invitation. The extent to which the web site visitors are representative of the target population and whether every visitor has a chance to be selected determine whether the procedure produces a nonprobability sample or a probability sample. Respondents accepting an open invitation posted on a web site to participate in a survey produces an opt-in, volunteer sample. A quota sample would be generated if "demographic balancing" is used by not accepting additional respondents once quotas set for specific demographic categories have been obtained. On the other hand, selecting web site visitors using simple random sampling or systematic sampling produces a probability sample.

Sampling From Recruited Panels

Panels of potential participants in future research projects may be compiled and respondents selected from these panels depending on the objectives of the research project. How a person becomes part of a panel and how a person is selected from the panel determines whether the ultimate sample is a nonprobability sample or a probability sample. The issue is whether every member of the target population has a chance to be selected in the sample. Generating frames via volunteer sampling and using quota sampling or demographic balancing to select a sample from the frame produces a nonprobability sample. On the other hand, generating the panel via probability sampling, such as random digit dialing, and selecting elements from the frame using stratified sampling generates a probability sample.

What Are the Strengths and Weaknesses of Web-Based Sampling?

The increase in the use of web-based surveys is partially due to their strengths when compared to personal interview surveys and other survey research modes. Strengths of web-based sampling and other aspects of web-based surveys include:

- Lower costs. The following costs of personal interview surveys either do not exist or are minimal with web-based surveys: printing of data collection instruments and coding forms; design and printing of training materials for interviewers, coders, and data entry personnel; postal costs; travel expenses for interviewers and payment of interviewers, coders, and data entry personnel. On the other hand, if the target population is a hidden or rare population with little online communications, the costs of reaching this population via web-based sampling may be higher than the costs of other sampling modes.
- Less time. Unlike personal interview surveys, travel time for interviewers is not relevant for web-based surveys. Moreover, unless computer-assisted data collection is used in the other modes, web-based surveys will take less time due to the lack of the need for data entry. Qualitative data may be easily converted to Microsoft Word files. The time between launching a survey and report writing is less for web-based surveys than other types of surveys.
- Wider geographical range. The target geographical area of a web survey can be global just as easy as it can be local. Global surveys may be done for as much as the same costs for local surveys.
- Greater accessibility of certain populations. Some populations may be more accessible via web-based surveys due to their memberships in newsgroups, listservs, etc.
- Larger sample size. Depending on the target population and considering the global range of the Internet, a web-based survey potentially can reach much larger numbers of potential respondents than other survey research modes.
- Wider range of design features of data collection instruments. Depending on the capabilities of the software employed, design features such as color, graphics, multimedia, randomized ordering of items, automatic branching with complex skip patterns, and other features can be incorporated into web-based survey instruments. Moreover, respondents may be given the option to suspend completing the data collection instrument and resume at a later time according to their schedule.

In spite of the above strengths, web-based sampling and web-based surveys yet have serious weaknesses that affect their usefulness for certain types of research. These weaknesses include:

- Greater coverage bias. Web-based surveys are likely to have a great deal more coverage bias than other survey modes. This is especially the case if the general population is the target population of a study. Web-based surveys are somewhat limited to persons who have access to both email and the web. Everyone in the general population does not have an email address, and there is no complete listing of everyone who does. Although decreasing, there is still a "digital divide" in the general population. On the other hand, a good sampling frame of the target population may be available if the target population of a study is a "closed organization," such as customers of a business; employees of an organization; students, faculty, or staff of a university; or members of a voluntary organization. Older persons, persons with no college education, and minorities are less likely than others to be Internet users or have email accounts. However, even if a person is Internet competent, there are still coverage problems due to persons changing their email addresses and having multiple email addresses. Moreover, it is noted that although the elderly are less likely than those younger to use the Internet, they are more likely to participate in web surveys, causing their overrepresentation in the sample.

- Potential hardware compatibility issues. Computers vary greatly in terms of processing power, screen configurations, and connection speeds. Some respondents either may not be able to respond at all to web surveys written with advanced design features, or their computer system may take a long time to process the features of the software. Frustration with the slow pace may encourage nonresponse.

- Problems calculating response rates. Often a web-based survey would not have a defined sampling frame, and as a result problems may exist in calculating the response rate.

- Lower response rates. Response rates are generally lower for web surveys than other survey modes. Techniques used to increase response rates for other survey modes may not be relevant to web surveys (e.g., matching interviewer-respondent characteristics, personalization, and type of stamp). On the other hand, the response rate of web surveys are likely to be affected by such factors as concern about viruses and spam, filtering software blocking pop-ups, respondents' computer capabilities, and computer-use patterns. As a result of their meta-analysis of electronic surveys, Cook, Heath, and Thompson (2000) indicated that factors likely to increase the response rate in these types of surveys include personalized correspondence, attention to the salience of the issues, multiple contacts, and prenotification.

- Incentives. It is more difficult to use incentives in web-based surveys than in other survey modes. A typical incentive that is used is participation in a lottery. This may backfire as many users of the Internet are suspicious of "get rich quick" schemes that fill their email folders. Some may place the incentive schemes of survey researchers in the same category.

- Multiple submissions. Given the ease in participating in web surveys, there is a greater need for the control of multiple submissions. Unique identifiers, passwords, and screening questions are used to control multiple submissions.
- Lack of assistance. An interviewer is not available to assist respondents in understanding the questions. Respondents with little computer experience may have problems completing the instruments.
- No counterpart to RDD in telephone-based sampling. Web-based sampling does not have an equivalent to RDD that is used in telephone-based sampling.
- As is the case of telephone surveys, compared to personal interview surveys, completion rates are likely to be low for long questionnaires.

Below are several research examples demonstrating the use of web-based sampling. Research Note 6.4 describes the nonprobability list-based, web-based sample design used in a study of the strategies used by teachers and counselors in handling school bullying incidents. Research Note 6.5 provides an example of a probability list-based, web-based sample design. In this study, an invitation to participate in a study of the prevalence of medical and non-medical use of prescription drugs was sent via postal mail to a random sample of college students attending a large university. The next two research notes provide examples of the nonprobability selection of web site visits. Research Note 6.6 describes the sample design of a study of identity and depression among African American women, and Research Note 6.7 describes the sample design used in a study of sexual aggression and HIV risk behavior among heterosexual men. Research Note 6.8 describes the sampling procedures used in a list-based sampling of email addresses in a study of sexual harassment victimization of college students.

RESEARCH NOTE 6.4

Example of Nonprobability List-Based, Web-Based Sampling: Study of Teachers' and Counselors' Strategies for Handling School Bullying Incidents

Bauman, Rigby, and Hoppac (2008) conducted a web-based survey of strategies used by teachers and counselors in handling school bullying incidents. They described their sampling as follows:

In order to reach a large sample and contain costs, the questionnaire was posted on a password-protected Internet site, and invitations to participate were distributed to teaching and school counseling listservs, email distributions lists, and via personal contacts. The decision to conduct the survey online was based on the benefits of Internet surveys over traditional survey methods. Although Internet surveys have lower response rates compared with traditional mail surveys, the benefits of Web surveys may outweigh the possibility of lower response rates. Internet surveys are beneficial because they require minimal (if any) expense, less time commitment, simplify data entry, and are relatively easy to execute.

Source: Bauman, Rigby, & Hoppac, 2008, p. 839. Reprinted with permission.

RESEARCH NOTE 6.5

Example of Probability List-Based, Web-Based Sampling: Study of the Prevalence of Medical and Nonmedical Use of Prescription Drugs Among College Students

McCabe (2008) utilized web-based sampling in his study of the use and abuse of prescription drugs among students attending a large, Midwestern 4-year university. He described his sampling procedures as follows:

This study was conducted from January 14, 2005, to February 28, 2005, drawing on a total undergraduate population of 20,738 full-time students (10,339 women and 9,799 men) attending a large US public research university. After the study received institutional review board approval, a random sample of 5389 full-time undergraduate students was drawn from the total undergraduate population. The entire sample was mailed $2.00 along with a prenotification letter that described the study and invited students to self-administer a Web survey by using a URL address and unique password. Informed consent was obtained online from each participant. Nonrespondents were sent up to 4 reminder e-mails. The Web survey was maintained on an Internet site running with the secure socket layer protocol to ensure privacy and security. By participating in the survey, students became eligible for a sweepstakes that included cash prizes, travel vouchers, tickets to athletic events, and iPods. The final response rate was 68%, and potential nonresponse bias was assessed by administering a short form of the questionnaire via telephone to a randomly selected sample of 159 students who did not respond to the original Web survey.

Source: McCabe, 2008, p. 2. Reprinted with permission.

RESEARCH NOTE 6.6

Example of Nonprobability Sampling of Web Site Visits: Study of Racial Identity and Depression Among African American Women

Settles, Navarrete, Pagano, Abdou, and Sidanius (2010) conducted a web-based survey of the relationship of racial identity and depression among African American women. They described their sampling as follows:

Participants were recruited on the Internet from postings on discussion groups and websites, including those related to African American women's interests.[1] Participants were invited to take part in an online survey for Black women. From an initial pool of 519 participants, observations were retained in the present analyses from respondents who (a) were 18 years of age or older, (b) were female, (c) had two Black parents and self-identified as Black or African American, (d) self-reported being a U.S. citizen, and (e) had completed all survey items necessary for our analyses. Using these criteria, we included 379 female respondents' data in the analyses.

Source: Settles, Navarrete, Pagano, Abdou, & Sidanius, 2010, p. 248. Reprinted with permission.

RESEARCH NOTE 6.7

Example of a Nonprobability Selection of Web Site Visits: Study of Sexual Aggression and HIV Risk Behavior Among Heterosexual Men

Peterson, Janssen, and Heiman (2010) used a nonprobability selection of web site visits in their study of sexual aggression and HIV risk behavior among heterosexual men. They described their sampling procedures as follows:

The present study used a large online convenience sample. . . . Participants for this study were 1,240 self-identified heterosexual men who completed an online questionnaire posted on the Web site of the Kinsey Institute for

Research in Sex, Gender, and Reproduction from October 2006 to May 2007. The Kinsey Institute Web site lists a variety of online studies that are available to any interested participants who visit the institute's site. No incentive was offered for participation.

Source: Peterson, Janssen, & Heiman, 2010, p. 542. Reprinted with permission.

RESEARCH NOTE 6.8

Example of a Nonprobability List-Based Sampling of Email Addresses: International Study of Diversion Programs in the Criminal Justice System

Hartford, Carey, and Mendonca (2007) used a nonprobability sampling of listings of email addresses and respondent-assisted sampling in their survey of diversion programs in the criminal justice system. They described their sampling procedures as follows:

> After pretesting the survey, it was converted into an electronic format accessible by multiple Web browsers. Prospective respondents were directed to the Web site by means of e-mails that explained the nature of the survey and that contained a hyptertext link to the Web site. In addition, PDF, Word, and Word-Perfect documents were attached with the e-mail, providing respondents with a range of response options. The Web site itself introduced the survey with a cover letter explaining the reason for and nature of the survey and provided assurances of confidentiality. Because many of the questions asked for detailed responses, individuals were able to cut and paste existing documents into the survey, send them as an e-mail attachment, or fax them, ensuring maximum flexibility. Respondents were asked if they wanted to receive a copy of the final report, and an automatic thank you was sent upon completion.
>
> Identifying the sample was a multistage effort. The first step involved searching for published, public e-mail addresses. The U.S. National Alliance for the Mentally Ill, and the Council of State Governments (2004), as well as the Council of State Governments (n.d.) documents provided an e-mail listing

(Continued)

(Continued)

of 228 police, court diversion, and mental health courts. After consideration of the new federal privacy legislation, the Canadian Association of Chiefs of Police released their membership directory that contained 129 e-mail addresses. The second step involved Web searches of public agencies. Police e-mail addresses or fax numbers in Australia and New Zealand were located; generic U.K. police, court, and National Health Service (NHS) e-mail addresses were also identified. The third step involved examining literature, using personal contacts known to the authors, and linking these to extensive searches on the Internet. From steps two and three, e-mail addresses of 518 individuals from Canadian, U.K., Australian, and New Zealand police, court diversion, and mental health courts were identified. Thus, an initial convenience sample of 875 persons/organizations was assembled. E-mails inviting prospective respondents to participate in the survey, and directing them to the survey Web site, were sent in four waves between May 24, 2004 and July 7, 2004.

Because many of the e-mail addresses in the original convenience sample proved unusable or inaccurate, we refined our sample throughout the survey by using snowball sampling and by deleting unusable addresses from our database. . . . If our original e-mail inviting a prospective participant to participate in the survey did not yield a response, we sent up to three follow-up e-mails as reminders. In some cases, e-mail recipients forwarded new contacts to us, which we then added to the sample. In other cases, recipients took the initiative to forward e-mails to people in their organizations whom they thought more likely or appropriate to complete the survey. Contacts whose e-mail addresses resulted in "bounce backs" were deleted from the sample. . . . After several months of revising our sample in this way, we arrived at 321 e-mail addresses we believed to be usable—that is, they were accurate addresses of people or associations involved in operative diversion programs. Nevertheless, because we have no way of distinguishing nonresponses from undelivered mail—some of our e-mail to addresses in the United Kingdom, for example, were treated as spam—it is therefore difficult for us to provide an accurate denominator to calculate the response rate. Thus, our final estimated response rate—47% (126/321)—is artificially high.

Source: Hartford, Carey, & Mendonca, 2007, pp. 39–40. Reprinted with permission.

RESEARCH NOTE 6.9

Example of a Probability List-Based Sampling of Email Addresses: Study of Sexual Harassment Victimization of College Students

Clodfelter, Turner, Hartman, and Kuhns (2010) used a probability list-based sampling of email addresses in their web-based study of sexual harassment of college students. They described their sampling procedures as follows:

> Participants comprised a random sample of 750 college students. Participant names were generated from the eligible campus population of a southeastern urban university. Eligibility included being enrolled during the fall semester of 2004. The target population either had assigned e-mail accounts that were provided by the university or had alternate e-mail addresses stored within the contact information provided to the school. E-mail addresses were used to initiate correspondence. All students first received a letter via electronic mail to introduce them to the study. A second letter was sent 2 weeks later with a link to a Web site that would host the survey. Two follow-up requests were e-mailed within 3-week intervals for those who did not initially respond. Once a student agreed to participate, he or she was directly routed to the Web address that housed the self-administered questionnaire.

Source: Clodfelter, Turner, Hartman, & Kuhns, 2010, p. 463. Reprinted with permission.

ADDRESS-BASED SAMPLING

What Is Address-Based Sampling?

Address-based sampling (ABS) is a set of sampling procedures that utilizes postal addresses as sampling units. Until recently, mail surveys targeting the general public were limited to naming the addressee "Current Resident" or using names obtained from telephone directories. With the availability of addresses through the Delivery Sequence File (DSF) of the United States Postal Service (USPS), during the 2000s there has been a resurgence of mail surveys. Utilizing the DSF, address-based sampling is used increasingly in national surveys (e.g., National Survey of Family Growth, General Social Survey, and the National

Election Study). Factors that are associated with the increased use of mail surveys and address-based sampling include:

- Increasing coverage bias of telephone surveys
- Added costs and effort in incorporating cell phone–only households in telephone surveys
- Required costs and effort in personal interview surveys
- Increasing nonresponse rates for other modes
- Increased employment of multimode and mixed-methods research
- Although decreasing, the coverage bias of web-based research
- The computerization of addresses by the USPS. The DSF is a computerized database of all delivery point addresses serviced by the USPS with the exception of general delivery. Mail carriers throughout the country update the database on a nearly continuous basis. The database includes listings of:
  o City-style addresses—addresses that contain a street name and number
  o Rural-style or simplified addresses—addresses that contain only the city, state, and zip code
  o Post office boxes
  o Multidrop addresses—addresses associated with more than one name
  o Certain types of addresses are flagged. These include:
    - Business addresses
    - Seasonal addresses
    - Throwback addresses—addressees whose mail is forwarded to another address
    - Addresses of vacant buildings

In conducting household surveys, seasonal addresses, throwback addresses, and business addresses are generally excluded. On the other hand, addresses to vacant units are included since they might be occupied by the time of data collection. Ninety percent of the addresses can be linked to names, and 65% can be linked to telephone numbers. The DSF file is made available only through certified vendors. Some vendors make available enhancements to the raw data file by including geographic information, household demographic information, a name, and a listed telephone number.

What Are the Strengths and Weaknesses of Address-Based Sampling?

The findings of recent studies have suggested that address-based sampling utilizing the DSF files is a viable option to RDD (Iannacchionee, Staab, & Redden, 2003;

Link, Battaglia, Frankel, Osborn, & Mokdad, 2008). Several strengths of the use of address-based sampling have been identified:

- ABS reaches cell phone–only households and households that do not have telephones without involving the cost and safety concerns tied to the dialing of cell phones.
- Using the auxiliary information that may augment the DSF, stratified sampling may be used.
- Using improved geocoding and mapping procedures, it is easier to match census data and other types of data to an address than to a telephone number. Telephone numbers selected using RDD may go beyond the targeted geographical area for a study, making it difficult to append census block data and other geographical data to the telephone number.
- If a cell phone number is provided by the respondent after having been contacted via mail, the number may be dialed using an automated dialer.
- Telephone numbers may be matched to sampled addresses in conducting mixed-methods research. However, it should be noted it is difficult to match post office boxes and telephone numbers.
- Given the problems of reaching younger persons in telephone surveys, especially since many of them are in the cell–phone only category, ABS improves the representation of younger persons.

Weaknesses of ABS include:

- Coverage in rural areas is lower than coverage in urban areas, partially due to the greater number of simplified addresses in rural areas. However, since the September 11 attacks, increasingly "rural-style" addresses have been converted to "city-style" in order to help direct emergency services to rural locations.
- If more than one person in a household is in the target population, the person to be included in the study should be selected utilizing probability methods. In using ABS, there is less control than that in personal interview studies and telephone interview studies in making such a selection.
- ABS relies on updates from mail carriers; as a result, updates and list management may vary.
- There is a lack of coverage of persons living in group quarters (i.e., dorms, assisted living facilities, etc.).
- ABS excludes households with no USPS mail delivery.
- The address frame must be purchased from vendors and cannot be obtained directly from USPS. The quality of the frame obtained from a vendor depends upon the auxiliary data in the frame, the updating practices of the vendor, and the sampling experience of the vendor.

- Response rates tend to be lower than telephone surveys due to the mailing to hard-to-reach elements in the population.
- Some vendors exclude addresses on request, thus creating coverage bias.
- The degree to which auxiliary information and enhancement to the raw data files maintained by USPS vary from vendor to vendor.
- The USPS frame contains post office boxes and multidrop addresses (i.e., multiple persons associated with the same address) which may be problematic for personal interview and telephone surveys, less for mail surveys.
- There may be duplicates in the sampling frame as some persons may have both a post office box address and a city-style address. In collecting data, it may be necessary to ask the respondents whether they have multiple addresses and to weight the data appropriately in the analysis phase of the study.
- ABS is more time-consuming than and not as timely as RDD.
- ABS has lower response rates than RDD.

Since 1998, Knowledge Networks has created online panels using RDD for a wide variety of research projects. Recently it switched from RDD to ABS in creating its online panels. This change is symbolic of the increased use of ABS. Knowledge Networks' description of its change to ABS is presented in Research Note 6.10.

RESEARCH NOTE 6.10

Example of Address-Based Sampling in Creating Online Panels: Practices of Knowledge Networks

Knowledge Networks (KN) utilized RDD to create online panels. However, due to decreasing response rates and the impact of cell phone–only households, it has begun using address-based sampling (ABS) to create its panels. It described its use of ABS as follows:

In 2009, KN initiated the use of an address-based sample (ABS) frame to first supplement the RDD frame and subsequently replace it. This was in response to the growing number of cell phone only households that are outside the traditional RDD landline telephone frame. Also, this switch was motivated by declining RDD response rates. ABS involves probability-based sampling of addresses from the U.S. Postal Service's Delivery Sequence File. Randomly sampled addresses are invited to join KnowledgePanel through a series of mailings (English and Spanish materials) and by telephone follow-up to non-responders when a telephone number can be matched to the sampled address. Invited households can join the panel by one of several means: completing and mailing back an acceptance form in a postage-paid envelope; calling a toll-free hotline staffed by bilingual recruitment agents; or going to a dedicated KN recruitment Web site and completing the recruitment information online.

Source: Knowledge Networks, 2010, p. 2. Reprinted with permission

TIME-BASED SAMPLING

What Is Time-Based Sampling?

Time-based sampling consists of a set of sampling procedures that utilize units of time as sampling units. It is used in studying repeated outcomes that vary a great deal over time. The units of time might be time of day, days of the week, month of the year, or some other time unit. Time intervals may be the sampling units. The length of the interval would depend in part on the rate of occurrence of that to be observed. Preparation for this type of sampling typically involves visits to the locations where the data will be collected, observing the density of the target population over time and gathering information from informants. Using the information obtained, a sampling frame of time units is developed. Data might be collected several times per day at time periods selected using simple random sampling or systematic sampling, upon the occurrence of a specific event, or at specifically scheduled time intervals.

What Are the Subtypes of Time-Based Sampling?

Special subtypes of time-based sampling have emerged as researchers sought to study ongoing experiences (Experience Sampling Method); events (Events Sampling Methodology); and the use of time by employees, equipment, and facilities (work sampling). Variables studied include social interactions, mood swings, level of stress, use of equipment and facilities, use of staff time, and factors impacting work experiences and productivity. Respondents may be alerted to complete an electronic or a paper questionnaire via beepers, pagers, watches, PDAs, palmtop computers, cell phones, or custom devices. Hektner, Schmidt, and Csikszentmihaly (2006) described the early beginning of the experience sampling method as follows:

> The first studies using pagers activated by electronic signals transmitted at random times from a central radio station were conducted in the laboratory of Mihaly Ciskszentmihalyi at the Committee of Human Development of the University of Chicago in the early 1970s. The original intent was to study "flow" experiences in everyday life. At first we asked informants to write down into diaries what they had done during the day and what the most enjoyable moments had been. However, we were soon disillusioned by the dry and generalized nature of such reports. It was obvious that people summarized the events of the day without much discrimination, according to predictable scripts. How could one obtain fresh accounts of cross sections from the stream of consciousness, short of following respondents throughout the day, which would be extremely intrusive and expensive? At the time we asked this question, certain categories of workers—physicians, plumbers, policeman—began to use electronic pagers as a way of staying connected with their dispatchers. One afternoon, as we were discussing the problems of getting timely reports of everyday experience, Suzanne Prescott—then a graduate student in Human Development—and Mihaly Csikszentmihalyi began to talk about the possibility of using pagers to trigger self-reports. We drafted a response sheet (similar to the ones still in use), rented two pagers, and tried out the method for ourselves for a week. The experience, while somewhat obtrusive at first, turned out to be quite fun—and the data produced, even from a single person, was unbelievably rich. The method quickly acquired a life of its own. (pp. 7–8)

What Are the Strengths and Weakness of Time-Based Sampling?

A strength of these time-based sampling procedures is that the effect of recall bias is minimized. However, the procedures are invasive and intrusive, and may impose a self-selection bias as many individuals in the target population may be unwilling to subject themselves to such intrusion, and instrument reactive effects may affect the internal validity of a study.

Research Note 6.11 and Research Note 6.12 illustrate the use of the Experience Sampling Method/Event Sampling Method in studying daily visual activities and work performance of human resource staff and teachers, respectively. At different time intervals the participants in these studies are paged and asked to answer questions relating to their behavior at the time they were paged.

RESEARCH NOTE 6.11

Example of the Experience Sampling Method: Study of Daily Visual Activities

Rah, Mitchell, Bullimore, Mutti, and Zadnik (2001) evaluated the Experience Sampling Method in studying daily visual activities. They described their sampling procedures as follows:

> Traditionally, direct observation, interviews, and work diaries have been used with limited success. For example, direct observation using video or trained observers can be costly and may alter the behavior of the subject. It may also be difficult for the observer to interpret the activities of the subject. Certain behaviors may not be observed due to the intrusive nature of the testing. Interviews rely heavily on recollection on the part of the subject, and diaries are, again, dependent on compliance. To best assess daily near-work activity, a more efficient method that provides prospective sampling without interrupting the daily activities of the subject to any substantial degree is needed. . . . A type of random work sampling known as the Experience Sampling Method (ESM) has been widely used to assess various types of daily activities, thoughts, and emotions. In the ESM, subjects are asked to carry a portable electronic pager, traditionally for 1 week, and they are paged randomly throughout the day. Each time a subject is paged, he or she is asked to complete a self-report survey of his or her activities at the moment of the page. The ESM "allows repeated assessment of the experience of subjects in their natural environment," and has been used "to obtain a comprehensive snapshot at each random moment." . . . After obtaining informed consent following the tenets of the Declaration of Helsinki, subjects were asked to complete a prestudy demographic questionnaire. A brief orientation was conducted to familiarize the subjects with the pagers and

(Continued)

(Continued)

> cellular phones, and a demonstration of the telephone survey was performed. A cellular phone and pager were then issued to each of the subjects. . . . After a run-in period, each subject was paged five times per day for 6 days. An automated dialing system was designed using Notify PCS and Paging software (AirMedia, New York, NY) installed on a laptop computer. This computer was used exclusively for this purpose during the testing period. A randomized list of paging times (restricted to between 7:00 a.m. and 10:00 p.m. and at least 45 minutes between pages) was generated, and each page was entered individually into the computer.

Source: Rah, Mitchell, Bullimore, Mutti, & Zadnik, 2001, p. 497. Reprinted with permission.

RESEARCH NOTE 6.12

Example of Event-Sampling Methodology: Study of the Effect of Stressors on the Work Performance of Human Resource Staff and Teachers

Daniels, Hartley, and Travers (2006) used an event-sampling methodology (ESM) in studying the effect of stressors on the work performance of human resource staff and teachers. They described their sampling procedures as follows:

> We used event-sampling methodology (ESM), in which participants provided reports, three times per day, on stressors experienced over the previous hour (hourly stressors) and state affect at that moment in time (momentary affect). ESM studies are able to capture data in context and close to changes in state affect and stressors, hence minimizing distortion due to recall bias (Bolger et al., 2003). Such methods can also control for temporal influences on dependent variables, previous levels of dependent variables, and stable factors associated with the individual. ESM methods can, therefore, allow stronger inferences of causality than can be obtained from many other non-experimental methods, whilst preserving high levels of ecological validity (Bolger et al., 2003; Tennen & Affleck, 2002). . . .Participants came from two samples, human resource and development (HR) staff at a UK university and teachers in a UK secondary school. These samples were chosen as it could reasonably be expected that: the samples would experience different kinds of stressors;

the incidence of those stressors would be frequent yet varying on a daily basis; and the nature of work would differ between the samples. Data were collected using Palm Tungsten E personal digital assistants (PDAs) using the iESP program (Intel Research, Seattle, WA: [http://seattlewev.intel-research .net/projects/ESM/index.html]) to administer questions three times daily over the course of one working week (Monday–Friday). An alarm on the PDAs signaled when questions were to be answered. Participants had 60 seconds to respond to the alarm, and 60 seconds to respond to each question. In cases where these times had elapsed, the PDA shut down and set off the alarm at the next measurement occasion. The HR staff responded at staggered intervals between 10–10.15am, 12.30–12.45pm and 15–15.15pm. The teachers responded in the midmorning break (11.05–11.10am), the lunch break (1.35–1.40pm), and just after students had left the school (4.05–4.10pm). Before commencement of the ESM period, participants completed a more extensive questionnaire. . . . In the week preceding the ESM period, participants were given a presentation on how to use the PDAs. The questionnaire was also distributed then. All questionnaires were completed and returned before the start of the ESM period. The PDAs were distributed to participants between 8.30–9.00am on the first day of the ESM period (a Monday). At the end of the ESM period, following the last alarm on the last day, the PDAs were collected from participants.

Source: Daniels, Hartley, & Travers, 2006, pp. 1266-1268. Reprinted with permission.

SPACE-BASED SAMPLING

What Is Space-Based Sampling?

Space-based sampling is a set of sampling procedures that utilize space as a sampling unit. This type of sampling is also referred to as area sampling, spatial sampling, location-based sampling, venue-based sampling, and facility-based sampling. The space may be geographical units (i.e., typical sampling units utilized in cluster sampling described above), the floor space of a shopping mall, grids on a map, or various locations or venues (i.e., **venue-based sampling** and location-based sampling). This sampling procedure is very useful when a sampling frame of the target population does not exist or is difficult to compile. It is the principal mode of sampling utilized in nationwide personal interview surveys, environmental sampling, and ecological sampling. Advances in global positioning systems (GPS), geographic information systems (GIS), and remote sensing (RS) have added new dimensions to spatial sampling. In environmental and ecological sampling, sampling frames of grids, vectors, or points may be laid over mapping of the target area. Next, grids, vectors, or points are randomly selected. Elements of the target population within the selected grids, or on the selected vectors or points are then included in the sample. As described in the discussion of multistage area sampling above, in area population sampling in national surveys of the United States, geographical areas such as states, counties, cities, census tracts, blocks, and dwelling units are used as sampling units. The costs and effort necessary to conduct nationwide personal interview surveys led to increased interest in telephone surveys.

The research notes listed below present examples of the use of time sampling and venue-based sampling. Research Note 6.13 presents a discussion of the use of location sampling in studying rare and mobile populations, and Research Note 6.14 describes the sampling procedures used in a study of patrons at nightclubs in New York City. The concern about the spread of HIV/AIDS and related issues has given rise to research on men who have sex with men. Venue-based sampling is often used in such research. Research Note 6.15 and Research Note 6.16 provide examples of the use of time/location/venue-based/ sampling in such research.

RESEARCH NOTE 6.13

Example of Location Sampling: Study of Rare and Mobile Populations

Kalton (2001) reviewed methods of sampling rare populations (e.g., "minority populations, specific age/sex groups such as males aged 18 to 24, the disabled population, or persons with rare diseases") and mobile populations (e.g., "international travelers, car passengers, visitors to museums or national parks, the homeless, voters at polling booths, hospital outpatients, and shoppers at a shopping mall"). He described location sampling as follows:

> Location sampling refers to methods used to sample individuals who visit specific locations such as libraries, museums, shopping centers, and polling places. Sampling is usually conducted either as the visitors enter or as they leave a location. Two distinct units of analysis need to be distinguished—visits and visitors (Kalton, 1991). Location sampling can readily produce

a probability sample of visits, with known selection probabilities, and hence visits are easily analyzed. Visits may be the appropriate unit of analysis for, say, a survey about satisfaction with visits to a museum. However, for many surveys using location sampling, the visitor is the appropriate unit of analysis. For example, the visitor is the appropriate unit of analysis in a survey of visitors to soup kitchens over a week to estimate the number of homeless, a survey of nomads visiting watering holes to estimate the size of the nomadic population, or a survey of men who have sex with men (MSM) visiting gay bars to study the characteristics of the MSM population.

The use of the visitor as the unit of analysis is complicated by the fact that a visitor may make multiple visits during the survey's time frame. If a standard sample of visits is selected, the increased selection probabilities associated with multiple visits need to be taken into account in developing the survey weights. The problem lies in estimating the multiplicities, both because a sampled person may be unable to accurately recall past visits since the start of the survey's reference period and because he or she is unable to forecast visits to be made from the time of interview until the end of the reference period. As a result, the multiplicities may be based on simple reports about general frequency of visits.

An alternative solution to the multiplicity problem is to uniquely identify one of the visits with the visitor, treating the other visits as blanks, thereby avoiding the problem. The natural choice for the uniquely identified visit is the first one in the survey reference period: each sampled person is asked if the visit is his or her first since the start of the survey, is selected if the answer is "Yes," and is rejected if the answer is "No." From the fieldwork perspective, an unattractive feature of this procedure is that most visits near the start of the time period will be first visits, leading to interviews, whereas most near the end will not. To some extent, this problem can be addressed by sampling the time periods with probabilities proportional to appropriate size measures, but determining these measures is problematic.

The usual sample design for a location sample is a two-stage design (Kalton, 1991). Primary sampling units are constructed as combinations of locations (entrances or exits) and time segments when the location is open (e.g., a given Monday from 10 a.m. to 2 p.m.). The PSUs are sampled with probabilities proportional to size, with careful stratification by location and time. Then some form of systematic sample is employed to select visitors entering (or exiting) the location.

Source: Kalton, 2001, p. 5. Reprinted with permission.

RESEARCH NOTE 6.14

Example of Venue-Based Sampling: Study of Patrons at Nightclubs in New York City

Parsons, Grov, and Kelly (2008) used a venue-based sample design in their study of patrons at nightclubs in New York City. They described their sample design as follows:

> To generate a proper sample of a venue-based population located at night-clubs in NYC, nightclubs served as the basic sampling unit. Rather than randomizing households or phone numbers as some other probability-based sampling methods do, we randomized both the days we recruited and the venues at which we recruited. . . . During the first variation of time-space sampling, three tiers of randomization were utilized: (1) the venues attended, (2) the days attending the venues, and (3) the young adults attending the venues (i.e., selecting every nth person who crossed a particular threshold). We first randomized "time and space" using a sampling frame of previously enumerated clubs and time periods of operation. Once at the venue, we randomized the individuals (i.e., every nth individual) . . . crossing a pre-determined imaginary threshold at the venue. . . . To construct the sampling frame, preliminary fieldwork was conducted to ascertain "socially viable" venues for each day of the week. Social viability was determined if a certain threshold of patron traffic existed at the venue on that given day of the week (e.g., a minimum of 10 "age eligible" individuals per recruitment hour per shift). For example, if a club is open on Thursdays but only three young adults usually show up, or it caters to an over-40 crowd, it was not consid-ered a socially viable venue on Thursday evenings. We generated lists of socially viable venues for each day of the week, for a total of 223 venues over the course of the project. For each day of the week, every socially viable venue was listed and assigned a number. Then, using a random digit gen-erator program, a random number was drawn for each recruitment day of that month. Each random number drawn corresponded to a given venue. This process ultimately yielded our schedule of venues for each month.
>
> Given that Friday and Saturday nights are the most common "party" nights, we weighted these recruitment days by sampling additional venues and adding additional recruitment shifts on these days. All Fridays and Saturdays were considered "weekend days." Also, during the year certain

other days were assigned "weekend" status depending on the specifics of those dates. The primary defining characteristic of a "weekend" night was that most individuals would not have to attend work/school the following day. For example, a Sunday night on a holiday weekend would have been assigned "weekend" status, even though most Sunday nights were not considered "weekend" nights.

During the first version of recruitment, three members of each recruitment team were assigned separate responsibilities: one served as a "counter" and two as "screeners." To achieve person-level randomization at each venue, the counter—typically the shift supervisor—tracked and counted every individual crossing a pre-determined threshold outside of the venue, e.g., the entrance. . . . . Every nth person to cross that threshold was selected for the survey. Thus, once a certain number in the count had been reached, the counter assigned a screener to the individual selected at random. The n was adjusted to match the level of patron traffic such that high-traffic nights (typically Friday and Saturdays) called for a higher n (e.g., every 76 person) and lower-traffic nights/venues called for a smaller n (e.g., every 56 person). The consideration of traffic flow allowed for individuals attending smaller venues and on "off nights" to be adequately represented in the sample. In the event that traffic flow dramatically changed during the course of the night, the counter was permitted to alter the n once during the night, by plus or minus two persons, in order to accommodate the variance in population.

For the duration of each recruitment shift, the counter continued to count patrons and assign the screeners at the designated random intervals to the young adults attending the venue. The screeners approached the assigned individual immediately, identified themselves, and requested verbal consent for participation in the anonymous brief survey. After obtaining verbal consent, the survey staff orally administered the survey and keyed the participant's responses onto a Palm Pilot PDA. If the patron refused, the screener noted their refusal and estimated their age, gender, and ethnicity. Although the estimated information for refusals was not included in this analysis, it was collected for the supervision and global tracking of refusal rates and demographic characteristics of those declining to participate. Field staff members were instructed not to administer surveys to any individuals who were visibly impaired by intoxicants.

Source: Parsons, Grov, & Kelly, 2008, pp. 1066–1067. Reprinted with permission.

RESEARCH NOTE 6.15

Example of Time-Space Sampling: Centers for Disease Control Study of Men Who Have Sex With Men

Karon (2005) assessed procedures for the analysis of data collected by the Centers for Disease Control (CDC) via time-location sampling in a study of men who have sex with men (MSM). He described features of time-location sampling and the steps he used as follows:

> Time-location sampling is used to sample a population for which a sampling frame cannot be constructed but locations are known at which the population of interest can be found, or for which it is more efficient to sample at these locations. Such populations include homeless persons, migrant workers, museum attendees, and blood donors. . . . I assume that sampling is to be done at more than one location. The sampling frame is the locations at which there is sufficient attendance by persons in the population of interest to make sampling worthwhile. A random sample of locations is chosen from this frame. If attendance depends on day of the week and time of day (as it does in studies of MSM), a sampling period is then chosen for each location in the sample. If locations vary in the frequency with which they have the necessary number of attendees, some care is required in constructing the sampling calendar, such as first choosing sampling periods for locations with the fewest available periods. Finally, a sample of attendees is chosen during each sampling event. If possible, this should be a random sample. The investigators should estimate the sampling fraction by recording the total number of persons at the location during the sampling period who meet, or appear to meet, the eligibility criteria for the study. . . . CDC used time-location sampling to obtain information about young MSM in the Young Men's Study Phase II, a study conducted in six metropolitan areas during 1998–2000 of 2942 MSM ages 23 to 29 years. Men were recruited at nine types of venues, including bars, dance clubs, businesses, health clubs, sex establishments, social organizations, street corners, and parks. Investigators asked men how often they attended bars or dance clubs during the last 6 months: never, less than once per month, once per month, 2 to 3 times per month, once per week, 2 to 3 times per week, or daily.

Source: Karon, 2005, pp. 3180–3182. Reprinted with permission.

RESEARCH NOTE 6.16

Example of Venue-Based Sampling: Study of the Differences by Race, Income, and Sexual Identity in the Locations Where Men Who Have Sex With Men Have Their First HIV Test

Lauby and Milnamow (2009) used venue-based sampling in their study of differences by race, income, and sexual identity in the locations where men who have sex with men (MSM) have their first HIV test. They described their sampling procedures as follows:

A venue-based sampling method was employed to enroll 451 men. Qualitative interviews with knowledgeable members of the target population and field observations by members of the study team were used to identify 65 recruitment venues in Philadelphia that are frequented by MSM. These venues included gay-identified and non-gay-identified dance clubs, bars, coffee houses, restaurants, community events, parks, bathhouses, street corners, bookstores, service organizations, and other indoor and outdoor spaces. Pairs of interviewers were assigned to visit the listed venues on different days of the week and at various times. Men were enrolled into the study by interviewers who used predetermined systematic selection procedures designed to minimize bias in the recruitment process. Selected men were approached by an interviewer, given a short description of the survey, and asked if they would be willing to participate.

To be eligible for inclusion in the study, participants had to be 18 years of age or older; live in one of nine counties in the Philadelphia metropolitan area, including six counties in Pennsylvania and three counties in southern New Jersey; and report having had a sexual experience with another man in the past 5 years. A total of 1600 men were approached by a survey administrator and asked to participate in the study. Of these men, 605 (38%) agreed to participate and 995 (62%) would not stop to hear about the survey or declined to participate for various reasons. Of the 605 men who agreed to participate, 471 (78%) met the eligibility criteria and were interviewed by a survey administrator. Subsequently, 20 completed surveys were discarded because of problems with missing data or because of concerns about the reliability of the data, resulting in a total sample of 451 MSM. Oversampling of places where Latino MSM could be located was necessary to ensure adequate representation in the study.

(Continued)

(Continued)

> Data collection was anonymous; no names, addresses, or other identifying information were collected. To maintain anonymity, signed consent forms were not used. Although it is possible that some men may have participated in the survey more than once, duplicate enrollment was minimized by employing a small number of interviewers and by limiting the number of visits to each of the 65 recruitment venues.

Source: Lauby & Milnamow, 2009, p. 51. Reprinted with permission.

MIXED-METHODS SAMPLE DESIGNS

What Is Mixed-Methods Sampling?

Researchers have the option of combining the various sampling procedures described in this text and using them in a single study. **Mixed-methods sampling** is a sampling method that combines different types of sampling methods into a single design. Whereas mixed-methods research designs tend to focus on the combination of qualitative and quantitative research designs, here the terminology "mixed-methods sample design" focuses on the extent to which different types of sampling procedures are used in the same study. Instead of choosing a single-method design, one may choose to combine different types of nonprobability sample designs, or different types of probability sample designs, or nonprobability sample designs and probability sample designs.

Mixed-methods research approaches were developed as alternatives to strict single-mode designs. The idea is that the weaknesses of one method may be compensated by the strengths of the other method that is used. The use of mixed-methods research designs was spurred by the application of two key concepts: *multimethod-multitrait matrix* and *triangulation*. The multimethod-multitrait matrix is an approach introduced by Campbell and Fiske in 1959 to assess the validity of a mixed set of items believed to measure an underlying construct. Denzin (2009) identified four types of triangulation: data triangulation (the use of different types of data); methodological triangulation (the use of different types of research method); investigator triangulation (the use of a research team composed of different types of investigators); and theory triangulation (the testing of competing and conflicting theories). In the spirit of Denzin, this section of the book explores different methods of sampling triangulation.

What Are the Subtypes of Mixed-Methods Sampling?

Mixed-methods sample designs may be divided into within-methods sample designs and cross-methods sample designs. Sample designs that combine different nonprobability sample designs or probability sample designs are within-methods sample designs. Sample designs that combine nonprobability sampling and probability sampling are cross-methods sample designs. Following the mixed-methods research and sampling models proposed by others (see, e.g., Creswell & Clark, 2007; Onwuegbuzie & Collins, 2007; Tashakkori & Teddlie, 1998), these three categories may be further broken into subcategories based on two additional dimensions: timing of the implementation of the different methods and the relationship of the different methods to each other. The time dimension recognizes that multiple designs might be used concurrently (implemented at the same time) or sequentially (implemented one after the other). The relationship dimension categorizes mixed-methods designs according to how the designs that are combined are related to each other. Three types of relationships have been identified: equivalent status, nested, and multilevel. Methods that have an equivalent status with each other have the same level of dominance. Nested designs are methods composed of one or more dominant designs and one or more subordinate designs. Multilevel designs combine methods targeting different levels of a target population. Cross-tabulating these dimensions for within-methods and cross-methods sample designs creates a typology of 16 subtypes of mixed-methods sample designs (see Table 6.1). They are briefly described below.

Table 6.1   Typology of Mixed-Methods Sample Designs

Time Order of Sampling and Relationship Among the Designs	Within-Methods Designs		Cross-Methods Designs
	Mixed-Nonprobability Sample Designs	Mixed-Probability Sample Designs	Mixed-Probability-Nonprobability Sample Designs
Concurrent Designs			
Equivalent	Design 1 Concurrent equivalent nonprobability design	Design 7 Concurrent equivalent probability design	Design 13 Concurrent equivalent probability-nonprobability design

(Continued)

Table 6.1 (Continued)

Time Order of Sampling and Relationship Among the Designs	Within-Methods Designs		Cross-Methods Designs
	Mixed-Nonprobability Sample Designs	Mixed-Probability Sample Designs	Mixed-Probability-Nonprobability Sample Designs
Nested	Design 2 Concurrent nested nonprobability design	Design 8 Concurrent nested probability design	Design 14 Concurrent nested probability-nonprobability design
Multilevel	Design 3 Concurrent multilevel nonprobability design	Design 9 Concurrent multilevel probability design	Design 15 Concurrent multilevel nonprobability-probability design
Sequential Designs			
Equivalent	Design 4 Sequential equivalent nonprobability design	Design 10 Sequential equivalent probability design	Design 16 Sequential equivalent probability-nonprobability design
Nested	Design 5 Sequential nested nonprobability design	Design 11 Sequential nested probability design	Design 17 Sequential nested probability-nonprobability design
Multilevel	Design 6 Sequential multilevel nonprobability design	Design 12 Sequential multilevel probability design	Design 18 Sequential multilevel nonprobability-probability design

Mixed-Nonprobability Sampling

Mixed-nonprobability sample designs combine different nonprobability sample designs. One may combine availability sampling with respondent-assisted sampling, combine different types of purposive sampling, or create some other combination of nonprobability sampling procedures. Taking into account the timing of the implementation of the different designs and their relationship to each other, the following subtypes may be identified:

Design 1: *Concurrent equivalent nonprobability design.* Two or more nonprobability sample designs with target populations of comparable status are selected at approximately the same point in time. For example, in a study of the attitudes of teachers toward a school policy, one may simultaneously select an availability sample of teachers at one school and a purposive sample of teachers at a different school.

Design 2: *Concurrent nested nonprobability design.* Using this design, a subset of a nonprobability sample is selected using a different nonprobability sampling procedure, at approximately the same point in time that the dominant sample is selected. For example, in a study of the attitudes of teachers toward a school policy, one may simultaneously select an availability sample of teachers, and using purposive sampling, select a sample of teachers with a reputation of being opinion leaders.

Design 3: *Concurrent multilevel nonprobability design.* Using this design, samples are selected from different levels of a target population at approximately the same point in time utilizing different nonprobability sampling procedures. For example, in a study of the attitudes of a school system's employees toward a school policy, one may simultaneously select a purposive sample of school administrators and principals and a quota sample of teachers.

Design 4: *Sequential equivalent nonprobability design.* Using this design, two or more nonprobability samples of comparable status in the study are selected at different points in time. For example, in a study of the attitudes of teachers and parents toward a school policy, one may first select an availability sample of teachers, and later, using the information collected via the first sampling, select a purposive sample of parents.

Design 5: *Sequential nested nonprobability design.* Using this design, a subset of a nonprobability sample is selected using a different nonprobability sampling procedure, at a time subsequent to the time that the dominant sample is selected. For example, in a study of the attitudes of teachers toward a school policy, one may select an availability sample of teachers, and using the information collected, at a later point in time, select a purposive sample of teachers identified to have a reputation of being opinion leaders.

Design 6: *Sequential multilevel nonprobability design.* Using this design, samples are selected from different levels of a target population at different points in time and utilizing different nonprobability sampling procedures. For example, in a study of the attitudes of a school system's employees toward a school policy, one may first select a purposive sample of school administrators and principals, and utilizing the information collected, at a later point in time select a quota sample of teachers.

Mixed-Probability Sampling

Mixed-probability sample designs combine different probability sample designs. Many applications of multistage cluster sampling and multiphase sampling fall into this category. A cluster sample of schools may be combined with element sampling of teachers. Different probability sampling procedures may be used for different categories of the population. Taking into account the timing of the implementation of the different designs and their relationship to each other, the following subtypes may be identified:

Design 7: *Concurrent equivalent probability design.* Two or more probability sample designs with target populations of comparable status are selected at approximately the same point in time. For example, in a study of the attitudes of teachers and parents toward a school policy, one may simultaneously select a stratified sample of teachers and a simple random sample of parents.

Design 8: *Concurrent nested probability design.* Using this design, a subset of a probability sample is selected using a different probability sampling procedure, at approximately the same point in time that the dominant sample is selected. For example, in a study of the attitudes of teachers toward a school policy, one may simultaneously select a stratified sample of teachers, and using systematic sampling, select a subsample of the teachers for more detailed data collection.

Design 9: *Concurrent multilevel probability design.* Using this design, samples are selected from different levels of a target population at approximately the same point in time utilizing different probability sampling procedures. For example, in a study of the attitudes of a school system's employees toward a school policy, one may simultaneously select a simple random sample of school administrators and principals and a stratified cluster sample of teachers.

Design 10: *Sequential equivalent probability design.* Using this design, two or more probability samples of comparable status in the study are selected at different points in time. For example, in a study of the attitudes of teachers and parents toward a school policy, one may first select a stratified sample of teachers, and later, using the information collected via the first sampling, select a simple random sample of parents.

Design 11: *Sequential nested probability design.* Using this design, a subset of a probability sample is selected using a different probability sampling procedure, at a point in time subsequent to the time the dominant sample was selected. For example, in a study of the attitudes of teachers toward a school policy, one may first select a stratified sample of teachers, and using the information collected, subsequently select a subsample of the teachers for more detailed data collection using simple random sampling.

Design 12: *Sequential multilevel probability design.* Using this design, samples are selected from different levels of a target population at different points in time, utilizing different probability sampling procedures. For example, in a study of the attitudes of a school system's employees toward a school policy, one may select a simple random sample of school administrators and principals, using the information collected, and at a subsequent point in time, select a stratified sample of teachers.

Mixed Nonprobability-Probability Sampling

Mixed-nonprobability-probability sample designs combine nonprobability sample designs and probability sample designs. One may combine availability sampling, respondent-assisted sampling, purposive sampling, and RDD in a study of a hidden population. Taking into account the timing of the implementation of the different designs and their relationship to each other, the following subtypes may be identified.

Design 13: *Concurrent equivalent nonprobability-probability design.* Using this design, a subset of a probability sample is selected using a nonprobability sampling procedure (or a subset of a nonprobability sample is selected using a probability sampling procedure), at approximately the same point in time. For example, in a study of the attitudes of teachers toward a school policy, one may simultaneously select a stratified sample of teachers, and using purposive sampling, select a sample of teachers with a reputation of being opinion leaders.

Design 14: *Concurrent nested nonprobability-probability design.* Using this design, a subset of a probability sample is selected using a nonprobability sampling procedure (or a subset of a nonprobability sample is selected using a probability sampling procedure), at approximately the same point in time. For example, in a study of the attitudes of teachers toward a school policy, one may simultaneously select a stratified sample of teachers, and using purposive sampling, select a subsample of the stratified sample targeting teachers with a reputation of being opinion leaders.

Design 15: *Concurrent multilevel nonprobability-probability design.* Using this design, samples are selected from different levels of a target population at approximately the same point in time utilizing both nonprobability sampling procedures and probability sampling procedures. For example, in a study of the attitudes of a school system's employees toward a school policy, one may simultaneously select a purposive sample of school administrators and principals and a stratified sample of teachers.

Design 16: *Sequential equivalent nonprobability-probability design.* Using this design, at different points in time, a subset of a probability sample is selected using a nonprobability sampling procedure (or a subset of a nonprobability sample is selected using a probability sampling procedure). For example, in a study of the attitudes of teachers toward a school policy, one may first select a stratified sample of teachers, and later, using the information previously selected, select a purposive sample of teachers with a reputation of being opinion leaders.

Design 17: *Sequential nested nonprobability-probability design.* Using this design, at different points in time, a subset of a probability sample is selected using a nonprobability sampling procedure (or a subset of a nonprobability sample is selected using a probability sampling procedure). For example, in a study of the attitudes of teachers toward a school policy, one may select a stratified sample of teachers, and using information collected, at a later point in time, select a purposive sample targeting teachers with a reputation of being opinion leaders.

Design 18: *Sequential multilevel nonprobability-probability design.* Using this design, samples are selected from different levels of a target population at different points in time utilizing both nonprobability sampling procedures and probability sampling procedures. For example, in a study of the attitudes of a school system's employees toward a school policy, one may first select a purposive sample of school administrators and principals, and later, using the information collected, select a stratified sample of teachers.

What Are the Strengths and Weaknesses of Mixed-Methods Sampling?

Mixed-methods sampling has a number of strengths and weaknesses when compared to single-method sampling (see Table 6.2). Compared to single-method sampling, mixed-methods sampling may be able to:

- Address a broader range of research questions
- Compensate for the weaknesses of one method via the strengths of another method
- Minimize cost, time, and effort by substituting, in part, a more expensive, time-consuming, and effort-demanding method, with one that takes less cost, time, and effort
- Provide a broader range of answers to research questions addressed
- Use the results of one method to enhance the utility of another method
- Improve the generalizability of results
- Add rigor, complexity, and depth to the study

- Compensate for limited auxiliary information in sampling frame
- Increase the likelihood that findings will be found credible
- Reduce the vulnerability of relying on one method

On the other hand, mixed-methods sampling has weaknesses when compared to single-method sampling. Compared to single-method sampling, mixed-methods sampling may:

- Be more time-consuming and costly, especially when compared to a single-method nonprobability design
- Be more administratively complicated
- Require greater methodological skills and requisite training

Table 6.2 Strengths and Weaknesses of Mixed-Methods Sampling Compared to Single-Method Sampling Procedures

Strengths	Weaknesses
Mixed-methods sampling:	
Addresses a broader range of research questions and objectives.	Could require greater time, money, effort, etc.
Provides a broader range of answers to the questions posed.	More administratively complicated.
Compensates for the weaknesses of one method via the strengths of other methods employed.	Requires greater methodological skills and requisite training.
Could minimize cost, time, and effort by substituting, in part, a more expensive, time-consuming, and effort-demanding method with one that takes less cost, time, and effort.	
Uses the results of the use of one method to enhance the use of another method.	
May improve the generalizability of results.	
Adds rigor, complexity, and depth to the study.	
Compensates for limited auxiliary information in sampling frame.	
Increases likelihood that findings will be found credible.	
Reduces the vulnerability of relying on one method.	

The research notes below provide examples of different types of mixed-methods sample designs. Research Note 6.17 through Research Note 6.22 provide various examples of mixed-nonprobability sampling. These studies cover the following topics: sexual risk-taking behavior among African American women; husbands who abused their spouse; the awarding of casino licenses in Philadelphia; mental health of lesbians, gays, and bisexuals and their siblings; perceptions of victimization risk and fear of crime among lesbians and gay men; and the effect of caregiving responsibilities on the careers of faculty members of schools of social work. Examples of mixed-probability sampling are presented in Research Note 6.23, Research Note 6.24, and Research Note 6.25. These studies include the California Health Interview Survey, which combines RDD landline telephone sampling and cell phone sampling; a study of police misconduct in Ohio; and a study of violence, crime, and victimization experienced by children. An example of mixed-nonprobability-probability sampling is presented in Research Note 6.26. This is a study of youth-based smoking cessation programs.

RESEARCH NOTE 6.17

Example of Mixed-Nonprobability Sampling: Study of Sexual Risk-Taking Behavior Among African American Women

Foreman (2003) utilized combinations of nonprobability sample designs in studying sexual risk-taking behavior among African American women. She described the sample design she used as follows:

> Recruitment criteria for study participants included being an African American female, attending the university, having had at least one male sex partner within the past year, and providing written informed consent to participate in the study. Research participants (N=15) were recruited using purposive convenience sampling through formal and informal networks. Snowball, also known as chain referral sampling, was also used as participants voluntarily encouraged their friends to participate in the study. A flyer detailing study inclusion criteria, study purpose, participation incentives, and information regarding how participants could contact the researcher was displayed and distributed in various locations throughout the university's campus. A female resident assistant (RA), knowledgeable

about the university community, assisted with recruitment by distributing flyers and serving as a gatekeeper.

All study participants were self-selected volunteers who contacted the researcher and met study inclusion criteria. Potential participants were screened during a brief telephone interview to discuss their involvement in the study. The screening interview was also used to develop rapport and answer any questions regarding study participation.

Source: Foreman, 2003, p. 641. Reprinted with permission.

RESEARCH NOTE 6.18

Example of Mixed-Nonprobability Sampling: Study of Husbands Who Were Abused by Their Spouse

Studying a population for which it is difficult to select a probability sample, Migliaccio (2002) utilized a referrals and a volunteer Internet sample in his study of husbands who had been abused by their spouse. He wanted to compare his findings to previous research on abused wives. He described his sampling procedures as follows:

A nonprobability-sampling procedure was used to contact 12 heterosexual men abused by their female partners. Although abuse does occur within homosexual relationships, this study focuses on those that are historically designated as the perpetrators of abuse: heterosexual men.

Two sampling techniques were used. The first was referrals of individuals connected with men's groups dealing with divorce and custody issues. Of the men, 2 approached the researcher and offered their stories; 2 other respondents, who were not connected to the groups, were referred by group members. All four of these face-to-face interviews were conducted at public establishments such as restaurants, lasting from 1 to 3 hours. The other sampling strategy used was posting on the Internet. The researcher's name, address, and phone number as well as a brief synopsis of the study, including a request for respondents, was inserted onto a Web page for battered men. Potential interviewees contacted the researcher through two different

(Continued)

(Continued)

forms of communication: 3 by e-mail and 4 by phone. Although the phone interviews were completed within the same time frame as those interviewed face to face, the e-mail interviews were conducted over the course of several weeks. Regardless, the same topics were covered in all of the interviews.

Source: Migliaccio, 2002, p. 32. Reprinted with permission.

RESEARCH NOTE 6.19

Example of Mixed-Nonprobability Sampling: Study of the Awarding of Casino Licenses in Philadelphia

Calvano and Andersson (2010) used a mixed-nonprobability sample design in their case study analysis of controversy in the awarding of casino licenses in Philadelphia in 2006. They described their sampling procedures as follows:

In order to examine and interpret current events that are embedded in a rich socio-political context, we used a case study approach, collected evidence from multiple sources and analyzed the evidence using creative analytical practice (CAP) ethnography. We gained the perspective of stakeholders involved in the casino controversy by conducting 19 in-depth, semi-structured interviews with 18 informants over a four-month period beginning in January 2007. In conversations lasting for an average of one hour, we asked informants to provide accounts of key events and interactions and comment on their significance. Our most important concern in selecting informants was to represent the perspectives of all stakeholder groups involved in the controversy. Thus, we used several techniques to ensure balance—key informant sampling (Deaux and Callahan, 1985), snowball sampling (Goodman, 1961) and targeted sampling (Watters and Biernacki, 1989). Beginning with key informant sampling, five individuals provided a broad overview of the casino controversy and generated lists of other potential informants. In order to ensure that we included the views of all sides, we specifically asked informants to recommend individuals who were both in favour of and opposed to casinos in Philadelphia. In addition, we used targeted sampling to contact pro-casino advocates as well as experts on particular aspects of the controversy.

Source: Calvano & Andersson, 2010, p. 588. Reprinted with permission.

RESEARCH NOTE 6.20

Example of Mixed-Nonprobability Sampling: Study of the Mental Health of Lesbians, Gays, and Bisexuals and Their Siblings

Balsam, Beauchaine, Mickey, and Rothblum (2005) described the problems of groups using traditional population-based, probability sampling procedures in sampling a sufficient number of lesbians, gays, and bisexuals (LGB) and a relevant heterosexual control group. Their solution was to use the siblings of the LGB respondents as a control group. They employed a mixed-methods sample design combining a convenience sample of LGBs and a respondent-assisted sample of their siblings. They described the problems and their solution as follows:

[N]ational representative studies yield small numbers of LGB respondents who are often combined into a single group to increase statistical power. Although convenience samples yield large numbers of LGB respondents, they are nonrepresentative and lack a heterosexual control group.

Large paid advertisements were placed in prominent national and state LGB periodicals and in periodicals for LGB people of color. In addition, announcements were sent to LGB organizations listed in the resource book Gayellow Pages (2001). The announcement was placed on LGB Web sites, sent to LGB electronic mailing lists, and distributed by LGB friends and colleagues. The text of ads and announcements stated: "University LGB research team is looking for volunteers to complete a survey about how the lives of adult sisters and brothers are similar or different. To participate, please contact . . . and indicate the number of siblings. You do not need to be out to your siblings to participate in this study." Thus, the ads did not indicate that the study was about mental health. When interested participants from these LGB resources contacted us, they were asked how many siblings might participate. We then mailed questionnaires and postage-paid return envelopes to the original respondents (index participants) and their siblings or, if they wished, mailed all questionnaires to the original respondents for them to mail to their siblings. In some cases, LGB participants had siblings who were themselves LGB. To cast a wide net and not exclude any siblings, we sent questionnaires to LGB siblings as well (such siblings were included in the pool of LGB participants). We did not specify that siblings had to be full biological siblings in order to participate in the study.

Source: Balsam, Beauchaine, Mickey, & Rothblum, 2005, p. 471–472. Reprinted with permission.

RESEARCH NOTE 6.21

Example of Mixed-Nonprobability Sampling: Study of Perceptions of Victimization Risk and Fear of Crime Among Lesbians and Gay Men

Otis (2007) used a mixed-methods nonprobability design in her study of perceptions of victimization risk and fear of crime among lesbians and gay men. She described their sampling procedures as follows:

Respondents for this study are a nonprobability sample of self-defined lesbians, gay men, and bisexuals living in households located in and around two metropolitan cities in a southern state (2000 county populations sizes were 250,000 and 683,000). Participants were recruited using a multipronged approach, including organizational mailing lists, snowball sampling, and a convenience sample at a local LGBT Pride gathering. Two hundred ninety-eight self-identified lesbians and gay men participated in the study.

Source: Otis, 2007, p. 203. Reprinted with permission.

RESEARCH NOTE 6.22

Example of Mixed-Nonprobability-Probability Sampling: Study of the Effect of Caregiving Responsibilities on the Careers of Faculty Members of Schools of Social Work

Young and Holley (2005) used a combination of nonprobability sampling and probability sampling in studying the effect of caregiving responsibilities on the careers of faculty members of schools of social work. They described their sampling procedures as follows:

The sample for this exploratory study comprised individuals who completed their doctorates in social work or social welfare in 1985 or later. Multiple probability and nonprobability sampling approaches were used to identify a diverse group of doctoral graduates who had selected various academic career paths. To recruit graduate-level faculty for the study, we randomly selected 13 schools from a list of Council on Social Work Education (CSWE)–accredited graduate social work schools and directly e-mailed all 168 faculty members who were listed on the selected schools' Web sites. Because fewer BSW programs had Web sites through which faculty members' e-mail addresses could be obtained, we took two steps to recruit faculty from such programs: posting an announcement on the Baccalaureate Program Directors' (BPD) listserv and mailing letters to the directors of a random selection of 79 CSWE-accredited baccalaureate programs asking them to forward information on the study to eligible faculty members. In an attempt to recruit doctoral graduates who had not sought positions in academia, we asked the respondents, via a survey question, to recommend others for participation, and these individuals were e-mailed when their e-mail addresses could be identified. Because early respondents were primarily White, heterosexual, and had no disabilities, we later sent e-mail messages to 23 members of three CSWE commissions (the Commission on Racial, Ethnic, and Cultural Diversity; the Commission on Sexual Orientation and Gender Expression; and the Commission on Disabilities and Persons with Disabilities) asking them to participate and to forward the survey to their colleagues.

Source: Young & Holley, 2005, p. 139. Reprinted with permission.

RESEARCH NOTE 6.23

Example of Mixed-Probability Sampling: RDD Landline and Cell Phone Sample Design of the California Health Interview Survey

The California Health Interview Survey (CHIS) is a population-based telephone survey of California's population conducted every other year since 2001. It is the largest state health survey ever undertaken in the United States. In 2007 the following mixed-methods sample design was used:

CHIS 2007 consisted of three samples: (1) a landline random digit dialing (RDD) sample combined with supplemental Korean and Vietnamese surname list samples, (2) a statewide RDD cell phone sample, and (3) an area

(Continued)

(Continued)

probability sample in Los Angeles County. The landline and cell phone samples were drawn using RDD approaches, whereas the list samples were drawn from separate surname lists of telephone numbers. The area probability sample was drawn in two stages. In the first stage, primary sampling units (PSUs) that represented geographic areas in Los Angeles County were selected with probability proportional to the number of occupied residential units; and in the second stage, residential addresses of households in the selected PSUs were drawn with equal probability. . . . Because of the need to produce reliable estimates at the county level, the sample allocation was not proportional to the population in the counties. With a proportional allocation, the estimates from the smaller counties would be based on small sample sizes and would not be adequate for the envisioned analyses. To achieve the goal of producing local or county estimates, the target sample sizes from medium and smaller counties was fixed at 500 or 600 interviews. The remaining sample was allocated proportional to the population size.

Source: California Health Interview Survey, 2009. Reprinted with permission.

RESEARCH NOTE 6.24

Example of Mixed-Probability Sampling: Study of the Prevalence of Police Misconduct in Ohio

Son and Rome (2004) examined the prevalence of police misconduct in the general police force in Ohio by analyzing data collected in a survey of citizens and a survey of police officers. An RDD sample was used in the survey of citizens and a two-stage cluster sample was used in the survey of police officers. They described their sampling procedures used in these two surveys as follows:

The citizen data analyzed in this study were obtained from a random sample of Ohio residents. Telephone interviews were conducted with 988 Ohio residents in the fall and winter of 1992 through random digit dialing.

The police data were collected in the winter and spring of 1993. The sample consisted of 665 Ohio police officers obtained by stratified cluster sampling. The cluster was a police department. The stratification was based on department size: small (fewer than 11 officers), medium-small (11 to 49 officers), medium-large (50 to 99 officers), and large (100 or more officers). From the selected departments, officers were chosen randomly for the survey. The number of officers in each stratum of the sample was proportionate to their numbers in the total population of officers.

Source: Son & Rome (2004), pp. 183–184. Reprinted with permission.

RESEARCH NOTE 6.25

Example of Mixed-Probability Sampling: Study of Violence, Crime, and Victimization of Children and Youth

Finkelhor, Ormrod, Turner, and Hamby (2005) examined a large range of violence, crime, and victimization experiences in a nationally representative sample of children and youth ages 2 to 17 years using a mixed-methods sample design. First, households were selected using list-assisted RDD; then, after collecting data from parents, one child was selected from eligible households. Their sample design was described as follows:

The sample selection procedures were based on a list-assisted random-digit (RDD) telephone survey design. List-assisted dialing confines the random digit selection from telephone exchanges that have known listed phone numbers. This design increases the rate of contacting eligible respondents by decreasing the rate of dialing business and nonworking numbers. . . .

A short interview was conducted with an adult caregiver (usually a parent) to obtain family demographic information. One child was randomly selected from all eligible children living in a household by selecting the child with the most recent birthday. If the selected child was age 2 to 9 years, the interview was conducted with the caregiver who was most familiar with the child's daily routine and experiences.

Source: Finkelhor, Ormrod, Turner, & Hamby, 2005, p. 7. Reprinted with permission.

RESEARCH NOTE 6.26

Example of Mixed-Nonprobability-Probability Sampling: Study of Community-Based Youth Smoking Cessation Programs

Emery et al. (2010) proposed a mixed-nonprobability-probability sample design for the study of community-based youth smoking cessation programs. Their proposed design has two stages: a probability sampling of counties in the first stage and a respondent-assisted sampling in the second stage. They described their sampling procedures as follows:

Our strategy for seeking and identifying community-based youth smoking cessation programs in the United States began with a clear operational definition of the target sample. We then developed a two-stage sampling design, with counties as the first-stage probability sampling units. The second stage used snowball sampling to identify individuals who administered youth smoking cessation programs. Cessation programs were profiled as they were identified. The goal of the snowball sampling strategy was to identify all contacts at the local level, who were knowledgeable about youth smoking cessation programs in their communities, or who could lead to such persons. Snowball sampling progressed through two "tiers" and ended with the identification of a program informant who administered a youth smoking cessation program in the community. The intent of this two-stage process was to contact the entire population of individuals within each county, who would have knowledge of, or be an administrator of, a youth smoking cessation program.

The critical elements of our methodology, described in detail below, were to

- Identify a proxy sample frame from which to search;
- Stratify the sample frame by key variables of interest;
- Use prior research and practical knowledge of youth smoking cessation treatment to identify likely sectors within the units of the sample frame from which to begin the search for programs;
- Develop lists of Tier 1 key informants within each sector, using publicly available information;
- Snowball sample for additional informants and program administrators, referred to as Tier 2 contacts; and
- Interview potential program administrators to screen for program eligibility for inclusion in the survey.

Source: Emery et al., 2010, p. 38. Reprinted with permission.

RESEARCH NOTE 6.27

Example of Mixed-Nonprobability-Probability Sampling: Study of Inmate-on-Inmate Sexual Assaults in California's Prisons

Jenness, Maxson, Sumner, and Matsuda (2010) conducted a survey of adult prisoners in California's prisons in a study of inmate-on-inmate sexual assaults. This study used a purposive sampling of prisons, simple random sampling of the general inmate population of the selected prisons, and a convenience sample of "transgendered" inmates housed in another prison. The simple random sampling procedure that was used is described in Research Note 5.1. The convenience sampling of the selection of the transgendered inmates is described below:

> In addition to the six prisons selected for the random sample of inmates, a seventh prison provided a research site from which to gather data from transgender inmates beyond the rare instances in which transgender inmates emerged in the random sample. This prison was chosen because it is known to house a concentrated population of transgender inmates . . . [It was used in] securing a convenience sample of transgender inmates. . . . For the purposes of this research, a "transgender" inmate was identified either through self-identification, identification of related medical needs (i.e., hormonal treatment), or participation in groups for transgender inmates. Once we received a list of inmates meeting one or more of these criteria from our liaison at this prison, we asked that they all be [prepared] for an interview. We made two trips to this facility to ensure that we provided all transgender inmates who were identified an opportunity to participate in the study.

Source: Jenness, Maxson, Sumner, & Matsuda, 2010, pp. 11-12. Reprinted with permission.

SUMMARY

Sampling procedures may be classified not only according to their operational procedures, but also according to the nature of the unit that is sampled. Often in population-based studies (i.e., studies using elements of the population as units of analysis), although the unit of analysis of a study is population-based, units of the population may not be available or practical to be used as sampling units. Alternative sampling units must be used. A number of sampling procedures characterized by the nature of the sampling unit have been developed. They include telephone-based sampling, web-based sampling, address-based sampling, time-based sampling, and space-based sampling. Telephone-based sampling utilizes telephone numbers as sampling units. It has three major subtypes: list-based sampling, basic random digit dialing, and list-assisted random digit dialing. Web-based sampling utilizes elements of electronic communications as sampling units. It has nonprobability and probability forms. Each has the following subtypes: list-based, selection of web site visits, and recruited panels. Address-based sampling utilizes addresses as sampling units. Time-based sampling utilizes units of time as the sampling unit. Space-based sampling utilizes space as sampling units. Venue-based sampling utilizes combinations of time and space as sampling units.

In addition to presenting descriptions of sample designs distinguished by the nature of the sample unit that is used, this chapter also presents a description of mixed-methods sample designs. Instead of implementing a single-method sample design, a researcher may combine multiple types of sample designs, creating mixed-methods sample designs. Mixed-methods research designs are typically characterized by the mixing of qualitative and quantitative research designs. Mixed-methods sample designs involve the use of different types of nonprobability sample designs, different types of probability sample designs, and combinations of nonprobability and probability sample designs. Within-methods designs either combine multiple nonprobability sample designs or combine multiple probability sample designs. Cross-methods designs combine nonprobability sample designs and probability sample designs. Subtypes of mixed-methods sample designs may be further classified utilizing the dimensions time ordering of the execution of the designs (concurrent and sequential) and the relationship of the designs to each other (equivalent, nested, and multilevel).

REVIEW QUESTIONS

1. Describe factors that affected the trends in the use of telephone-based sampling, web-based sampling, and address-based sampling.

2. What are the major subtypes of telephone sampling, the steps involved in using them, and their strengths and weaknesses?

3. How has the cell phone influenced telephone sampling?

4. What are the major subtypes of web-based sampling and their strengths and weaknesses?

5. What is address-based sampling, and what factors have influenced its use?

6. What is time-based sampling? Describe examples of its applications.

7. Describe possible applications of time-space (venue-based) sampling.

8. What is mixed-methods sampling?

9. What do you consider to be the most critical guidelines for choosing among the various types of mixed-methods sampling? Why?

10. What alternative sample designs would you propose for the sample designs described in the research notes in this chapter?

11. Oldfield (2001) provides a critical assessment of the use of time sampling in observational research. Oldfield indicates that a major limitation of time sampling is the reliability in estimating frequency and duration of observed behavior. Give examples of situations in which these limitations would be important.

12. Has the time come for mixed-methods research? See Johnson and Onwuegbuzie (2004) listing in References for more information.

13. Are representative Internet surveys possible? Why or why not? Once you have answered this question, consider Smith's "Are Representative Internet Surveys Possible?" (2002).

14. If you wanted to conduct a study of travel behavior of the U.S. population, would you use web-based sampling or address-based sampling? Why? Once you have answered these questions, consider Nadkarni and Harmon's "Accuracy of Travel Data Samples: Utilizing Online vs. Mail Tethodologies" (2008).

15. Random digit dialing (RDD) can be very costly as many telephone numbers dialed are likely to be either nonworking, disconnected, or non-household telephone numbers. List-assisted RDD methods attempt to reduce these costs. Is list-assisted RDD likely to be more cost effective than sampling from electronic white pages? Why or why not? Once you have answered this question, consider Yang and Eyeson-Annan's "Does Sampling Using Random Digit Dialing Really Cost More Than Sampling From Telephone Directories: Debunking the Myths" (2006).

KEY TERMS

Define and give examples of the following concepts:

address-based sampling

list-assisted RDD sampling

mixed-methods sampling

sequential mixed-methods sampling

space-based sampling

telephone-based sampling

time-based sampling

venue-based sampling

web-based sampling

REFERENCES FOR FURTHER STUDY

Bergman, M. (Ed). (2008). *Advances in mixed methods research.* London: Sage.

Blumberg, S. J., & Luke, J. (2007). Coverage bias in traditional telephone surveys of low-income and young adults. *Public Opinion Quarterly, 71,* 734–749.

Bradley, N. (1999). Sampling for Internet surveys: An examination of respondent selection for Internet research. *Journal of the Market Research Society, 41,* 387–395.

Bryant, B. E. (1975). Respondent selection in a time of changing household composition. *Journal of Marketing Research, 12,* 129–135.

Collins, K. M. T., Onwuegbuzie, A. J., & Jiao, Q. G. (2006). Prevalence of mixed-methods sampling designs in social science research. *Evaluation and Research in Education, 19,* 83–101.

Collins, K. M. T., Onwuegbuzie, A. J., & Jiao, Q. G. (2007). A mixed methods investigation of mixed methods sampling designs in social and health science research. *Journal of Mixed Methods Research, 1,* 267–294.

Cooper, S. L. (1964). Random sampling by telephone: An improved method. *Journal of Marketing Research, 1,* 45–48.

Creswell, J. W., & Plano Clark, V. L. (2007). *Designing and conducting mixed methods research.* Thousand Oaks, CA: Sage.

Curtin, R., Presser, S., & Singer, E. (2005). Changes in telephone survey nonresponse over the past quarter century. *Public Opinion Quarterly, 69,* 87–98.

Czaja, R., Blair, J., & Sebestik, J. P. (1982). Respondent selection in a telephone survey: A comparison of three techniques. *Journal of Marketing Research, 19,* 381–385.

Dutwin, D., Keeter, S., & Kennedy, C. (2010). Bias from wireless substitution in surveys of Hispanics. *Hispanic Journal of Behavioral Sciences, 32,* 309–328.

Groves, R. M., & Kahn, R. L. (1979). *Surveys by telephone: A national comparison with personal interviews.* New York: Academic Press.

Hnatiuk, S. H. (1991). Experience sampling with elderly persons: An exploration of the method. *International Journal of Aging and Human Development, 33,* 45–64.

Iannacchionee, V. G., Staab, J. M., & Redden, D. T. (2003). Evaluating the use of residential mailing addresses in a metropolitan household survey. *Public Opinion Quarterly, 76,* 202–210.

Johnson, R. B., & Onwuegbuzie, A. J. (2004). Mixed methods research: A research paradigm whose time has come. *Educational Researcher, 33,* 14–26.

Keeter, K. (2006). The impact of cell phone noncoverage bias on polling in the 2004 presidential election. *Public Opinion Quarterly, 70,* 88–98.

Lavrakas, P. J. (1993). *Telephone survey methods: Sampling, selection, and supervision.* Thousand Oaks, CA: Sage.

Lavrakas, P. J., Shuttles, C. D., Steeh, C., & Fienberg, H. (2007). The state of surveying cell phone numbers in the United States. *Public Opinion Quarterly, 71,* 840–854.

Link, M. W., Battaglia, M. P., Frankel, M. R., Osborn, L., & Mokdad, A. H. (2008). A comparison of address-based sampling (ABS) versus random-digit dialing (RDD) for general population surveys. *Public Opinion Quarterly, 72,* 6–27.

Mann, J., Have, T., Plunkett, J., & Meisels, S. (1991). Time sampling: A methodological critique. *Child Development, 62,* 227–241.

Nadkarni, N., & Harmon, G. (2008). Accuracy of travel data samples: Utilizing online vs. mail methodologies. Proceedings of Statistics Canada Symposium 2001. Available at: http://www.statcan.gc.ca/bsolc/olc-cel/olc-cel?catno=11-522-X&chropg=1&lang=eng

Parsons, J. T., Grov, C., & Kelly, B. C. (2008). Comparing the effectiveness of two forms of time-space sampling to identify club drug-using young adults. *Journal of Drug Issues, 38*, 1061–1082.

Peytchev, A., Carley-Baxter, L. R., & Black, M. C. (2010). Coverage bias in variances, associations, and total error from exclusion of the cell phone-only population in the United States. *Social Science Computer Review, 28*, 287–302.

Pratesi, M., Manfreda, K. L., Biffignandi, S., Vehovar, V. (2004). List-based Web surveys: Quality, timeliness, and nonresponse in the steps of the pa/rticipation flow. *Journal of Official Statistics, 20*, 451–465.

Smith, T. W. (2002). Are representative Internet surveys possible? Proceedings of Statistics Canada Symposium 2001. Available at: http://www.statcan.gc.ca/bsolc/olc-cel/olc-cel?catno=11-522-X&chropg=1&lang=eng

Tashakkori, A., & Teddlie, C. (1998). *Mixed methodology: Combining qualitative and quantitative approaches.* Thousand Oaks, CA: Sage.

Teddlie, C., & Yu, F. (2007). Mixed methods sampling: A typology with examples. *Journal of Mixed Methods Research, 1*, 77–100.

Tuckel, P., & O'Neill, H. (2002). The vanishing respondent in telephone surveys. *Journal of Advertising Research, 42*, 26–48.

Waksberg, J. (1978). Sampling methods for random digit dialing. *Journal of the American Statistical Association. 73*, 40–46.

Yang, B., & Eyeson-Annan, M. (2006). Does sampling using random digit dialing really cost more than sampling from telephone directories: Debunking the myths. *BMC Medical Research Methodology, 6*, 6–14.

Yu, F. (2007). Mixed methods sampling. *Journal of Mixed Methods Research, 1*, 77–100.

CHAPTER 7
CHOOSING THE SIZE OF THE SAMPLE

> *What you will learn in this chapter:*
>
> - How to determine sample size
> - Guidelines for choosing an appropriate sample size for nonprobability sample designs
> - Guidelines for choosing an appropriate sample size for probability sample designs

INTRODUCTION

The choice of sample size is a very important decision. One should carefully assess all of the relevant factors, but should not waste time and money by selecting a sample size too large, nor fail to satisfy the objectives on one's study because the sample size is too small. This chapter includes a description of guidelines for determining sample size.

GUIDELINES FOR CHOOSING SAMPLE SIZE

Determination of sample size should begin with a review of the factors covered in Chapter 1. One should have a clear understanding of the following:

- Objectives of the study:
  - Exploratory versus nonexploratory objectives
  - Importance to have credible results
  - Need to describe or compare subpopulations
  - Need to include rare or very small categories of the population in the study

- Ethical and legal considerations
- Nature of the population
- Availability of resources
- Nature of the research design including:
  o Type of research design
  o Type of data analysis design
  o Type of sample design

Moreover, one should determine whether one will use a fixed approach or a sequential approach. When using a fixed approach, one would set a specific sample size target before commencing data collection. On the other hand, using a sequential approach, instead of preselecting a specific sample size target, one would preselect a set of decision rules or stopping rules to govern when sampling will stop. Sample size determination involves a number of critical choices. A flow chart of considerations in determining sample size is displayed in Figure 7.1.

Objectives of the Study

> **Guideline 7.1.** *Objectives of the study.* If a research study has an exploratory objective, and/or has a low level of importance, consider using a small sample size rather than a large sample size. On the other hand, if the objective of a research study is to provide a description of a population, a prediction, an evaluation, or an explanation, a relatively large sample size may be required. Moreover, generally, the greater the importance of a study, the need to conduct detailed analyses of subpopulations, and the need to include rare or very small segments of a population, the larger the sample size is required.

In conducting an exploratory study, the researcher is not attempting to make conclusive analyses, and a small sample size may suffice. On the other hand, if a study concerns critical business decisions or scientific issues, and requires great precision, its research design should be more rigorous. For such circumstances, a large sample size may be justified. For explorative research, a small sample size may suffice.

Moreover, generally, the more important a study is, the larger the sample size required in order to satisfy the objectives. A large sample size would minimize random sampling error and make for a more rigorous analysis of the data collected.

Figure 7.1   Factors Consider in Determining Sample Size

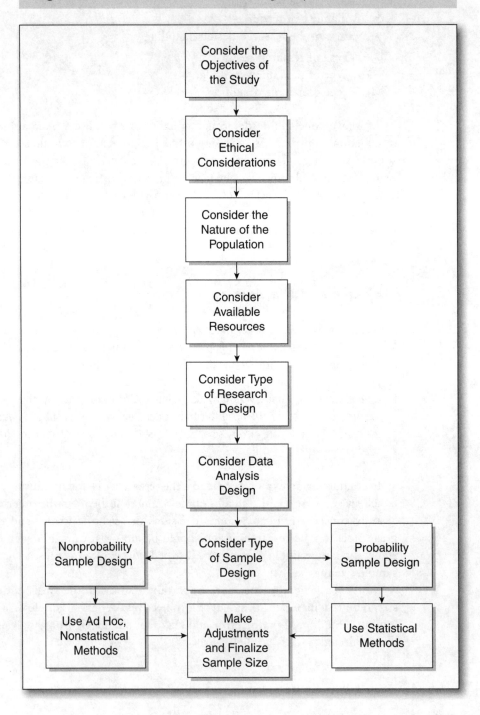

A study that requires one to describe or compare detailed subpopulations generally requires a larger sample size than a study that requires one only to describe population parameters. Research frequently has multiple target populations, each critically important to the objectives of the study. A health survey may target all persons who have chronic and acute conditions, women within their reproductive years, families with infants, families with children aged 13 to 17, or families with persons 65 years or older. In order to have equally reliable results for each of these subpopulations, the sample size of the study may have to be much larger than the sample size for a health survey that does not have such concerns.

If the objectives require the inclusion of rare or hidden populations in one's study, or if a sampling procedure such as respondent-assisted sampling is not used, a large sample size may be required to obtain a sufficient sample size. Generally, the more rare and hidden the target population, the larger the required sample size.

Ethical Considerations

Guideline 7.2. *Ethical considerations.* Taking the burden on study participants into consideration, one should choose the smallest sample necessary to satisfy the objectives of a study.

Participation in research imposes a burden on participants. Although this burden is greater in some research than in others, it is unethical to subject participants to any unnecessary burden. From an ethical point of view, a sample is too large if it has more participants than necessary and too small if it is not large enough to detect a significant effect that has practical relevance. An extremely large sample may indicate that a very small difference is statistically significant even though the difference may be meaningless from a practical or clinical perspective. One should choose the smallest sample that satisfies the study's objectives.

Nature of the Population

Several characteristics of a target population are relevant in determining the sample size. These include:

- Size of the population
- Homogeneity/heterogeneity of the population
- Spatial distribution of the population

Guideline 7.3. *Size of the population.* For large populations, size of the population is not a critical factor in determining sample size; on the other hand, for small populations, the size of the population should be considered in determining sample size.

Population size is usually not a factor in determining sample size. However, if the sample is more than 5% of the population size, the size of the population should be taken into consideration.

Guideline 7.4. *Homogeneity/heterogeneity of the population.* The more homogeneous the population in terms of the variables of interest, the more consideration should be given to choosing a smaller sample rather than a larger sample; the more heterogeneous the population in terms of the variables of interest, the more consideration should be given to choosing a larger sample rather than a smaller sample.

The rule of homogeneity holds that the more homogeneous the population, the fewer elements are necessary to represent the population. If a population is perfectly homogeneous in terms of the study variables, only one element would be necessary to have a representative sample. Inferences based on homogeneous samples have smaller margins of error than inferences based on heterogeneous samples. It is not unusual for a research project to have multiple key variables with differing variances. In such a situation, one should choose the sample size based on the variable for which the greatest precision is required.

Guideline 7.5. *Spatial distribution of the population.* Due to the relationship between the spatial distribution of the population and data collection costs, the more scattered a population, the more consideration should be given to choosing a smaller sample rather than a larger sample.

The spatial distribution of a population significantly affects the data collection costs of a study; as a result, the spatial distribution of the population is a critical factor in determining sample size. Given availability of funds, a larger sample may not be an option in studying a widely dispersed population. Using cluster sampling may reduce such costs. However, as noted earlier, cluster sampling would yield higher sampling errors, necessitating the sampling of a larger number of clusters and a larger overall sample size.

Availability of Resources

Guideline 7.6. *Availability of resources.* The more limited one's resources (i.e., money, time, facilities, personnel, etc.), the more consideration should be given to choosing a smaller sample rather than a larger sample.

The number of elements selected for a research project will primarily be determined by the availability of resources. There is a direct relationship between amount of money, time, facilities, and personnel available to conduct a study and sample size. It will be a waste of effort to identify a large number of elements for participation in the study if one does not have the facilities, personnel, and other resources to involve them in the study. If immediate results are required, a large sample size may be out of the question. There must be a balance between resources and sample size. Using only budget considerations, the sample size may be determined by dividing the available funds for data collection by the average data collection cost per element.

Research Design Considerations

Several factors relating to the research design of a study should be considered in determining sample size. These include considerations relating to:

- Type of research design
- Data analysis design
- Type of sample design

Type of Research Design

Guideline 7.7. *Type of research design.* Quantitative research designs tend to require larger sample sizes than qualitative research designs; nonexperimental designs tend to require larger sample sizes than experimental research designs; and longitudinal research designs tend to have larger sample sizes than cross-sectional research designs.

Sampling in qualitative research tends to differ from sampling in quantitative research in that quantitative research designs tend to require larger sample sizes. Although a specific sample size may be prescribed in employing availability sampling and quota sampling, often specific sample sizes are not targeted in purposive sampling and respondent-assisted sampling.

Experimental research designs also tend to have smaller sample sizes than survey research designs. Experimental research designs focus on variable and relationships external validity, and the internal validity of the study. More attention is given to controlling for measurement error and controlling for extraneous variables than factors affecting population generalizability. When different types of experimental designs are compared, quasi-experimental designs should have larger sample sizes than true experimental designs because, since randomization is not used, a larger sample size is needed to control for extraneous variables via statistical analyses.

Longitudinal research designs, or more specifically, panel longitudinal research designs, tend to have larger sample sizes than cross-sectional research designs. In panel longitudinal designs, data are collected from the same population elements at different points in time. In order to compensate for problems in recruiting population elements for long-term studies and the problem of mortality, elements leaving the study, often a larger sample size is used than what would have been used with a different research design.

Data Analysis Design

Guideline 7.8. *Data analysis design.* The sample size should be set taking into consideration:

- The assumptions of the statistical procedures that are to be used in the study.
- The complexity and amount of details the data analysis design required. For example, one should take into account the required sample size per cell of cross-tabulations that may be part of one's analysis design.
- The strength of the expected relationship of relationships studies, and the size of the differences between categories for comparative studies. The stronger the expected relationship the data analysis is expected to reveal, the smaller the sample size necessary to reveal the result; while the fainter the relationship the data analysis is expected to reveal, the larger the sample size necessary to reveal the result. Moreover, the smaller the differences between categories that are expected, the larger the sample size that is necessary.

Statistical procedures vary in terms of their sample size requirements. Violation of the sample size assumptions of the statistical procedures that are used will affect the internal validity of a study.

Analyses that are complex, include a large number of variables, and include detailed subgroup analyses require larger sample sizes than other analyses. The strength of the relationship analyzed will also affect the sample size requirements of a study. Generally, the stronger the expected relationships, the smaller the sample size necessary to detect it.

Type of Sample Design

The sample size required differs from one sample design to the other. The type of sample design affects the relevance of different factors in determining sample size. The calculations of the margin of error of estimates and the significance of differences between estimates assume the use of probability sampling. Such calculations are irrelevant if nonprobability sampling is used. Considerations relating to the type of sample design are described below.

Guideline 7.9. *Nonprobability sample designs.* If nonprobability sampling is used, consider using adhoc, nonstatistical methods in determining sample size.

If a researcher uses nonprobability sampling, although statistical theories are not applicable in determining sample size, one may consider using various conventions, "rules of thumb," and adhoc, nonstatistical methods. Typical sample sizes for various types of research designs include:

- Case study research: 3 to 5 participants
- Phenomenological research: 6 to 10 participants
- Grounded theory research: 15 to 30 participants
- Ethnographic research: 35 to 50 participants
- Focus group research: 3 to 12 focus groups depending upon type of participants, 6 to 12 participants per group
- Experimental research: 15 to 30 participants per group
- Survey research, single topic community or national study: 400 to 2,500 participants
- Survey research: multipletopic, national study: 10,000 to 15,000 participants
- Exploratory research, pilot study, pretest: 20 to 150 participants
- Correlation research: 30 participants
- Analysis of major subgroup: 100 participants
- Analysis of minor subgroup: 30 participants
- Marketing research, product testing: 200 to 2,500 participants
- Population size over 400: 200 to 1,500 participants

Guideline 7.10. *Probability sample designs.* If probability sampling is used, consider using statistical formulas in determining sample size.

If probability sampling is used, it is not necessary to rely on conventions and rules of thumb in determining sample size. One may use statistical formulas based on probability theories. The formulas for calculating sample size vary from problem to problem. If one is conducting a descriptive study with the purpose of estimating population parameters, one should use formulas for calculating the confidence of intervals for these estimates. The confidence level describes the level of confidence that the population figure is within the confidence interval around the estimate. If one is conducting an analytical study or experimental research with the purpose of estimating the significance of the difference between subgroups, one would use formulas for testing the significance of such differences.

If an objective of the research is to estimate population parameters, one may determine the sample size necessary for such a study by using formulas for calculating the confidence intervals for the statistic used in the study (the confidence interval approach of determining sample size). Steps that may be used for a simple random sample design include:

1. Identify the major study variable(s) and determine whether they are categorical or continuous. It is not unusual for a study to have more than one variable of interest. The sample size should be sufficient for all the important analyses that must be done. One may calculate the sample size for all of the important variables, and then use the one that requires the largest sample size.

2. Determine the statistic to estimate. Typically, if the variables are categorical, percentages (or proportions) are used; if the variables are continuous, means are used.

3. Identify the formula (equation) for computing confidence intervals for the statistic selected in Step 2, and solve the equation for the sample size. Depending upon the formulas used, the equations below may result:

   - Proportions: $n = z^2\,pq/e^2$
   - Means: $n = z^2 s^2/e^2$

Where:

n = the sample size

z = the z score corresponding with the desired level of confidence or probability of error. The level of confidence is equal to 1 minus the significance level (α). Typically, a level of confidence of 95% (i.e., one can be 95% certain that the true figure is within the margin of error) is set. A z score of 1.96 is used for the .95 level of confidence, and a z score of 2.58 is used for the .99 level of confidence.

p = the estimated proportion in the population. This estimate might be based on prior research, pilot study, estimates from experienced researcher(s) who studied similar populations and research questions, and/or industry conventions. The most conservative estimate is .50. It is used if there is little basis for making an estimate.

$q = 1 - p$

e = the tolerable margin of error or precision of the estimate. It should be driven by the purposes of the study. The more important the study, the higher the level of precision desired, and the smaller the tolerable margin of error that should be targeted.

s = estimated variability of the statistic in the target population. The estimate may be based on prior research, pilot study, estimates from experienced researcher(s) who studied similar populations and research questions, and/or industry conventions. If information on the range is available, the range method for estimating the standard deviation may be used by dividing the range by a value of 4 to 6.

Example 1: What sample size is necessary to estimate the proportion of voters likely to vote for a political candidate if prior research indicates that it is likely that the candidate will receive 54% of the vote, and it is desired that the margin of error is .04 and the level of confidence is .95?

Answer:

$$n = z^2 \, pq/e^2$$
$$= (1.96^2)(.54)(.46)/ \, .04^2$$
$$= 596$$

Example 2: What sample size is necessary to estimate mean number of hours per week students at a local high school study if prior research suggests a standard deviation of 2 hours; it is desired that the margin of error is .5 hours; and the level of confidence is .95?

Answer:

$$n = z^2 s^2/e^2$$
$$= ((1.96^2)(2^2)/.5)^2$$
$$= 62$$

Using the above formula for calculating the sample size for a study whose variables of interest are measured in terms of proportions, the sample size for various values of a proportion and margin of error were calculated and presented in Table 7.1. The 95% level of confidence was used for these calculations. The formula used assumes simple random sampling is used, and study is descriptive study with a purpose to estimate population parameters. Different formulas would be appropriate for studies with different purposes, data analytic requirements, and more complex sample designs. The discussion of these formulas is beyond the scope of this text. (For more information, see Kish, 1965; Levy & Lemeshow, 2008; Lohr, 2009; Scheaffer, Mendenhall, & Ott, 2006; Thompson, 2002.)

Table 7.1 Sample Size for Various Values of a Proportion and Margin of Error

Value of Proportion	Margin of Error (+/−)									
	.01	.02	.03	.04	.05	.06	.07	.08	.09	.10
.01	380	95	42	24	15	11	8	6	5	4
.02	753	188	84	47	30	21	15	12	9	8
.03	1118	279	124	70	45	31	23	17	14	11
.04	1475	369	164	92	59	41	30	23	18	15
.05	1825	456	203	114	73	51	37	29	23	18
.06	2167	542	241	135	87	60	44	34	27	22
.07	2501	625	278	156	100	69	51	39	31	25
.08	2827	707	314	177	113	79	58	44	35	28
.09	3146	787	350	197	126	87	64	49	39	31
.10	3457	864	384	216	138	96	71	54	43	35
.15	4898	1225	544	306	196	136	100	77	60	49
.20	6147	1537	683	384	246	171	125	96	76	61
.25	7203	1801	800	450	288	200	147	113	89	72
.30	8067	2017	896	504	323	224	165	126	100	81
.35	8740	2185	971	546	350	243	178	137	108	87
.40	9220	2305	1024	576	369	256	188	144	114	92
.45	9508	2377	1056	594	380	264	194	149	117	95
.50	9604	2401	1067	600	384	267	196	150	119	96

Note: The 95% level of confidence was used for these calculations.

Guideline 7.11. *Sequential sampling approaches.* One may apply the above formulas prior to data collection, fixing the sample size at that time, or a sequential sampling or adaptive sampling approach may be used. In using a sequential approach, the number of sampling units to be included in the study is not fixed in advance of data collection. Instead of setting a fixed sample size, a researcher would set a "stopping rule," such as a targeted margin of error or "data saturation," and continue to sample until the rule is satisfied. If probability sampling is used, the researcher may continue to add cases until a targeted margin of error is satisfied. If nonprobability sampling is used, the researcher may continue to sample until additional elements do not provide new information; that is, one has "data saturation," "theoretical saturation," or "informational redundancy," or exhausted the social network being studied. Sequential sampling has been found to result in smaller samples than the sample size generated via a fixed approach, and as a result is completed in a shorter period of time (Anscombe, 1963; Armitage, 1975; Birt & Brogren, 1964; Howe, 1982).

The following research notes provide examples of sample size determination in qualitative research. The task is such that research is often not to make inferences to population parameters but to bring about an understanding of the subject matter of the study. Theoretical saturation is one of the criteria used to determine whether a sample is too small or too large. Research Notes 7.1 and 7.2 provide illustrations of theoretical saturation. Research Note 7.1 concerns a study of nursing support for family members of critically ill adults, and Research Note 7.2 concerns a study of the effect of spirituality on the self-management of diabetes among African Americans.

RESEARCH NOTE 7.1

Example of Theoretical Saturation: Study of Nursing Support for Family Members of Critically Ill Adults

Vandall-Walker, Jensen, and Oberle (2007) used theoretical sampling in their grounded theory study of nursing support for family members of critically ill adults. They used theoretical saturation in determining sample size of the study. They described their sampling procedures as follows:

> To be included, participants had to be adult family members who (a) visited an adult patient admitted to a critical care unit, (b) were able to speak and understand English, and (c) were cognitively able to reflect on and verbalize their experiences and their perceptions of nursing support. At the time of the

(Continued)

(Continued)

initial face-to-face meeting, a written consent was obtained after an explanation of the study both verbally and in written form.

Sampling was engaged in until theoretical saturation was reached; that is, until what was being revealed in the data was not new information but confirmatory of the categories already developed. This approach resulted in a convenience sample of 20 family members from 14 families who were involved in one or two interviews held in a quiet room in the ICU, the social worker's office, or the first author's office.

Ideally in grounded theory, after the first few interviews, data collection is guided by theoretical sampling, in which the interviewer purposively samples "people, places, or events, that will maximize opportunities to discover variations among concepts and to densify categories in terms of their properties and dimensions" (Strauss & Corbin, 1998, p. 201). In this study, theoretical sampling was constrained somewhat by the nature of the ethically approved recruitment process, wherein participants self-selected. However, this self-selection did result in participants being recruited from most of the critical care units, so there was breadth of appropriate "places" represented. As well, from within this pool of participants, theoretical sampling for incidents and experiences was addressed. Partway through the study, some family members who had heard of the study by word of mouth were recruited. These individuals added information that significantly influenced the evolving theory and constituted a serendipitous theoretical sample: individuals the first author would have approached had the ethically approved recruitment protocol included this option.

Source: Vandall-Walker, Jensen, & Oberle, 2007, pp. 1208–1209. Reprinted with permission.

RESEARCH NOTE 7.2

Example of Theoretical Saturation: Study of the Effect of Spirituality on the Self-Management of Diabetes Among African Americans

Polzer and Miles (2007) used theoretical sampling in their development of a theoretical model about how the spirituality of African Americans affects their self-management of diabetes. Their sample size was determined by theoretical saturation. They described their sampling procedures as follows:

Participants were men and women with diabetes, as well as 5 Protestant ministers. The inclusion criteria for participants with diabetes were (a) African American men and women, (b) diagnosed with type 2 diabetes for at least a year, (c) under the care of a health care provider for type 2 diabetes, (d) ages 40 to 75 years, (e) of low socioeconomic status, (f) able to perform most of the activities of self-management themselves, (g) cognitively intact, and (h) able to speak English. In addition, participants had (a) no other health problems that required considerable self-management and (b) no other health problems for which the person was undergoing current major medical treatment (e.g., chemotherapy). The only eligibility criterion for the ministers was that they be ministers of churches with primarily African American congregations.

Sampling began with purposeful sampling, whereby individuals who were deemed information rich were chosen for the study (Patton, 2001). As typologies began to emerge in data analysis, we used theoretical sampling to refine the differences and similarities between these groups. Data collection and analysis stopped once informational redundancy had been achieved.

The sample of persons with diabetes consisted of 10 African American men and 19 African American women. All had been diagnosed with type 2 diabetes for a mean of 13 years (range 1 to 35).

Source: Polzer & Miles, 2007, p. 178. Reprinted with permission.

Final Adjustments

Once a targeted sample size has been determined either by "rules of thumb" or statistical formulas, further adjustments should be made. Where relevant, adjustments should be made for:

- Ineligibility/incidence rate
- Nonresponse
- Finite population correction factor
- Design effect
- Attrition/mortality rate

Guideline 7.12. *Ineligibility/incidence rate.* The targeted sample size should be adjusted to take into account the ineligibility or incidence rate.

It should be anticipated that when contact is made with the sampled elements, some will not be members of the target population. They should be excluded from the study. The targeted sample size should be adjusted to account for ineligibles.

- Gross incidence rate: the percentage of the general population that are members of the finite population, for example, the percentage of the general population who are 18 years of age or older.
- Reachable rate: Reflects how good the sampling frame is.
- Net incidence rate: The percentage of contacts who qualify for inclusion in the study. Gross incidence × qualification percentage.
- Completion rate: Percentage of elements in the target population from whom a completed data collection instrument is obtained.
- Contacts = n / R × I × C

Guideline 7.13. *Nonresponse.* The targeted sample size should be adjusted to take into account the unit nonresponse rate and the item nonresponse rate for key variables.

One should anticipate unit nonresponse and item nonresponse for key variables. Previous similar research and/or a pilot study might assist in estimating the nonresponse one is likely to encounter. The targeted sample size should be adjusted for anticipated nonresponse.

Guideline 7.14. *Finite population correction factor.* If the probability sampling is used and the calculated targeted sample size is greater than 5% of the population, the targeted sample size should be adjusted to take into account the finite population correction factor.

If sampling without replacement is used and the sample is large relative to the population (the sample size is greater than 5% of the population size), an adjustment should be made to the targeted sample size using a finite population correction factor (fpc). The fpc may be computed using the formula: fpc = square root of $(N - n) / N - 1)$, where N = the population size, and n = the sample size. The fpc has little effect when the sample size is less than 5% of the population. The finite population correction takes into account that unlike the assumption made in standard statistical theory that population is infinite, the population is finite in size and the sample is selected without replacement. The higher the sampling fraction (n/N), the lower the fpc and the standard error of estimates based on the sample.

> **Guideline 7.15.** *Design effect.* If probability cluster sampling is used, the targeted sample size should be adjusted taking into account the design effect.

The formulas presented in the above discussion of the confidence interval and the hypothesis testing approaches in determining the size of a sample assume that simple random sampling will be used. On the other hand, other formulas must be used for alternative sample designs. A review of these formulas is beyond the scope of this text. Yet, an adjustment may be made via the targeted sample size by applying the design effect. The design effect (DEFF) is the ratio of the variances of sample design employed to the variances of a comparable simple random sample design. The DEFF of a stratified sample design tends to be a little less than one, indicating that if stratification is used the sample size may be smaller than the sample size simple random sampling at the same margin of error. Technically, the DEFF indicates how much less (or more) the precision of a nonsimple random design used when it is compared to the precision of simple random sample design. From a sample size perspective, it indicates how many more (or fewer) elements should be selected in the planned sample design compared to the sample size required for a simple random sample to achieve the same level of sampling variance. If the DEFF of a cluster sample is greater than 2 (a DEFF of 2.0 is typically a default value), the sample size for the sample must be more than twice the sample size of a comparable simple random sample at the same margin of error.

> **Guideline 7.16.** *Attrition/mortality rate.* The targeted sample size should be adjusted to take into account the attrition or mortality rate.

If a longitudinal study is planned, in particular a panel study, attrition should be anticipated. The initial sample size should be adjusted to take this factor into account.

SUMMARY

The choice of sample size is a very important decision. Guidelines for choosing the size of a sample indicate that such factors as having an exploratory research objective, the minimization of the burden on study participants, homogeneous population, scattered population, and limited resources suggest a smaller sample size rather than a larger sample size. On the other hand, such factors as quantitative, nonexperimental, and longitudinal research designs and a complex and detailed data analysis design suggest a larger sample size rather than a smaller sample size. "Rules of thumb" are suggested for nonprobability sample designs, and statistical formulas are suggested for probability sample designs. The statistical formulas take into account such factors as confidence intervals, level of significance, level of power, and effect size. The final sample size should be calculated after making adjustments for the incidence rate, the nonresponse rate, the finite population correction factor, the design effect, and the attrition/mortality rate.

REVIEW QUESTIONS

1. How does sample size determination in nonprobability sampling differ from sample size determination in probability sampling?

2. What guidelines should be used in determining the appropriate sample size for nonprobability sampling?

3. What guidelines should be used in determining the appropriate sample size for probability sampling?

4. Illustrate the confidence interval approach of determining sample size.

5. Illustrate the hypothesis-testing approach of determining sample size.

6. In determining sample size, how might one decide on the level of confidence desired and the level of accuracy to use?

7. Is it necessary to make a determination of the size of a sample before beginning to select elements for the sample? Justify your answer.

8. What is sequential sampling, and its strengths and weaknesses?

9. Is a larger sample size always better? Why or why not?

10. Qualitative researchers tend to consider factors in determining sample size that are different from the factors that quantitative researchers tend to consider. What do you consider to be the key factors that a qualitative researcher should consider? What are the reasons for your answer? Once you have answered these questions, consider Small's "'How Many Cases Do I Need?' On Science and the Logic of Case Selection in Field-Based Research." (2009).

11. Suppose you desired to conduct a study of 1,000 lesbians. What procedures would you use to achieve this goal and why? Once you have answered these questions, consider Fish's "Sampling Lesbians: How to Get 1000 Lesbians to Complete a Questionnaire" (1999).

KEY TERMS

Define and give examples of the following concepts:

confidence interval

data saturation

design effect

finite population correction factor

margin of error

REFERENCES FOR FURTHER STUDY

Armitage, P. (1975). *Sequential medical trials.* New York: Wiley & Sons.

Birt, E. M., & Brogren, R. H. (1964). Minimizing number of interviews through sequential sampling. *Journal of Marketing Research, 1,* 65–67.

Dattalo, P. (2009). A review of software for sample size determination. *Evaluation and the Health Profession, 32,* 229–248.

Fish, J. (1999). Sampling lesbians: How to get 1,000 lesbians to complete a questionnaire. *Feminism & Psychology, 9,* 229–238.

Hektner, J., Schmidt, J. A., & Csikszentmihalyi, M. (2006). *Experience sampling method.* Thousand Oaks, CA: Sage.

Henry, G. T. (1990). *Practical sampling.* Thousand Oaks, CA: Sage.

Kish, L. (1965). *Survey sampling.* New York: Wiley & Sons.

Moore, S. R. (1998). Effects of sample size on the representativeness of observational data used in evaluation. *Education and Treatment of Children, 21,* 209–226.

Scheaffer, R. L., Mendenhall, W., & Ott, L. (2006). *Elementary survey sampling.* Belmont, CA: Duxbury Press.

Small, M. L. (2009). How many cases do I need? On science and the logic of case selection in field-based research. *Ethnography, 10,* 5–38.

Thompson S. K., & Seber, G. A. F. (1996). *Adaptive sampling.* New York: Wiley & Sons.

GLOSSARY

Address-based sampling: Address-based sampling is a set of sampling procedures that utilize postal addresses as sampling units.

Availability sampling: Nonprobability sampling procedure in which elements are selected from the target population on the basis of their availability, convenience of the researcher, and/or their self-selection. Also referred to as convenience sampling, accidental sampling, chunk sampling, grab sampling, opportunistic sampling, fortuitous sampling, incidental sampling, straw polling, opt-in online sampling, volunteer sampling, and nonprobability systematic sampling.

Bellwether case sampling: Nonprobability sampling procedure in which elements are selected from the target population on the basis of their track record in predicting trends and future events.

Case control sampling: See matched sampling.

Census: Total enumeration of the target population.

Chain sampling: See respondent-assisted sampling.

Cluster sampling: Probability sampling procedure in which elements of the population are randomly selected in naturally occurring aggregates or clusters.

Clustered frame bias: Bias due to the use a sampling frame that includes units with more than one element of the target population.

Cohort study: A longitudinal research design that tracks over time population elements that have a common experience.

Concurrent mixed-methods sample design: A sample design incorporating the use of two or more different sampling procedures at roughly the same time.

Confidence interval: A range of values within which the true value of the population is likely to fall.

Confirmatory sampling: Nonprobability sampling procedure in which elements are selected from the target population on the basis of their consistency with the hypotheses of a study.

Consecutive sampling: Nonprobability sampling procedure in which elements are selected from the target population on a first-come, first-chosen basis.

Coverage bias: The lack of a one-to-one correspondence between the elements in the target population and the elements encompassed by the respondent selection procedures used in a study.

Critical case sampling: Nonprobability sampling procedure in which elements are selected from the target population on the basis of their particular importance to the subject matter that is studied.

Cross-sectional research design: A research design in which data are collected within one time period.

Data saturation: The point at which the informational needs of a researcher have been satisfied and there is no added value in collecting additional information.

Descriptive research: Research that seeks to describe the parameters of a population, subpopulation, or relationships among variables.

Design effect: The ratio of the variances of sample design employed to the variances of a comparable simple random sample design. It measures how much sampling variability in a sample differs from the variability if simple random sampling were used.

Deviant case sampling: Nonprobability sampling procedure in which elements are selected from the target population on the basis of their differences from the modal or typical case. Also referred to as rare element sampling, extreme case sampling, intensity case sampling, and outlier sampling.

Dimensional sampling: A special case of nonproportional quota sampling in which the researcher selects elements so that there will be at least one element in the sample representing each possible combination of dimensions of the variables targeted in the study.

Disconfirming case sampling: Nonprobability sampling procedure in which elements are selected from the target population on the basis of their inconsistency with the hypotheses of a study. Also referred to as negative case sampling.

Disproportionate allocation: Stratified sampling procedure in which the number of elements allocated to the various strata is not proportional to the representation of the strata in the target population.

Diversity sampling: See maximum variation sampling.

Equal allocation disproportionate allocation: Disproportionate stratified sampling procedures in which the number of elements sampled from each stratum is equal.

Equal probability selection method (EPSEM): Probability selection procedure in which every element in the target population has an equal probability of being selected.

Evaluation research: Research that seeks to determine the need for an intervention, the form an intervention should take, the processes of an intervention, and the outcome of an intervention.

Experimental research: A research design in which the researcher controls exposure to the key independent variable of a study.

Expert sampling: Nonprobability sampling procedure in which elements are selected from the target population on the basis of their known or demonstrable experience and expertise.

Explanatory research: Research that seeks to explain the patterns of population parameters and the relationships among variables.

Exploratory research: Research that targets information seeking to better understand a population, theoretical issues, or methodological issues relating to a study.

Extreme case sampling: See deviant case sampling.

Finite population correction factor (fpc): An adjustment in determining sample size when sampling without replacement is used and the sample is large relative to the population (the sample size is greater than 5% of the population size).

Heterogeneity sampling: See maximum variation sampling.

Homogeneous sampling: Nonprobability sampling procedure in which elements are selected from the target population so as to minimize the variability of elements within the sample. Also referred to as heterogeneity sampling and diversity sampling.

Informant sampling: Nonprobability sampling procedure in which elements are selected from the target population on the basis of their ability to provide information about the subject matter of the study.

Intensity case sampling: See deviant case sampling.

Item nonresponse bias: Bias resulting from the failure to obtain the desired information on an item for which information is sought.

Judgment sampling: Nonprobability sampling procedure in which elements are selected from the target population on the basis of the opinion of the researcher or his/her informants.

Linear systematic sampling: Selection of a single systematic sample.

List-assisted RDD sampling: List-assisted RDD sampling represents a set of sampling procedures that involve a combination of list-based sampling and RDD sampling.

List-based sampling: List-based sampling is a set of sampling procedures that involves the sampling from a listing of telephone numbers of the target population.

Longitudinal research design: A research design in which data are collected over multiple time periods.

Margin of error: The radius of the confidence interval of a statistic.

Matched sampling: Nonprobability sampling procedure in which elements are selected from the target population on the basis of their similarity to elements used as a comparison group. Also referred to as case control sampling.

Maximum variation sampling: Nonprobability sampling procedure in which elements are selected from the target population so as to maximize the variability of elements within the sample. Also referred to as heterogeneity sampling and diversity sampling.

Mixed-methods sampling: Sampling method that combines different types of sampling methods into a single design.

Modal instance sampling: See typical case sampling.

Multiple-coverage bias: Bias due to the use of a sampling frame that includes elements more than once.

Multiplicity sampling: A form of network sampling in which sampled elements provide information on others with whom they have relationships.

Multistage cluster sampling: Cluster sampling with more than two stages, each sampling being made on aggregates (or clusters) in which the clusters already obtained by the preceding sampling have been divided. A sampling procedure in which sampling occurs at two or more steps or stages (e.g., a sample of school districts, then a sample of schools from the selected school districts, and then a sample of pupils from the selected schools).

Negative case sampling: See disconfirming case sampling.

Network sampling: See respondent-assisted sampling.

Nonexperimental research: A research design in which the researcher does not control exposure to the key independent variable of a study.

Nonprobability sampling: A sampling procedure that does not give every element in the target population a known and nonzero chance of being selected.

Nonproportional quota sampling: A quota sampling design in which the allocation of the number of elements to be selected for each quota category is not based on their proportions in the target population.

Nonresponse bias: Bias due to systematic differences in study variables between study participants and those who were selected for inclusion in the study but did not participate.

Opportunistic sampling: See availability sampling.

Optimum allocation: Stratified sampling procedure in which the number of elements allocated to the various strata is set so as to minimize the overall variance in a sample and/or the overall data collection costs.

Outlier sampling: See deviant case sampling.

Overcoverage bias: Bias due to the use of a sampling frame or sampling procedures that include elements that are not members of the target population of a study.

Panel study: A longitudinal research design that collects data from the same elements over time.

Politically important cases: Nonprobability sampling procedure in which elements are selected from the target population on the basis of their politics or political importance.

Population specification bias: A poor fit between the research questions a study attempts to answer and the population that is chosen to be studied.

Prediction research: Research that seeks to predict the parameters of a population, subpopulation, or relationships among variables.

Primary sampling unit: The sampling units in the first stage of a multistage sample.

Probability sampling: A sampling procedure that gives every element in the target population a known and nonzero probability of being selected.

Proportional quota sampling: A quota sampling design in which the allocation of the number of elements to be selected for each quota category is based on their proportions in the target population.

Proportionate allocation: Stratified sampling procedure in which the number of elements allocated to the various strata is proportional to the representation of the strata in the target population.

Purposive sampling: Nonprobability sampling procedure in which elements are selected from the target population on the basis of their fit with the purposes of the study and specific inclusion and exclusion criteria.

Qualitative research: Research that primarily involves the collection and analysis of non-numerical data.

Quantitative research: Research that primarily involves the collection and analysis of numerical data.

Quota sampling: Nonprobability sampling procedure in which the population is divided into mutually exclusive subcategories, and interviewers or other data collectors solicit participation in the study from members of the subcategories until a target number of elements to be sampled from the subcategories has been met.

Random sampling error: Difference between a sample estimate and the true population value that is due to chance variation of multiple samples.

Rare element sampling: See deviant case sampling.

Referral sampling: See respondent-assisted sampling.

Repeated systematic sampling: Selection of multiple samples from the target population and then combining them into a single sample.

Reputational sampling: Nonprobability sampling procedure in which elements are selected from the target population on the basis of their public image or standing.

Respondent-assisted sampling: Nonprobability sampling procedure in which elements are selected from a target population with the assistance of previously selected population elements. Subtypes include snowball sampling, network sampling, chain sampling, referral sampling, and respondent-driven sampling.

Respondent-driven sampling: Subtypes of respondent-assisted sampling in which previously selected respondents seek out and invite other members of the target population to participate in the study. Respondents are given coupons that may be turned in for a monetary incentive for their participation. Data collection takes place at a central location.

Response bias: Bias due to the collection of invalid or inappropriate data from sampled elements.

Rotating panel design: A longitudinal research design involves the collection of data from multiple panels of population elements with each being used a fixed number of times.

Sample: Subset of the target population.

Sampling: The selection of a subset of a population for inclusion in a study instead of the entire population.

Sampling frame: Listing of the target population.

Sampling frame bias: The extent to which there are differences between the elements that are listed in the frame and the elements that make up the target population.

Sampling with replacement: After an element has been selected from the sampling frame, it is returned to the frame and is eligible to be selected again.

Sampling without replacement: After an element is selected from the sampling frame, it is removed from the population and is not returned to the sampling frame

Secondary sampling unit: Sampling unit sampled from within a primary sampling unit at the second sampling stage of a multistage cluster sample design.

Selection bias: Bias due to systematic differences in the characteristics of population elements that are selected to be included in the study and population elements that are not selected.

Sequential mixed-methods sampling: A sample design incorporating the use of two or more different sampling procedures in which they are implemented one after another.

Simple random sampling: A probability sampling procedure that gives every element in the target population, and each possible sample of a given size, an equal chance of being selected.

Single-stage cluster sample design: Probability sampling procedure in which elements of the population are randomly selected in naturally occurring groupings (clusters) with no subsequent sampling.

Snowball sampling: See respondent-assisted sampling.

Space-based sampling: Space-based sampling is a set of sampling procedures that utilize space as a sampling unit.

Stratified sampling: A probability sampling procedure in which the target population is first separated into mutually exclusive, homogeneous segments (strata), and then a simple random sample is selected from each segment (stratum).

Subjective sampling: See judgment sampling.

Surrogate information error: Discrepancy between the information required for a study to achieve its objectives and the information sought by the researcher.

Systematic error: Difference between a sample estimate and the true population value that is due to factors other than random error.

Systematic sampling: Probability sampling procedure in which a random selection is made of the first element for the sample, and then subsequent elements are selected using a fixed or systematic interval until the desired sample size is reached. Also referred to as interval sampling.

Target population: The set of elements to which a researcher desires to apply the findings of a study.

Telephone-based sampling: Sampling procedures that utilize telephone numbers are sampling units.

Theoretical sampling: Nonprobability sampling procedure in which elements are selected from the target population on the basis of their likelihood to inform a theory of interest.

Time-based sampling: Sampling procedures that utilize units of time as sampling units.

Trend study: A longitudinal research design that examines the same variables over time.

Two-stage cluster sample design: Cluster sampling design that is conducted in two stages. In the first stage, primary sampling units are selected. For each primary sampling unit selected, secondary sampling units are selected.

Typical case sampling: Nonprobability sampling procedure in which elements are selected from the target population on the basis of their representation of the average, typical, or highest frequency case. Also referred to as modal instance sampling.

Undercoverage bias: Differences between the elements of a target population encompassed by the sampling procedures of a study and elements of the target population not encompassed by those procedures.

Unequal allocation disproportionate allocation: Disproportionate stratified sampling procedures in which the number of elements sampled from each stratum is equal.

Unit nonresponse bias: Bias resulting from the failure of a researcher to successfully collect any data or a sufficient amount of data from elements selected to be included in a study.

Venue-based sampling: A location-based sampling that typically combines time-based sampling and space-based sampling.

Web-based sampling: Sampling procedures that utilize email addresses, web site visits, and recruited users of the Internet as sampling units.

REFERENCES AND SUGGESTED READINGS

Abbassi, A., & Singh, R. N. (2006). Assertiveness in marital relationships among Asian Indians in the United States. *The Family Journal, 14,* 392–399.

Abell, N. (2001). Assessing willingness to care for persons with AIDS: Validation of a new measure. *Research on Social Work Practice, 11,* 118–130.

Aday, L. A., & Cornel, L. J. (2006). *Designing and conducting health surveys* (2nd ed.). San Francisco: Jossey-Bass.

Alderson, W. (1946). Trends in public opinion research. In A. B. Blankenship (Ed.), *How to conduct consumer and opinion research: The sampling survey in operation* (pp. 289–300). New York: Harper & Brothers.

Alexander, C. H. (1988). Cutoff rules for secondary calling in a random digit dialing survey. In R. M. Groves, P. P. Biemen, L. E. Lyberg, J. T. Massey, W. L. Nicholls, & J. Waksberg (Eds.), *Telephone survey methodology* (pp. 113–126). New York: John Wiley & Sons.

Allison, P. D. (2001). *Missing data.* Thousand Oaks, CA: Sage.

Alreck, P. L., & Settle, R. B. (2004). *The survey research handbook* (3rd ed). Boston: McGraw-Hill.

Anderson, T., Daly, K., & Rapp, L. (2009). Clubbing masculinities and crime: A qualitative study of Philadelphia nightclub scenes. *Feminist Criminology, 4,* 302–332.

Armitage, P. (1975). *Sequential medical trials.* New York: Wiley & Sons.

Anscombe, F. J. (1963). Sequential medical trials. *Journal of the American Statistical Association, 58,* 365–383.

Asher, H. (1995). *Polling and the public: What every citizen should know* (3rd ed). Washington, DC: Congressional Quarterly.

Ashkar, P. J., & Kenny, D. T. (2007). Moral reasoning of adolescent male offenders: Comparison of sexual and nonsexual offenders. *Criminal Justice and Behavior, 34,* 108–118.

Assael, H., & Deon, J. (1982). Nonsampling vs. sampling errors in survey research. *Journal of Marketing, 46,* 114–123.

Auslander, W. F., Sterzing, P. R., Zayas, L. E., & White, N. H. (2010). Psychosocial resources and barriers to self-management in African American adolescents with type 2 diabetes: A qualitative analysis. *The Diabetes Educator, 36,* 613–622.

Babbie, E. (1990). *Survey research methods.* Belmont, CA: Wadsworth.

Babbie, E. (2009). *The practice of social research.* Belmont, CA: Wadsworth.

Balsam, K. F., Beauchaine, T. P., Mickey, R. M., & Rothblum, E. D. (2005). Mental health of lesbian, gay, bisexual, and heterosexual siblings: effects of gender, sexual orientation, and family. *Journal of Abnormal Psychology, 114,* 471–476.

Battaglia, M. P., Link, M. W., Frankel, M. R., Osburn, L., & Mokdad, A. H. (2008). An evaluation of respondent selection methods for household mail surveys. *Public Opinion Quarterly, 72,* 459–469.

Bauman, S., Rigby, K., & Hoppac, K. (2008). US teachers' and school counselors' strategies for handling school bullying incidents. *Educational Psychology, 28,* 837–856.

Beaulaurier, R., Seff, L., Newman, F., & Dunlop, B. (2007). External barriers to help seeking for older women who experience intimate partner violence. *Journal of Family Violence, 22,* 747–755.

Berenson, W. M., Elifson, K. W., & Tollerson, T., III. (1976). Preachers in politics: A study of political activism among the Black ministry. *Journal of Black Studies, 6,* 373–392.

Bergman, M. (Ed). (2008). *Advances in mixed methods research.* London: Sage.

Bergman, M. E., Langhout, R. D., Palmieri, P. A., Cortina, L. M., & Fitzgerald, L. F. (2002). The (un)reasonableness of reporting: Antecedents and consequences of reporting sexual harassment. *Journal of Applied Psychology, 87,* 230–242.

Berry, C. C., Flatt, S. W., & Pierce, J. P. (1996). Correcting unit nonresponse via response modeling and raking in the California Tobacco Survey. *Journal of Official Statistics, 12,* 349–363.

Biemer, P. P., & Lyberg, L. E. (2003). *Introduction to survey quality.* New York: Wiley & Sons.

Biemer, P., Groves, P., Lyberg, L., & Mathiowetz, N. (2004). *Measurement errors in surveys.* New York: Wiley & Sons.

Bimber, B. (1996). *Government and politics on the net project.* Available at University of California, Santa Barbara web site: www.sscf.ucsb.edu/survey1/main.html

Binson, D., Canchola, J. A., & Catania, J. A. (2000). Random selection in a national telephone survey: A comparison of the Kish, next birthday, and last-birthday methods. *Journal of Official Statistics, 16,* 53–59.

Birt, E. M., & Brogren, R. H. (1964). Minimizing number of interviews through sequential sampling. *Journal of Marketing Research, 1,* 65–67.

Blankenship, A. B. (1977a). Listed versus unlisted numbers in telephone-survey samples. *Journal of Advertising Research, 17,* 39–42.

Blankenship, A. B. (1977b). *Professional telephone surveys.* New York: McGraw-Hill.

Blumberg, S. J., & Luke, J. (2007). Coverage bias in traditional telephone surveys of low-income and young adults. *Public Opinion Quarterly, 71,* 734–749.

Botman, S. L., & Allen, K. (1990). Some effects of undercoverage in a telephone survey of teenagers. *Proceedings of the survey research methods section, American Statistical Association,* 396–400.

Boyle, J., Bucuvalas, M., Piekarski, L., & Weiss, A. (2009). Zero banks: Coverage error and bias in RDD samples based of hundred banks with listed numbers. *Public Opinion Quarterly, 73,* 729–750.

Bradley, N. (1999). Sampling for internet surveys: An examination of respondent selection for internet research. *Journal of the Market Research Society, 41,* 387–395.

Braunstein, M. S. (1993). Sampling a hidden population: Noninstitutionalized drug users. *AIDS Education and Prevention, 5,* 131–139.

Brick, J. M., & Kalton, G. (1996). Handling missing data in survey research. *Statistical Methods in Medical Research, 5,* 530–535.

Brick, J. M., & Waksberg, J. (1991). Avoiding sequential sampling with random digit dialing. *Survey Methodology, 17,* 27–42.

Brick, J. M., Waksberg, J., Kulp, D., & Starer, A. (1995). Bias in list-assisted telephone samples. *Public Opinion Quarterly, 59,* 218–235.

Brown, L.D., Eaton, M. L., Freedman, D. A., Klein, S. P., Olshen, R. A., Wachter, K. W., et al. (1999). *Statistical controversies in Census 2000* (Technical Report 537). Department of Statistics, University of California, Berkeley. Available at http://www.stat.berkeley.edu/~census/537.pdf

Brunner, J. A., & Brunner, G. A. (1971). Are voluntary unlisted telephone subscribers really different? *Journal of Marketing Research, 8,* 121–124.

Bryant, B. E. (1975). Respondent selection in a time of changing household composition. *Journal of Marketing Research, 12,* 129–135.

Bryson, Maurice C. (1976). The Literary Digest poll: Making of a statistical myth. *American Statistician, 30,* 184–185.

Burke, T. W., Jordan, M. L., & Owen, S. S. (2002). A cross-national comparison of gay and lesbian domestic violence. *Journal of Contemporary Criminal Justice 18,* 231–257.

Burke, J., Morganstein, D., & Schwartz, S. (1981). Toward the design of an optimal telephone sample. *Proceedings of the survey research methods section, American Statistical Association,* 448–453.

Burke, T. W., Owen, S. S., & Jordan, M. L. (2001). Law enforcement and gay domestic violence in the United States and Venezuela. *ACJS Today, 24,* 4–6.

Burnam, M. A., & Koegel, P. (1988). Methodology for obtaining a representative sample of homeless persons: The Los Angeles Skid Row Study. Evaluation Review, 12, 117–152.

Cahalan, D. (1989). The digest poll rides again. *Public Opinion Quarterly 53,* 129–133.

California Health Interview Survey. (2009). *CHIS 2007 methodology series: Report 1—sample design.* Los Angeles: UCLA Center for Health Policy Research.

Calvano, L., & Andersson, L. (2010). Hitting the jackpot (or not): An attempt to extract value in Philadelphia's casino controversy. *Organization, 17,* 583–597.

Campbell, J. C., & Soeken, K. I. (1999). Women's responses to battering over time: An analysis of change. *Journal of Interpersonal Violence, 14,* 21–40.

Carlson, R. G., Wang, J., Siegal, H. A., Falck, R. S., & Guo, J. (1994). An ethnographic approach to targeted sampling: Problems and solutions in AIDS prevention research among injection drug and crack-cocaine users. *Human Organization, 53,* 279–386.

Casady, R. J., & Lepkowski, J. M. (1991). Optimal allocation for stratified telephone survey designs. *Proceedings of the section on survey research methods. American Statistical Association,* 111–116.

Casady, R. J., & Lepkowski, J. M. (1993). Stratified telephone survey designs. *Survey Methodology, 19,* 103–113.

Centers for Disease Control and Prevention. (n.d.). *Ambulatory health care data, scope and sample design: NAMCS scope and sample design.* Retrieved April 21, 2010, from http://www.cdc.gov/nchs/ahcd/ahcd_scope.htm#namcs_scope

Centers for Disease Control and Prevention. (n.d.). *National Health Interview Survey: About the National Health Interview Survey.* Retrieved April 21, 2010, from http://www.cdc.gov/nchs/nhis/about_nhis.htm#sample_design

Centers for Disease Control and Prevention. (n.d.). National Health and Nutrition Examination Survey: NHANES I web tutorial, sample design in NHANES I, key concepts about NHANES I sample design. Retrieved April 21, 2010, from http://www.cdc.gov/nchs/tutorials/nhanes/surveydesign/SampleDesign/Inf01.htm

Centers for Disease Control & Prevention. (2006, December 12). *Behavioral risk factor surveillance system: Operational and user's guide* (Version 3.0). Retrieved April 21, 2010, from http://www.cdc.gov/brfss/pdf/userguide.pdf

Centers for Disease Control and Prevention. (2007). *National home and hospice care survey: Sample design*. Retrieved April 21, 2010, from http://www.cdc.gov/nchs/nhhcs/nhhcs_sample_design.htm

Chandek, M. S., & Porter, C. O. L. H. (1998). The efficacy of expectancy disconfirmation in explaining crime victim satisfaction with the police. *Police Quarterly, 1,* 21–40.

Chen, A. C.-C., Keith, V. M., Airriess, C., Li, W., & Leong, K. J. (2007). Economic vulnerability, discrimination, and Hurricane Katrina: Health among Black Katrina. *Journal of the American Psychiatric Nurses Association, 13,* 257–266.

Chu, D., Song, J. H.-L., & Dombrink, J. (2005). Chinese immigrants' perceptions of the police in New York City. *International Criminal Justice Review, 15,* 101–114.

Clodfelter, T. A., Turner, M. G., Hartman, J. L., & Kuhns, J. B. (2010). Sexual harassment victimization during emerging adulthood: A test of routine activities theory and a general theory of crime. *Crime & Delinquency, 56,* 455–481.

Collins, K. M. T., Onwuegbuzie, A. J., & Jiao, Q. G. (2006). Prevalence of mixed-methods sampling designs in social science research. *Evaluation and Research in Education, 19,* 83–101.

Collins, K. M. T., Onwuegbuzie, A. J., & Jiao, Q. G. (2007). A mixed methods investigation of mixed methods sampling designs in social and health science research. *Journal of Mixed Methods Research, 1,* 267–294.

Cook, C., Heath, F., & Thompson, R. (2000). A meta-analysis of response rates in web or Internet-based surveys. *Educational & Psychological Measurement, 60,* 821–836.

Cooper, S. L. (1964). Random sampling by telephone—an improved method. *Journal of Marketing Research, 1,* 45–48.

Cornfield, J. (1942). On certain biases in samples of human populations. *Journal of the American Statistical Association, 37,* 63–68.

Couper, M. (2000). Web surveys: A review of issues and approaches. *Public Opinion Quarterly, 64,* 464–494.

Couper, M. P., Traugott, M. W., Lamias, M. J. (2001). Web survey design and administration. *Public Opinion Quarterly, 65,* 230–253.

Cowles, M. (2000). *Statistics in psychology: An historical perspective.* Mahwah, NJ: Lawrence Erlbaum.

Cox, B. G., & Cohen, S. B. (1985). *Methodological issues for health care surveys.* New York: Marcel Dekker.

Coyle, S. L., Boruch, R. F., & Turner, C. F. (Eds.). (1991). *Evaluating AIDS prevention programs.* Washington, DC: National Academy Press.

Craft, S. M., & Serovich, J. M. (2005). Family-of-origin factors and partner violence in the intimate relationships of gay men who are HIV positive. *Journal of Interpersonal Violence, 20,* 777–791.

Creswell, J. W., & Plano Clark, V. L. (2007). *Designing and conducting mixed methods research.* Thousand Oaks, CA: Sage.

Crossley, A. M. (1957). Early days of public opinion research. *Public Opinion Quarterly, 21,* 159–164.

Cuddeback, C. B., Orme, J. G., & Le Prohn, N. S. (2007). Measuring foster parent potential: Casey Foster applicant inventory-worker version (CFAI-W). *Social Work Practice, 17,* 93–109.

Cummings, K. M. (1979). Random digit dialing: A sampling technique for telephone surveys. *Public Opinion Quarterly, 43,* 233–244.

Curtin, R., Presser, S., & Singer, E. (2005). Changes in telephone survey nonresponse over the past quarter century. *Public Opinion Quarterly, 69,* 87–98.

Czaja, R., Blair, J., & Sebestik, J. P. (1982). Respondent selection in a telephone survey: A comparison of three techniques. *Journal of Marketing Research, 19,* 381–385.

Daniel, W. W. (1975). Nonresponse in sociological surveys: A review of some methods for handling the problem. *Sociological Methods & Research, 3,* 291–307.

Daniels, K., Hartley, R., & Travers, C. J. (2006). Beliefs about stressors alter stressors' impact: Evidence from two experience-sampling studies. *Human Relations, 59,* 1261–1285.

Dattalo, P. (2009). A review of software for sample size determination. *Evaluation and the Health Profession, 32,* 229–248.

Deaux, E., & Callaghan, J. W. (1985). Key informant versus self-report estimates of health behavior. *Evaluation Review, 9,* 365–368.

De Leeuw, E. D. (2005). To mix or not to mix: Data collection modes in surveys. *Journal of Official Statistics, 21,* 233–255.

DeMaio, T. (1980). Refusals: Who, where, and why. *Public Opinion Quarterly, 44,* 223–233.

Denzin, N. K. (2009). *The research act in sociology.* Chicago: Aldine.

Department of Defense 1995 Sexual Harassment Survey [CD-ROM]. (1997). Arlington, VA: Defense Manpower Data Center [Producer and distributor].

Diehr, P., Koepsell, T. D., Cheadle, A., & Psaty, B. M. (1992). Assessing response bias in random-digit dialing surveys: the telephone-prefix method. *Statistics in Medicine 11,* 1009–1021.

Dillman, D. A. (1978). Mail and telephone surveys: The total design method. New York: Wiley & Sons.

Dillman, D. (2007). *Mail and internet surveys: The tailored design method* (2nd ed.). New York: Wiley & Sons.

Dillman, D., Gallegos, J., & Frey, J. (1976). Reducing refusals rates for telephone interviews. *Public Opinion Quarterly, 40,* 66–78.

Draucker, C. B., Martsolf, D. S., Ross, R. & Rusk, T. B. (2007). Theoretical sampling and category development in grounded theory. *Qualitative Health Research, 17,* 176–188.

Dutwin, D., Keeter, S., & Kennedy, C. (2010). Bias from wireless substitution in surveys of Hispanics. *Hispanic Journal of Behavioral Sciences, 32,* 309–328.

Eastlack, J. O., Jr., & Assael, H. (1966). Better telephone surveys through centralized interviewing. *Journal of Advertising Research, 6*(1), 2–7.

Edwin, R. (1960). Gallup polls public opinion for 25 years. *Editor & Publisher, 93,* 62–63.

Efron, B. (1994). Missing data, imputation and the bootstrap. *Journal of the American Statistical Association, 89,* 463–479.

Ellis, J., & Fox, P. (2001). The effect of self-identified sexual orientation on helping behavior in a British sample: Are lesbians and gay men treated differently? *Journal of Applied Social Psychology, 31,* 1238–1247.

Ellsberg, M., & Heise, L. (2005). *Researching violence against women: A practical guide for researchers and activists.* Washington DC: World Health Organization, PATH.

Emery, S., Lee, J., Curry, S. J., Johnson, T., Sporer, A. K., Mermelstein, R. et al. (2010). Finding needles in a haystack: A methodology for identifying and sampling community-based youth smoking cessation programs. *Evaluation Review, 34,* 35–51.

Ezzati-Rice, T. M., Rohde, F., & Greenblatt, J. (2008). *Sample design of the medical expenditure panel survey household component, 1998–2007* (Methodology Report No. 22). Rockville, MD: Agency for Healthcare Research and Quality. Available at http://www.meps.ahrq.gov/mepsweb/data_files/publications/mr22/mr22.pdf

Fagan, J., & Chin, K. (2006). Violence as regulation and social control in the distribution of crack. In M. De La Rosa, E. Y. Lambert, & B. Gropper (Eds.), *Drugs and violence: Causes, correlates, and consequences* (NIDA Research Monograph No. 103, pp. 8–43). Washington, DC: U.S. Government Printing Office.

Fahimi, M., Kulp, D., & Brick, J. M. (2009). A reassessment of list-assisted RDD methodology. *Public Opinion Quarterly, 73,* 751–760.

Field, L., Pruchno, R. A., Bewley, J., Lemay, E. P., Jr., & Levinsky., N. G. (2006). Using probability vs. nonprobability sampling to identify hard-to-access participants for health-related research: Costs and contrasts. *Journal of Aging and Health, 18,* 565–583.

Finkelhor, D., Ormrod, R., Turner, H., & Hamby, S. L. (2005). The victimization of children & youth: A comprehensive, national study. *Child Maltreatment, 10,* 5–25.

Fish, J. (1999). Sampling lesbians: How to get 1,000 lesbians to complete a questionnaire. *Feminism & Psychology, 9,* 229–238.

Ford, E. S. (1998). Characteristics of survey participants with and without a telephone: Findings from the third National Health and Nutrition Examination Survey. *Journal of Clinical Epidemiology 51,* 55–60.

Foreman, F. E. (2003). Intimate risk: Sexual risk behavior among African American college women. *Journal of Black Studies, 33,* 637–653.

Forsman, G., & Danielsson, S. (1997). Can plus digit sampling generate a probability sample? *Proceedings of the Section on Survey Research Methods, American Statistical Association,* 958–963.

Fox, R. J., Crask, M. R., & Kim, J. (1988). Mail survey response rates: a meta-analysis of selected techniques for inducing response. *Public Opinion Quarterly, 52,* 467–491.

Frankel, M. R., & Frankel, L. R. (1987). Fifty years of survey sampling in the United States. *Public Opinion Quarterly, 51,* S127–S138.

Frankel, M. R., Srinath, K. P., Battaglia, M. P., Hoaglin, D. C., Wright, R. A., & Smith, P. J. (1999). Reducing nontelephone bias in RDD surveys. *Proceedings of the Section on Survey Research Methods, American Statistical Association,* 934–937.

Frerichs, R. R., & Shaheen, M. A. (2001). Small-community-based surveys. *Annual Review of Public Health, 22,* 231–247.

Frey, J. H. (1989). *Survey research by telephone* (2nd ed.). Beverly Hills, CA: Sage.

Fricker, R. D., Jr. (2008). Sampling methods for web and e-mail surveys. In N. G. Fielding, R. M. Lee, & G. Blank (Eds.), *The handbook of online research methods* (pp. 195–216). Thousand Oaks, CA: Sage.

Fricker, R. D., & Schonlau, M. (2002). Advantages and disadvantages of internet research surveys: Evidence from the literature. *Field Methods, 14,* 347–367.

Fuchs, M. (2008). Mobile web surveys. In F. G. Conrad & M. F. Schober (Eds.), *Envisioning the survey interview future* (pp. 77–94). New York: John Wiley & Sons.

Fuller, C. H. (1974). Weighting to adjust for survey nonresponse. *Public Opinion Quarterly, 38,* 239–246.

Gallup, G. (1957). The changing climate for public opinion research. *Public Opinion Quarterly, 21*, 23–27.

Gayellow pages. (2001). New York: Renaissance House.

Ghosh, D. (1984). Improving the plus 1 method of random digit dialing. *Proceedings of the Section on Survey Research Methods, American Statistical Association*, 285–288.

Gile, K. J., & Handcock, M. S. (2010). Respondent-driven sampling: An assessment of current methodology. In T. F. Liao (Ed.), *Sociological methodology 2010* (Vol. 40, pp. 285–327). Washington, DC: American Sociological Association.

Glaser, B. G. (1978). Theoretical sensitivity: Advances in the methodology of grounded theory. Mill Valley, CA: Sociology Press.

Glaser, B. G., & Strauss, A. L. (1967). The discovery of grounded theory: Strategies for qualitative research. New York: Aldine.

Glasser, G. J., & Metzger, G. D. (1972). Random digit dialing as a method of telephone sampling. *Journal of Marketing Research, 9*, 59–64.

Glasser, G. J., & Metzger, G. D. (1975). National estimates of nonlisted telephone households and their characteristics. *Journal of Marketing Research, 12*, 359–361.

Glicken, M. D. (2003). *Social research: A simple guide*. Boston: Allyn & Bacon.

Goodman, L. A. (1961). Snowball sampling. *Annals of Mathematical Statistics, 32*, 148–170.

Goritz, A. A. (2006). Incentive in web studies: Methodological issues and a review. *International Journal of Internet Science, 1*, 58–70.

Goyder, J. C. (1987). The silent minority: Nonrespondents on sample surveys. Boulder, CO: Westview Press.

Grayman, N. (2009). "We who are dark . . . :" The Black community according to Black adults in America: An exploratory content analysis. *Journal of Black Psychology, 35*, 433–455.

Groves, R. M. (1989). *Survey error and survey costs*. New York: Wiley & Sons.

Groves, R. M. (2006). Nonresponse rates and nonresponse bias in household surveys. *Public Opinion Quarterly, 70*, 646–675.

Groves, R. M., Cialdini, R. B., & Couper, M. P. (1992). Understanding the decision to participate in a survey. *Public Opinion Quarterly 56*, 475–495.

Groves, R. M., & Couper, M. P. (1998). *Nonresponse in household interview surveys*. New York: Wiley & Sons.

Groves, R. M., Dillman, D. A., Eltinge, J. L., & Little, R. J. A. (2001). *Survey nonresponse*. New York: Wiley & Sons.

Groves, R., Fowler, F., Couper, M., Lepkowski, J., Singer, E., & Tourangeau, R. (2009). *Survey methodology* (2nd ed.). New York: Wiley & Sons.

Groves, R. M., & Kahn, R. L. (1979). Surveys by telephone: A national comparison with personal interviews. New York: Academic Press.

Groves, R. M., & Peytcheva, E. (2008). The impact of nonresponse rates on nonresponse bias: A meta-analysis. *Public Opinion Quarterly, 72*, 187–189.

Groves, R. M., Presser, S., & Dipko, S. (2004). The role of topic interest in survey participation decisions. *Public Opinion Quarterly 68*, 2–31.

Groves, R. M., Singer, E., & Corning, A. (2000). Leverage-saliency theory of survey participation: Description and an illustration. *Public Opinion Quarterly 64*, 299–308.

Hagan, D. E., & Collier, C. M. (1983). Must respondent selection procedures for telephone surveys be invasive? *Public Opinion Quarterly, 47*, 547–556.

Hansen, M. H. (1987). Some history and reminiscences on survey sampling. *Statistical Science, 2*, 180–190.

Harden, J., Schafenacker, A., Northouse, L., Mood, D., Pienta, K., Hussain, M., & Baranowski, K. (2002). Couples' experiences with prostate cancer: Focus group research. *Oncology Nursing Forum, 29*, 701–715.

Hartford, K., Carey, R., & Mendonca, J. (2007). Sampling bias in an international Internet survey of diversion programs in the criminal justice system. *Evaluation Health Professions, 30*, 35–46.

Hauck, M., & Cox, M. (1974). Locating a sample by random digit dialing. *Public Opinion Quarterly 38*, 253–260.

Hays, K. L., Regoli, R. M., & Hewitt, J. D. (2007). Police chiefs, anomia, and leadership. *Police Quarterly, 10*, 3–22.

Heckathorn, D. D. (1997). Respondent driven sampling: A new approach to the study of hidden populations. *Social Problems, 44*, 174–199.

Heckathorn, D. D. (2002). Respondent driven sampling II: Deriving valid population estimates from chain-referral samples of hidden populations. *Social Problems, 44*, 11–34.

Hektner, J., Schmidt, J. A., & Csikszentmihalyi, M. (2006). *Experience sampling method*. Thousand Oaks, CA: Sage.

Henry, G. T. (1990). *Practical sampling*. Thousand Oaks, CA: Sage.

Herrenkohl, T. I., McMorris, B. J., Catalano, R. F., Abbott, R. D., Hemphill, S. A., & Toumbourou, J. W. (2007). *Journal of Interpersonal Violence, 22*, 386–405.

Hnatiuk, S. H. (1991). Experience sampling with elderly persons: An exploration of the method. *International Journal of Aging and Human Development, 33*, 45–64.

Hogue, C. R., & Chapman, D. W. (1984). An investigation of PSU cutoff points for a random digit dialing survey. *Proceedings of the Section on Survey Research Methods, American Statistical Association*, 286–291.

Holt, D., & Elliot, D. (1991). Methods of weighting for unit non-response. *The Statistician, 40*, 333–342.

Homsi, J., Walsh, D., Lasheen, W., Nelson, K. A., Rybicki, L. A., Bast, J., & LeGrand, S. B. (2010). A comparative study of 2 sustained-release morphine preparations for pain in advanced cancer. *American Journal of Hospice and Palliative Medicine, 27*, 99–105.

Howe, H. L. (1982). Increasing efficiency in evaluation research: The use of sequential analysis. *American Journal of Public Health, 72*, 690–697.

Hultsch, D. F., MacDonald, S. W. S., Hunter, A., Maitland, S. B., & Dixon, R. A. (2002). Sampling and generalizability in developmental research: Comparison of random and convenience samples of older adults. *International Journal of Behavioral Development, 26*, 345–359.

Iachan, R., & Dennis, M. L. (1993). A multiple frame approach to sampling the homeless and transient population. *Journal of Official Statistics, 9*, 747–764.

Iannacchionee, V. G., Staab, J. M., & Redden, D. T. (2003). Evaluating the use of residential mailing addresses in a metropolitan household survey. *Public Opinion Quarterly, 76*, 202–210.

Ibo, S. E. (2006). A gold mine and a tool for democracy: George Gallup, Elmo Roper, and the business of scientific polling, 1935–1955. *Journal of the History of Behavioral Sciences, 42*, 109–134.

Ilies, R., Hauserman, N., Schwochau, S., & Stibal, J. (2003). Reported incidence rates of work-related sexual harassment in the United States: Using meta-analysis to explain reported rate disparities. *Personnel Psychology, 56*, 607–631.

Inglis, K. M., Groves, R. M., & Heeringa, S. G. (1987). Telephone sample designs for the U.S. Black household population. *Survey Methodology, 13*, 1–14.

Jenness, V., Maxson, C. L., Sumner, J. M., & Matsuda, K. N. (2010). Accomplishing the difficult but not impossible: Collecting self-report data on inmate-on-inmate sexual assault in prison. *Criminal Justice Policy Review, 21,* 3–30.

Johnson, B. M. (2003). Emergency department utilization among Hispanic and African-American under-served patients with type 2 diabetes. *Ethnicity & Disease, 13,* 369–375.

Johnson, M. B., Lange, J. E., Voas, R. B., Clapp, J. D., Lauer, E., & Snowden, C. B. (2006). The sidewalk survey: A field methodology to measure late-night college drinking. *Evaluation Review, 30,* 27–43.

Johnson, R. B., & Onwuegbuzie, A. J. (2004). Mixed methods research: A research paradigm whose time has come. *Educational Researcher, 33,* 14–26.

Johnson, T. J., & Kaye, B. K. (1998). The internet: Vehicle for engagement or a haven for the disaffected? In T. J. Johnson, C. E. Hays, & S. P. Hays (Eds.), *Engaging the public: How the government and media can reinvigorate American democracy* (pp. 123–135). Lanham, MD: Rowman & Littlefield.

Kalsbeek, W. D., Boyle, W. R., Agans, R., & White, J. E. (2007). Disproportionate sampling for population subgroups in telephone surveys. *Statistics in Medicine, 26,* 657–674.

Kalton, G. (1991). Sampling flows of mobile human populations. *Survey Methodology, 17,* 183–194.

Kalton, G. (2001, August). *Practical methods for sampling rare and mobile populations.* Proceedings of the annual meeting of the American Statistical Association, Rockville, MD.

Karon, J. M. (2005). The analysis of time-location sampling study data. *Proceedings of the Section on Survey Research Methods, American Statistical Association,* 3180.

Katz, D., & Cantril, H. (1937). Public opinion polls. *Sociometry* 1, 155–179.

Kaye, B. K., & Johnson, T. J. (1999). Research methodology: Taming the cyber frontier—techniques for improving online surveys. *Social Science Computer Review, 17,* 323–337.

Keeter, K. (2006). The impact of cell phone noncoverage bias on polling in the 2004 presidential election. *Public Opinion Quarterly, 70,* 88–98.

Kerner J., Breen, N., Tefft, M., & Silsby, J. (1998). Tobacco use among multi-ethnic Latino populations. *Ethnicity & Disease, 8,* 167–183.

Kiesler, S., & Sproull, L. S. (1986). Response effects in electronic surveys. *Public Opinion Quarterly, 50,* 402–413.

Kish, L. (1949). A procedure for objective respondent selection within the household. *Journal of the American Statistical Association, 44,* 380–387.

Kish, L. (1965). *Survey sampling.* New York: Wiley & Sons.

Kish, L. (1995). The hundred year wars of survey sampling. *Statistics in Transition, 2,* 813–830.

Knowledge Networks. (2010). *Knowledge panel® design summary.* Retrieved August 2, 2010, from http://www.knowledgenetworks.com/knpanel/docs/KnowledgePanel (R)-Design-Summary-Description.pdf

Koerber, A., & McMichael, L. (2008). Qualitative sampling methods: A primer for technical communication. *Journal of Business and Technical Communication, 22,* 454–473.

Kruskal, W., & Mosteller, F. (1980). Representative sampling, IV: The history of the concept in statistics, 1895–1939. *International Review of Statistics, 48,* 169–195.

Kumar, N. (2007). Spatial sampling design for a demographic and health survey. *Population Research and Policy Review, 26,* 581–599.

Kuzel, A. (1999). Sampling in qualitative inquiry. In B. Crabtree & W. Miller (Eds.), *Doing qualitative research* (pp. 33–45). Thousand Oaks, CA: Sage.

Langhout, R. D., Bergman, M. W., Cortina, L. M., Fitzgerald, L. F., Drasgow, F., & Williams, J. H. (2005). Sexual harassment severity: Assessing situational and personal determinants and outcomes. *Journal of Applied Social Psychology, 35*, 975–1007.

Lauby, J. L., & Milnamow, M. (2009). Where MSM have their first HIV test: Differences by race, income, and sexual identity. *American Journal of Men's Health, 3*, 50–59.

Lavrakas, P. J. (1993). Telephone survey methods: Sampling, selection, and supervision. Thousand Oaks, CA: Sage.

Lavrakas, P. J., Bauman, S. L., & Merkle, D. M. (1993). The last-birthday method and within-unit coverage problems. *Proceedings of the Section on Survey Research Methods, American Statistical Association*, 1107–1112.

Lavrakas, P. J., & Shuttles, C. D. (2005). Cell phone sampling: RDD surveys and marketing research implications. *Alert!, 43*, 4–5.

Lavrakas, P. J., Shuttles, C. D., Steeh, C., & Fienberg, H. (2007). The state of surveying cell phone numbers in the United States. *Public Opinion Quarterly, 71*, 840–854.

LeCompte, M. D., & Preissle, J. (1993). *Ethnography and qualitative design in educational research* (2nd ed.), San Diego, CA: Academic Press.

Lee, J., Pomeroy, E. C., Yoo, S., & Rheinboldt, K. T. (2005). Attitudes toward rape: A comparison between Asian and Caucasian college students. *Violence Against Women, 11*, 177–196.

Lepkowski, J. M., & Groves, R. M. (1986). A mean squared error model for dual frame, mixed mode survey design. *Journal of the American Statistical Association, 81*, 930–937.

Lepkowski, J. M., Mosher, W. D., Davis, K. E., Groves, R. M., & Van Hoewyk, J. (2010, June). The 2006–2010 National Survey of Family Growth: Sample design and analysis of a continuous survey. *Vital and Health Statistics, 2*(150), 1–36. Available from National Center for Health Statistics web site: http://www.cdc.gov/nchs/data/series/sr_02/sr02_150.pdf

Lessler, J. T., & Kalsbeek, W. D. (1992). *Nonsampling error in surveys*. New York: Wiley & Sons.

Leuthold, D. A., & Scheele, R. (1971). Patterns of bias in samples based on telephone directories. *Public Opinion Quarterly, 35*, 249–257.

Levy, P. S., & Lemeshow, S. (2008). *Sampling of populations: Methods and applications*. New York: Wiley & Sons.

Lim, S., & Cortina, L. M. 2005. Interpersonal mistreatment in the workplace: The interface and impact of general incivility and sexual harassment. *Journal of Applied Psychology, 90*, 483–496.

Link, H. C. (1947). Some milestones in public opinion research. *Journal of Applied Psychology, 313*, 225–234.

Link, M. W., Battaglia, M. P., Frankel, M. R., Osborn, L., & Mokdad, A. H. (2008). A comparison of address-based sampling (ABS) versus random-digit dialing (RDD) for general population surveys. *Public Opinion Quarterly, 72*, 6–27.

Link, M. W., Mokdad, A., Kulp, D., & Hyon, A. (2006). Has the national "do not call" registry helped or hurt state-level response rates? *Public Opinion Quarterly, 70*, 794–809.

Little, R. J. A., & Wu, M. M. (1991). Models for contingency tables with known margins when target and sampled populations differ. *Journal of the American Statistical Association, 86*, 87–95.

Lohr, S. L. (2009). *Sampling: Design and analysis*. Belmont, CA: Duxbury Press.

Lynch, C. F., Logsden-Sackett, N., Edwards, S. L., & Cantor, K. P. (1994). The driver's license list as a population-based sampling frame in Iowa. *American Journal of Public Health, 84,* 469–472.

MacKellar, D. A., Gallagher, K. M., Finlayson, T., Sanchez, T., Lansky, A., & Sullivan, P. S. (2007). Surveillance of HIV risk and prevention behaviors of men who have sex with men: A national application of venue-based, time-space sampling. *Public Health Reports, 122,* 39–47.

Malm, D., & Hallberg, L. R.-M. (2006). Patients' experiences of daily living with a pacemaker: A grounded theory study. *Journal of Health Psychology, 11,* 787–798.

Mandell, L. (1975). When to weight: Determining nonresponse bias in survey data. *Public Opinion Quarterly, 38,* 247–252.

Marcus, A., Mullins, L. C., Brackett, K. P., Tang, Z., Zongli, A., Allen, A. M., & Pruett, D. W. (2003). Perceptions of racism on campus. *College Student Journal, 37,* 611–626.

Mason, R. E., & Immerman, F. W. (1998). Minimum cost sample allocation for Mitosky-Waksberg random digit dialing. In R. Groves, P. Biemer, L. Lyberg, J. Massey, W. Nicholls, & J. Waksberg (Eds.), *Telephone survey methodology* (pp. 127–142). New York: Wiley & Sons.

Mason, R., Lesser, V., & Traugott, M. (2002). Effect of item nonresponse on nonresponse error and inference. In R. M. Groves, D. Dillman, J. Eltinge, & R. Little (Eds.), *Survey nonresponse* (pp. 149–162). New York: Wiley & Sons.

McCabe, S. E. (2008). Screening for drug abuse among medical and nonmedical users of prescription drugs in a probability sample of college students. *Archives of Pediatrics & Adolescent Medicine, 162,* 225–231.

Melnik, T. A., Hosler, A. S., Sekhobo, J. P., Duffy, T. P., Tierney, E. F., Engelgau, M. M., & Geiss, L. S. (2000). Diabetes prevalence among Puerto Rican adults in New York City. *American Journal of Public Health, 94,* 435–437.

Migliaccio, T. A. (2002). Abused husbands: A narrative analysis. *Journal of Family Issues, 23,* 26–52.

Miles, M. B., & Huberman, A. M. (1994). *Qualitative data analysis: An expanded sourcebook* (2nd ed.). Thousand Oaks, CA: Sage.

Montgomery, S. B., Hyde, J., DeRosa, C. J., Rohrbach, L. A., Ennett, S., Harvey, S. M., et al. (2002). Gender differences in HIV risk behaviors among young injectors and their social network members. *American Journal of Drug and Alcohol Abuse, 28,* 453–475.

Moore, S. R. (1998). Effects of sample size on the representativeness of observational data used in evaluation. *Education and Treatment of Children, 21,* 209–226.

Morrow, K. M., Vargas, S., Rosen, R. K., Christensen, A. L., Salomon, L., Shulman, L., Barroso, C., & Fava, J. L. (2007). The utility of non-proportional quota sampling for recruiting at-risk women for microbicide research. *AIDS Behavior, 11,* 586–595.

Morton-Williams, J. (1993). *Interviewer approaches.* Aldershot: Dartmouth Publishing.

Nadkarni, N., & Harmon, G. (2008). Accuracy of travel data samples: Utilizing online vs. mail methodologies. Proceedings of Statistics Canada Symposium 2001. Available at: HYPERLINK http://www/ http://www.statcan.gc.ca/bsolc/olc-cel/olc-cel?catno= 11-522-X&chropg=1&lang=eng

Neyman, J. (1934). On the two different aspects of the representative method: The method of stratified sampling and the method of purposive selection. *Journal of the Royal Statistical Society, 97,* 558–606.

Nguyen, P. (2004). Some notes on biased statistics and African Americans. *Journal of Black Studies, 34,* 514–531.

Norris, D. A., & Paton, D. G. (1991). Canada's General Social Survey: Five years of experience. *Survey Methodology, 17,* 227–240.

Northrop, A. (1971). The rise of the polls: Bloopers amid improving aim. *National Journal, 3,* 1703.

Oldendick, R. W., Bishop, G. F., Sorenson, S. B., & Tuchfarber, A. J. (1988). A comparison of the Kish and last birthday methods of respondent selection in telephone surveys. *Journal of Official Statistics, 4,* 307–318.

Oldfield, S. J. (2001). A critical review of the use of time sampling in observational research. *Nursing Times Research, 6,* 597–608.

Onwuegbuzie, A., & Collins, K. M. T. (2007). A typology of mixed methods sampling designs in social science research. *The Qualitative Report, 12,* 281–316.

O'Rourke, D., & Blair, J. (1983). Improving random respondent selection in telephone surveys. *Journal of Marketing Research, 20,* 428–432.

Ostrove, J. M., Feldman, P., & Adler, N. E. (1999). Relations among socioeconomic status indicators and health for African-Americans and whites. *Journal of Health Psychology, 4,* 451–463.

Otis, M. D. (2007). Perceptions of victimization risk and fear of crime among lesbians and gay men. *Journal of Interpersonal Violence, 22,* 198–217.

Palit, C. D. (1983). Design strategies in RDD sampling. *Proceedings of the Section on Survey Research Methods, American Statistical Association,* 627–629.

Palit, C. D., & Blair, J. (1986). Some alternatives for the treatment of first phase telephone numbers in a Waksberg-Mitofsky RDD sample. *Proceedings of the Section on Survey Research Methods, American Statistical Association,* 363–369.

Parker, D., & Jensen, D. (1997, March). *Texas poll of elementary school teachers: Survey sampling procedures and questionnaire design.* Paper presented at the annual meeting of the National Association for Research in Science Teaching, Chicago, IL.

Parsons, J. T., Grov, C., & Kelly, B. C. (2008). Comparing the effectiveness of two forms of time-space sampling to identify club drug-using young adults. *The Journal of Drug Issues, 38,* 1061–1082.

Patton, M. Q. (2001). *Qualitative research and evaluation methods.* Thousand Oaks, CA: Sage.

Penrod, J., Preston, D. B., Cain, R. E., & Starks, M. T. (2003). A discussion of chain referral as a method of sampling hard-to-reach populations. *Journal of Transcultural Nursing, 14,* 100–107.

Perry, J. B. (1968). A note on the use of telephone directories as a sample source. *Public Opinion Quarterly 32,* 691–695.

Peterson, Z. D., Janssen, E., & Heiman, J. R. (2010). The association between sexual aggression and HIV risk behavior in heterosexual men. *Journal of Interpersonal Violence, 25,* 538–556.

Peterson, J. A., Penrod, J., Preston, D. B., Cain, R. E., & Starks, M. T. (2003). A discussion of chain referral as a method of sampling hard-to-reach populations. *Journal of Transcultural Nursing, 14,* 100–107.

Peytchev, A., Carley-Baxter, L. R., & Black, M. C. (2010). Coverage bias in variances, associations, and total error from exclusion of the cell phone-only population in the United States. *Social Science Computer Review, 28,* 287–302.

Polzer, R. L., & Miles, M. S. (2007). Spirituality in African Americans with diabetes: Self-management through a relationship with God. *Qualitative Health Research, 17,* 176–188.

Potter, F. J., McNeill, J. J., Williams, S. R., & Waitman, M. A. (1991). List-assisted RDD telephone surveys. *Proceedings of the Section on Survey Research Methods, American Statistical Association*, 117–122.

Pratesi, M., Manfreda, K. L., Biffignandi, S., & Vehovar, V. (2004). List-based web surveys: Quality, timeliness, and nonresponse in the steps of the participation flow. *Journal of Official Statistics, 20*, 451–465.

Prewitt, K. (1999). Census 2000: Science meets politics. *Science, 283*, 935.

Rah, M. J., Mitchell, G. L., Bullimore, A., Mutti, D. O., & Zadnik, K. (2001). Prospective quantification of near work using the experience sampling method. *Optometry and Vision Science, 78*, 496–502.

Rahman, M. M., Luong, N. T., Divan, H. A., Jesser, C., Golz, S. D., Thirumalai, K., et al. (2005). Prevalence and predictors of smoking behavior among Vietnamese men living in California. *Nicotine & Tobacco Research*, 7(1), 103–109.

Reisinger, H. S., Schwartz, R. P., Mitchell, S. G., Kelly, S. M., Brown, B. S., & Agar, M. H. (2008). Targeted sampling in drug abuse research: A review and case study. *Field Methods, 20*, 155–170.

Rich, C. L. (1977). Is random digit dialing really necessary? *Journal of Marketing Research, 14*, 300–305.

Rim, K. H. (2009). Racial context effects and the political participation of Asian Americans. *American Politics Research, 37*, 569–592.

Rosenthal, R., & Rosnow, R. L. (1969). *Artifact in behavioral research*. New York: Academic Press.

Roslow, S., & L. Roslow. (1972). Unlisted phone subscribers are different. *Journal of Advertising Research, 7*, 35–38.

Salganik, M. J. (2006). Variance estimation, design effects, and sample size calculations for respondent driven sampling. *Journal of Urban Health, 83*, 98–112.

Salmon, C. T., & Nichols, J. S. (1983). The next-birthday method of respondent selection. *Public Opinion Quarterly, 47*, 270–276.

Sandelowski, M. (2000). Combining qualitative and quantitative sampling, data collection, and analysis techniques in mixed-methods studies. *Research Nursing Health, 23*, 246–255.

Santster, R. L. (2003). Can we improve our methods to reduce nonresponse bias in RDD surveys? *Proceedings of the Section on Survey Research Methods, American Statistical Association*, 3642–3649.

Savage, J., Giarratano, G., Bustamante-Forest, R., Pollock, C., Robichaux, A., & Pitre, S. (2010). Post-Katrina perinatal mood and the use of alternative therapies. *Journal of Holistic Nursing, 28*, 123–132.

Scheaffer, R. L., Mendenhall, W., & Ott, L. (2006). *Elementary survey sampling*. Belmont, CA: Duxbury Press.

Schillewaert, N., Langerak, F., & Duhamel, T. (1998). Non-probability sampling for WWW surveys: A comparison of methods. *Journal of the Market Research Society, 6*, 36–44.

Schulenberg, J. L., & Warren, D. M. (2009). Content and adequacy of specialized police training to handle youth-related incidents: Perceptions of trainers, supervisors, and frontline officers. *International Criminal Justice Review, 19*, 456–477.

See, L. A. L. (1989). Tensions between Black women and White women: A study. *Affilia, 4*, 31–45.

Semaan, S., Lauby, J., & Liebman. J. (2002). Street and network sampling in evaluation studies of HIV risk-reduction interventions. *AIDS Review, 4,* 213–223.

Settles, I. H., Navarrete, C. D., Pagano, S. J., Abdou, C. M., & Sidanius, J. (2010). Depression and ethnic identity among African American women. *Cultural Diversity & Ethnic Minority Psychology, 16,* 248–255.

Shaver, F. M. (2005). Sex work research: Methodological and ethical challenges. *Journal of Interpersonal Violence, 20,* 296–319.

Shin, H., & Abell, N. (1999). The homesickness and contentment scale: Developing a culturally sensitive measure of adjustment for Asians. *Research on Social Work Practice, 9,* 45–60.

Singer, E. (2006). Nonresponse bias in household surveys. *Public Opinion Quarterly, 70,* 637–645.

Skinner, C. J. (1991). On the efficiency of raking ratio estimation for multiple frame surveys. *Journal of the American Statistical Association, 86,* 779–784.

Small, M. L. (2009). How many cases do I need?: On science and the logic of case selection in field-based research. *Ethnography, 10,* 5–38.

Smith, A. W. (1987). Problems and progress in the measurement of Black public opinion. *American Behavioral Scientist, 30,* 441–455.

Smith, T. W. (1995). Trends in non-response rates. *International Journal of Public Opinion Research, 57,* 157–171.

Smith, T. W. (2002). Are representative Internet surveys possible? Proceedings of Statistics Canada Symposium 2001. Available at: HYPERLINK http://www.statcan.gc.ca/bsolc/olc-cel/olc-cel?catno=11-522- http://www.statcan.gc.ca/bsolc/olc-cel/olc-cel?catno=11-522-X&chropg=1&lang=eng

Sommer, R., & Sommer, B. (2001). *A practical guide to behavioral research: Tools and techniques.* New York: Oxford University Press.

Son, I. S., & Rome, D. M. (2004). The prevalence and visibility of police misconduct: A survey of citizens and police officers. *Police Quarterly, 7,* 179–204.

Song, J. H. (1992). Attitudes of Chinese immigrants and Vietnamese refugees toward law enforcement in the United States. *Justice Quarterly, 9,* 703–719.

Spence, J. M., Bergmans, Y., Strike, C., Links, P. S., Ball, J. S., Rhoade, A. E., et al. (2008). Experiences of substance-using suicidal males who present frequently to the emergency department. *CJEM: The Journal of the Canadian Association of Emergency Physicians, 10,* 339–346.

Squire, P. (1988). Why the 1936 Literary Digest poll failed. *Public Opinion Quarterly, 52,* 125–133.

Srivenkataramana, T., & Saisree, M. (2009). Web-based surveys: An emerging tool. *Bhavan's International Journal of Business, 3,* 51–56.

Stephan, F. F. (1948). History and uses of modern sampling procedures. *Journal of the American Statistical Association, 43,* 12–39.

Stephan, F. F. (1949). Development of election forecasting by polling methods. In F. Mosteller, H. Hyman, P. J. McCarthy, E. S. Marks, & D. B. Truman (Eds.), *The pre-election polls of 1948: Report to the committee on analysis of pre-election polls and forecasts, social science research council* (Bulletin No. 60, pp. 8–14). New York: Social Science Research Council.

Stephan, F. F. (1957). Advances in survey methods and measurement techniques. *Public Opinion Quarterly, 21,* 79–90.

Strauss, A., & Corbin, J. (1990). Basics of qualitative research grounded theory procedures and techniques. London: Sage.

Strauss, A., & Corbin, J. (1994). Grounded theory methodology: An overview. In N. Denzin & Y. Lincoln (Eds.), *Strategies of qualitative inquiry* (pp. 158–183). Thousand Oaks, CA: Sage.

Sudman, S. (1976). *Applied sampling.* New York: Academic Press.

Sudman, S., & Blair, E. (1999). Sampling in the twenty-first century. *Journal of the Academy of Marketing Science, 27,* 269–277.

Surratt, H. L., Inciardi, J. A., Kurtz, S. P., & Kiley, M. C. (2004). Sex work and drug use in a subculture of violence. *Crime & Delinquency, 50,* 43–59.

Swartz, J. A., Lurigio, A. J., & Weiner, D. A. (2004). Correlates of HIV-risk behaviors among prison inmates: Implications for tailored AIDS prevention programming. *The Prison Journal, 84,* 486–504.

Tanguma, J. (2000, November). *A review of the literature on missing data.* Paper presented at the annual meeting of the Mid-South Educational Research Association, Bowling Green, KY.

Tashakkori, A., & Teddlie, C. (1998). Mixed methodology: Combining qualitative and quantitative approaches. Thousand Oaks, CA: Sage.

Teddlie, C., & Yu, F. (2007). Mixed methods sampling: A typology with examples. *Journal of Mixed Methods Research, 1,* 77–100.

Thompson, S. K. (2002). *Sampling.* New York: Wiley & Sons.

Thompson, S. K., & Seber, G. A. F. (1996). *Adaptive sampling.* New York: Wiley & Sons.

Tomaskovic-Davey, D., Leiter, J., & Thompson, S. (1995). Item nonresponse in organizational surveys. *Sociological Methodology, 25,* 77–110.

Traugott, M. W., Groves, R. M., & Lepkowski, J. M. (1987). Using dual frame designs to reduce nonresponse in telephone surveys. *Public Opinion Quarterly, 51,* 522–539.

Troldahl, V. C., & Carter, R. E. (1964). Random selection of respondents within households in phone surveys. *Journal of Marketing Surveys, 1,* 71–76.

Tuckel, P., & O'Neill, H. (2002). The vanishing respondent in telephone surveys. *Journal of Advertising Research, 42,* 26–48.

Tucker, C., Casady, R. J., & Lepkowski, J. (1993). A hierarchy of list-assisted stratified sample design options. *Proceedings of the Section on Survey Research Methods, American Statistical Association,* 982–987.

Tucker, C., Lepkowski, J. M., & Piekarski, L. (2002). The current efficiency of list-assisted telephone sampling designs. *Public Opinion Quarterly, 66,* 322–338.

Tucker, C., & Lepkowski, J. M. (2008). Telephone survey methods: Adapting to change. In J. M. Lepkowski, et al. (Eds.), *Advances in telephone survey methodology* (pp. 3–26). Hoboken, NJ: Wiley & Sons.

Turell, S. C. (2000). A descriptive analysis of same-sex relationship violence for a diverse sample. *Journal of Family Violence, 15,* 281–293.

Tyler, K., Whitbeck, L. B., Hoyt, D. R., & Cauce, A. M. (2004). Risk factors for sexual victimization among male and female homeless and runaway youth. *Journal of Interpersonal Violence, 19,* 503–520.

U.S. Census Bureau. (2000). Cities with 100,000 or more population in 2000 ranked by population per square mile, 2000 in rank order. *County and city data book: 2000, Table C-1.* Available at http://www.census.gov/statab/ccdb/cit1040r.txt

United States Postal Service. (2005). *Delivery sequence file.* Available at http://www.usps.com/ncsc/addressservices/addressqualityservices/deliverysequence.htm

Vandall-Walker, V., Jensen, L., & Oberle, K. (2007). Nursing support for family members of critically ill adults. *Qualitative Health Research, 17,* 1207–1218.

Volz, E., & Heckathorn, D. D. (2008). Probability based estimation theory of respondent driven sampling. *Journal of Official Statistics, 24,* 79–97.

Voogt, R., & Saris, W. (2005). Mixed mode designs: Finding the balance between nonresponse bias and mode effects. *Journal of Official Statistics, 21,* 367–387.

Waksberg, J. (1978). Sampling methods for random digit dialing. *Journal of the American Statistical Association, 73,* 40–46.

Wallace, H. A., & McCamy, J. L. (1940). Straw polls and public administration. *Public Opinion Quarterly, 4,* 221–223.

Walsh, W. A., Jones, L. M., Cross, T. P., & Lippert, T. (2010). Prosecuting child sexual abuse: The importance of evidence type. *Crime & Delinquency, 56,* 436–454.

Wang, Y., Tussing, L., Odoms-Young, A., Braunschweig, C., Flay, B., Hedeker, D., & Hellison, D. (2006). Obesity prevention in low socioeconomic status urban African-American adolescents: Study design and preliminary findings of the HEALTH-KIDS study. *European Journal of Clinical Nutrition, 60,* 92–103.

Watters, J. K., & Biernacki, P. (1989). Targeted sampling: Options for the study of hidden populations. *Social Problems, 36,* 416–430.

Weber, L., & Higginbotham, E. (1997). Black and White professional-managerial women's perceptions of racism and sexism in the workplace. In E. Higginbotham & M. Romero (Eds.), *Women and work: Exploring race, ethnicity, and class practice* (pp. 153–175). Thousand Oaks, CA: Sage.

Weisberg, H. F. (2005). The total survey error approach: A guide to the new science of survey research. Chicago: The University of Chicago Press.

Weiss, N. J. (1983). *Farewell to the party of Lincoln.* Princeton, NJ: Princeton University Press.

Wimmer, R. D., & Dominick, J. R. (1991). *Mass media research.* Belmont, CA: Wadsworth.

Wingood, G., & DiClemente, R. (1998). Pattern influences and gender-related factors associated with noncondom use among young adult African American women. *American Journal of Community Psychology, 26,* 29–53.

Wright, J. D., Allen, T. L., & Devine, J. A. (1995). Tracking non-traditional populations in longitudinal studies. *Evaluation and Program Planning, 18,* 267–277.

Wright, T. (1998). Sampling and Census 2000: The concepts. *American Scientist, 86,* 245.

Wu, W., & Weaver, D. (1997). Online democracy or online demagoguery: Public opinion "polls" on the Internet. *Harvard International Journal of Press/Politics, 2,* 71–86.

Wunsch, D. R. (1986). Survey research: Determining sample size and representative response. *Business Education Forum, 40,* 31–34.

Young, D. S., & Holley, L. C. (2005). Combining caregiving and career: Experiences of social work faculty. *Affilia, 20,* 136–152.

Yu, F. (2007). Mixed methods sampling. *Journal of Mixed Methods Research, 1,* 77–100.

Yang, B., & Eyeson-Annan, M. (2006). Does sampling using random digit dialing really cost more than sampling from telephone directories: Debunking the myths. *BMC Medical Research Methodology, 6,* 6–14.

Zhang, Y. (2000). Using the internet for survey research: A case study. *Journal of Education for Library and Information Science, 5,* 57–68.

INDEX

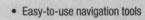